To Deliver Me of My Dreams

To Deliver Me of My Dreams

Elizabeth Avakian

LES FEMMES
MILLBRAE, CALIFORNIA

The Anaïs Nin quotes are from *The Diary of Anaïs Nin, Volume I*, New York: Harcourt Brace Jovanovich, 1966, and *Volume II*, 1967.

Published by CELESTIAL ARTS
231 Adrian Road, Millbrae, California 94030

First printing: September, 1975
Made in the United States of America

Library of Congress Cataloging in Publication Data

Avakian, Elizabeth, 1943-
To deliver me of my dreams.

1. Women--Psychology. 2. Self-actualization.
3. Avakian, Elizabeth, 1943- I. Title.
HQ1206.A87 155.6'33 75-10577
ISBN 0-89087-906-0

To Jeffrey . . .
and to all who remember . . .

Preface

This book began as my Master's thesis in Psychology at Sonoma State College, written in the Spring of 1972 at the end of a year of introspection and reflection; a year in which I had a chance to take a giant step backwards from my life and put certain events and experiences in perspective; a year in which I was given new tools for exploring myself and the time to learn to use them. It seemed appropriate that the written culmination of such a year—my thesis—should be about me. It seemed equally appropriate that it reflect my growing consciousness of myself as a woman—of what my experiences have in common with those of other women —and of my growing concern that these experiences be expressed and shared.

At Sonoma State I was encouraged to look to myself for both the questions and the answers, to trust my own perceptions, reactions, conclusions. One perception and reaction that kept recurring was how male-oriented the whole field of Psychology—even Humanistic Psychology—was, and how frustrating it then became to try to find explanations, information, analyses of human behavior that applied to me. In a department of twenty-some instructors, only three were women, and one of them was on two-fifths time. None of the graduate professors that year were women. But that doesn't really say what I mean when I speak of male domination; it was the lack of a feminine point of view, a feminine way of seeing things, that I became increasingly and painfully aware of as the year progressed. I would be having difficulty understanding how a concept related to me, and suddenly I would realize that the concept had been developed by a man to explain male behavior (or what is possibly worse, female behavior) and was now being explained to me by another man who, quite rightly, refused to attempt to translate it into feminine terms, but suggested that that had best be done by a woman. I found little to read in the area of psychology that spoke to my own experience as a woman.

At the same time, I was becoming increasingly involved with groups of women, both informal and formal, who shared their personal experiences freely, avidly. I began to gravitate towards the then infant (now healthily adult) Women's Studies program and towards the women poets, writers, artists, composers who were expressing our reality. Finally, I concluded that the least I could do toward developing a psychology and a body of literature that did speak to women was to write something of my own.

Although I wrote my thesis with this awareness, I was actually writing mostly for myself—to clear my own vision, to get as straight with myself as I could over the issues that concerned me. I did not expect very many people to read it, outside of my thesis committee, a few close friends, and perhaps some future graduate students who might be curious as to what a Psychology thesis was like. Assuming it would not have much exposure freed me, I think, to write more honestly, more personally, than if I had expected it to be read by large numbers of people.

In the year after I wrote it, however, I was asked to do some readings for various Women's Studies and Psychology classes. At first I was terrified of sharing my writing with strangers. I felt exposed, fearful of criticism or even ridicule. But once I got past my stagefright, I began to look forward to the readings, because they turned into such honest, personal exchanges that always left me turned on, eager to write more.

Some dedicated and energetic women mimeographed the thesis and it was distributed on campus. Copies found their way as far afield as Carbondale, Illinois, Cape Elizabeth, Maine, and even New Zealand, as people sent them to their friends and relatives. Needless to say, I was flattered by this response, but having just barely conquered my embarrassment at reading aloud from it, I found my complete loss of control over who read it and which sections they read to be as anxiety-producing as my first reading had been. It has taken me almost two years to let go of my thesis; to allow it to speak for itself and trust that it will not betray me.

Publishing it is the last step in this process of letting go, and as I do it, I am experiencing many of the same fears I felt when I began to write—do I dare to make the personal *this* public? But here I am answered by the wonderful realization that in the two years since I wrote it, the literature that I craved and couldn't find—the many and varied and, at the same time, strikingly similar stories of what it means to be a woman, has come fully into flower. No longer is it so strange to see these kinds of words in print; these sentences that unashamedly start with "I" and bravely explore the ambivalences and struggles inherent in growing up female.

I feel much moved to be part of such a flowering. My hope is that by publishing my thesis I may scatter some seeds which will sprout more words that describe our lives as they are really lived and felt, for we can never have enough of those.

Elizabeth Avakian
Petaluma, California
January, 1974

CONTENTS

And what I have to say is really distinct from the artist and art. It is the woman who has to speak. *And it is not only the woman Anaïs who has to speak, but I who have to speak for many women. As I discover myself, I feel I am merely one of many . . . The mute ones of the past, the inarticulate, who took refuge behind wordless intuitions; and the women of today, all action, and copies of men. And I, in between.*

—from *The Diary of Anaïs Nin*

Introduction

We are all giving birth to each other.

Anaïs Nin, December 1971

I used to think life went like this: you were born (why *you* and not somebody else I still don't know); you were a child for awhile doing child things; and then you entered the state of bliss called being a teenager, after which you went to college and got married (probably in that order) and became a grownup, at which time you began doing whatever it was you were going to be when you grew up—which for me, since I was a little girl, naturally included being a mommy, but, since I also came from a family of professionals with high expectations for their daughters, also included some kind of career. In those days, the age of twenty seemed a long time away, and, as far as I could see, any growing or changing or learning or exploring was all going to be done by then. At about the age of twenty, you became a grownup, which is to say, you died and went to the heaven of marriage and a career, where you lived quite happily and uneventfully ever after. I fully expected to be giving birth to children somewhere in my twenties, but I never expected to be giving birth to myself.

And yet that is the best way I can describe the painful, exciting, and apparently never-ending process of discovering who I really am underneath all these layers of accumulated disguises, and letting the real Elizabeth stand up and breathe. Everyone—at least everyone who hasn't accepted the static existence I once anticipated—experiences this struggle in some way. Paradoxically, women, the natural child-bearers, givers and sustainers of life, seem to have the hardest time giving birth to and nurturing themselves. That is, we have more difficulty finding out who we really are and then allowing ourselves to be the people we have discovered; because, in addition to all the rest of the expectations and patterns that are laid on children by adults, little girls are taught, by example and precept, that they exist *in relation to* men, that their most basic and important function, bearing and raising children, is to be fulfilled through a strong and lasting bond with a man. To enable us to find and keep this man, we are taught the art of relating—of subordinating our own needs to the needs of others, and in fact, of suppressing those parts of ourselves which might interfere with the fulfillment of our prescribed role.

"A woman should try to be whatever her man wants her to be," sings Marvin Gaye, and Anaïs Nin quotes Otto Rank in her *Diary:* "Man is always trying to create a woman who will fill his needs, and that makes her untrue to herself." My own struggle, and the struggle of many women I know to create ourselves, rather than be born of Adam's rib, is complicated by a desire to remain related—to continue to exist *in relation to* others, including male partners. I don't want to give up romantic love, intimacy, sex, or even motherhood for the right to be me, but often it is difficult not to compromise one for the other. This work is about my own continuing struggle with this problem, and I hope it will give some indication of how "we are all giving birth to each other," of how relationships with others can feed rather than stifle growth. With Anaïs, I believe that "woman does not forget . . . that everything that is born of her is planted in her."

I have quoted Anaïs Nin several times in this introduction, an indication of her importance for me right now in my attempt to keep track of who I am, how I feel, and where I'm going. I had started to keep a journal on a fairly regular basis before I picked up Volume One of her published *Diary*. As I write this, some five months later, I am still not quite finished with Volume Two, primarily because whenever I read the *Diaries,* I am seized by an overwhelming urge to write in my own, sometimes to respond directly to what she says, other times to reflect upon my experiences in the way she reflects upon hers.

When I met her recently at an Esalen-sponsored discussion group, I apologized for not having finished reading the *Diaries* (which I had fully intended to do before coming), and explained why. Her face lit up with pleasure: "Oh, but that's what I hoped would happen," she said. And instead of autographing a copy of one of the *Diary* volumes, she wrote her name and address into mine.

Anaïs, I have not written to you directly because I am so busy writing to your diary in my diary. And this, my thesis, is being written in my diary too, because it is the medium in which the seeds that are being planted by my dreams, your words, the words of my friends and lovers, current experiences and memories, germinate and begin to sprout. The diary is like a greenhouse, a warm, enclosed, safe place where new, tentatively emerging parts of my self can begin to grow.

By publishing your diary you have taught me the value of making the personal public, and in my thesis, I want to do just that—to transplant the seedlings from the diary into the open air, where they will have more room to grow and breathe and hopefully nourish others as well. I too want to publish my diary, although as I write that, I experience a tremor of fear. Do I really want to expose that much of myself? And who would want to read about *me,* anyway? I'm not famous and I don't have famous friends. But I had never heard of Anaïs before I read her *Diaries,* and she is important to me not because she knew Henry Miller and Lawrence Durrell, but because she is a woman writing very personally about the same questions I struggle with. And since none of the questions have final answers anyway, there is still plenty of room for all of us to write about them: questions such as, is it possible for me to live a full, rich, creative life without a deep, lasting relationship with a man? Or,on the other hand, is it possible to live such a life *with* one? What does having children mean to me? How would it change me, and what am I willing or not willing to sacrifice to fulfill my biological potential? How can women give each other energy and encouragement, instead of competing for male attention and protection, as we've done in the past? Who are the women I can look to for guidance and sustenance in my attempt to become more whole?

I don't really expect to provide the answers to these questions, but to share my thoughts about the conflicts they suggest and some of the ways I'm working to resolve them. For it is the story of a personal quest that I am writing, and as with all adventure stories, what happens along the way is at least as important as how it turns out. In fact, what happens along the way is all there is to tell.

MEN TRAVEL: WOMEN HAVE LOVE AFFAIRS

I am caught today by the image of man as wanderer and adventurer as opposed to the image of woman as stationary, confined within the home. Perhaps this is where our self-limitation begins–with the archetypal image of woman as keeper of the hearth.

from my journal, 3/19/72

"A woman's place . . ."

We all know how that one ends. Archaic though it sounds in these days of women's liberation, it expresses a deeply rooted cultural expectation that sets psychological as well as physical boundaries to woman's experience. Not only does it imply that I am to devote my life to the care and feeding of my husband and children, but it tells me that I must keep my "place," thereby limiting my aspirations, cutting me off from feeling the possibilities within me for creativity and adventure.

> I am restless. Adventure is pulling me out. When a man feels this, it is no crime, but let a woman feel this and there is an outcry.
>
> Nin, II, 46

Adventure means moving out—beyond the limits of the familiar, the safe, the known. It is exciting and dangerous and exhilarating. It involves risk and struggle, and it tests the limits of one's strength, endurance, ingenuity. Although it may be fashionable, as well as accurate, to equate the "inner quest" with the old-fashioned, swashbuckling, heroic romance, the imagery of the quest, the struggle, the adventure, remains masculine, leaving woman no model with which to identify. For in all the old adventure stories, it is the man who is the mover, the doer, the wanderer, the seeker, the hero. Woman, if she is good, supports and encourages, waits patiently and faithfully; or, if she is bad, entangles, bewitches, tempts or betrays, but whether she is good or bad, always, always stays in one place. And, on either the psychic or the physical level, staying in one place suggests safety and security at the price of stagnation and decay.

It feels as if part of what keeps women—myself included—from all kinds of adventuring, growing, risking, testing, and defining ourselves against outside reality as men do, is this imagery which pervades our culture. We see ourselves at best as the beautiful mortal visited by the masculine god in animal form at night—the unconscious recipient of the divine seed—giving birth to genius without ever conceiving in the mind what we conceive in the womb. We are Calypso hiding Odysseus in her cave until he has the strength to venture forth again, then helping him to continue his journey home; and Penelope, waiting patiently for

struggle is a state of movement
a search for life and curiosity to
believe in unknowns

his return, faithful despite the persistence of the suitors during the twenty years of his absence. At worst, we are Circe, turning men to swine by arousing their passions; Delilah, sapping Samson's strength with sex; Hera scheming to punish Zeus for his infidelity; Lady Macbeth, invoking the spirits to strip her of her femininity that she may spur her husband on to murder for power. Always the beautiful is she who is chaste—and chased—or at least discreet and undemanding. Feminine power is most often used to bind, manipulate, control, and is therefore seen as ugly. Is there no other choice? Where is the positive image of the adventurous, powerful woman that will encourage us to move out, to leave the protected safety of the dolls' houses our men have built for us, the walls that have become our prisons?

This imagery exists not only in mythology and classical literature; it pervades pop culture as well. In modern novels and rock music, man is active, aggressive, mobile. He's the fox, the midnight creeper, the easy rider, the backdoor man, the whistling gypsy. He can stick his thumb out on any highway and be gone before he knows where he's going. Wherever he is can be home until it gets too tight, too constricting—then he's gone again. It is an image of freedom and self-sufficiency, of lonely strength and irresponsibility. How many novels are there like *On the Road,* written by and about men? There are few picaresque heroines, but how many wandering heroes and anti-heroes, from Tom Jones to Frodo Baggins; how many songs like Dylan's bitter, sarcastic, "Don't Think Twice," or its complement, Buffy Ste. Marie's ballad of the "liberated" woman, gracefully accepting the inevitability of her lover's eventual departure, "Until It's Time For You To Go."

And what of the woman, she who waits, passive, stationary, alone in her house, who waits to receive the wanderer, to feel for an instant a connection with adventure, mystery, danger? For her it must all be contained within their sexual union—in the moment of male climax when she will receive his strength, his seed, and possibly his child to keep for when he will go away again.

There is an idealized picture of this union in Steve Miller's "Baby's House." A woman sits alone in a colorless house: and is attracted by the song of a young wanderer passing by her window. His song is the song of the free spirit with no ties to anyone. He can come and go as he pleases.

She receives him, and he brings her to life: temporarily ending her loneliness.

The woman finds life and meaning through the man and child, and, according to Miller, she is happy—filled and fulfilled by the wanderer who is "born to be free." There is no hint of the hardship and struggle that is to follow as she remains alone to care for the child after he has gone his "easy" way. This is a man's song, written out of an imperfect understanding of woman's experience.

If you listen to The Joy of Cooking, a fine rock band led by two strong women, who have left the kitchen for the joy of cooking musically, you hear the woman's side of the story, sung in deep, throaty harmonies; the wistful fantasy and painful reality of women who have sought fulfillment through men, as well as the determination and strength of the woman who is ready to move out on her own.

In "Red Wine at Noon," the rich woman with "everything money can buy" sings of her absent husband and her empty life:

The man that I married,
He travels in Europe,
He brings me back presents
From over the sea.

He meets with officials
And shakes hands with strangers,
And comes home to visit me.

The song paints a poignant picture of an aging, once-vital woman, deceived by the American dream of what is supposed to bring women happiness, a dream which has left her lonely and bored, drinking "White wine in the morning sun/Red wine at noon." The wine and her wealth are all that separate her from the poverty-stricken woman of "Too Late, But Not Forgotten," whose song begins with these images of stagnation and immobility:

Low tide, river gone down,
Got no car to drive into town,
And the dry wind blows
Through the cracks in the walls,
And out in the trees
A forgotten bird calls.

There is the hint of a lost hope for something better:

New light, a silhouette,
Something that I never could get . . .

And the silhouette sharpens into a memory of the man who is gone:

And I remember you, daddy,
When you stood in the door,
Crazy with whiskey
And askin' for one more.

I see him standing in the doorway, ready to split, laughing, charming in his craziness. Who could resist that magic; who could refuse him "one more"—of anything? I always hear in those lines the conception of their child; the baby who is still with her long after he has left, to remind her of him; the baby, who keeps growing like the "corn . . . in the sunshine," who now ties her irrevocably to the house—her prison and her fragile protection from the extremes of weather. Trapped inside the reality which grew from the dream she once believed, she denies herself any further foolish dreams, even as she reveals that she still hasn't let go of the old one:

Dreams go, but memories keep,
Today I'm wishin' for a good night's sleep,
And the only thing that I ever did need,
Was a good man's lovin' and a baby to feed.
. . .

Too late, but not forgotten,
And the storms keep blowin' up the river . . .
Time's gone and the baby keeps growin'
And I can't help knowin'
Daddy, I loved you . . .

Somehow, it feels as if her strength lies in her very vulnerability to the changing seasons, the storms and droughts without and within. Even as she is swept downstream by forces she cannot control, she is in contact with those forces, with the basic life rhythms, just as she is in contact with her own feelings, her pain and her loss.

I have the sense that she is rooted to the ground in a way that her man is not—that those roots are limiting, keeping her stuck in one place, a forgotten bird, singing in a tree —but also that they keep her in touch with reality in a way that he may never be. The difference between the depth of her experience and his is the difference between the deeply moving quality of this song and the superficiality of the Steve Miller song.

I had a similar feeling the night I had a group of women over to talk about how they had dealt with unplanned pregnancies. In every case, whether the woman had kept her child and raised it alone, or given it up for adoption, or arranged to have an abortion, having taken responsibility for another human life had changed her, transformed her, so that she was no longer a child but a woman; whereas the men, who, without exception, had run away from the responsibility, had apparently remained little boys.

To be sensitive, responsible, caring, involved with someone else is to change and grow yourself. Hesse wrote of this in *Narcissus and Goldmund* when he described the wandering Goldmund's feelings about his chaste sojourn with Lydia:

> Sometimes Goldmund asked himself why he had not left long ago. . . . Why was he staying and accepting it all, all these entanglements and confused emotions? . . . Had he not the right of the homeless, of the non-possessing, to extricate himself from these delicate complications and to laugh at them? . . . And yet . . . he not only put up with it, but was secretly happy to do so. It was foolish, difficult, a strain to live this way, but it was also wonderful . . . and he felt he himself had become another person in these few weeks: much older; not more intelligent, yet more experienced; not happier, yet much more mature, much richer in his soul. He was no longer a boy.

With the freedom to split, the ability to disengage, comes superficiality of experience, shallowness, an atrophy of feeling. And men are, for the most part, more cut off from their feelings than are women, both a cause and an effect of the ability to split.

Perhaps it is this too that I fear when I fear the adventurous life: In addition to the real challenges and dangers that may be waiting for me, and the difficulty of finding a positive image of feminine power to model myself upon, and the fear that I will no longer be loved, for, as Anaïs says, "no one has ever loved an adventurous woman as they have loved adventurous men," there is also the fear that I will become cut off from deep feeling, from sustaining and sustained relationships, that I will live superficially with many instead of intimately with one, that I will have no home, no center, no children. I wonder if it is necessary to sacrifice one for the other; to sever ties, destroy relationships, remain alone and disconnected, in order to remain true to myself and my own quest.

I take courage from women like Anaïs who seem to be able to move out, create, venture into unknown territory, without sacrificing the deep connections, intimate relationships, without becoming shallow or uncaring. In fact, her adventures seem to lead her into deeper levels of experience rather than away from them. She writes in Volume Two:

> Henry's creation (*Tropic of Capricorn*) at times resembles insanity, because it is experience disconnected from feeling. . . . Where are the deep sources of feeling in my father and in Henry which life succeeded in atrophying? Why is it that I never get cut off from pity, sympathy, participation, in spite of the fact that I am living out my own dream, my interior vision . . . I listen to all, I hear all that is said . . . I am open to wounds, open to love. I am rooted to my devotions, I am never separate, never cut off, never blind, deaf, absent . . .

Nin, II, 269

I see women around me living out their dreams without losing touch with others: Corrine, the woman I live with, developing her own classes in women's studies and batik, making her home into a weaving studio, learning the "masculine" craft of carpentry and teaching it to her girl students so that they can build their own looms. She ventures out of her home, but does not leave it; it is becoming the site of new projects rather than a museum for old achievements or a cemetery for old dreams. And still she maintains close and deep ties with the man she lives with, her child, her women friends.

And I think of Geri, my co-student in the M.A. program, so much stronger than her delicate form suggests at first; her very feminine quality lending itself to quiet and effective leadership; so creative with her needles, yarns, patches, pies, fantasies and images, taking her domestic arts beyond her home, her inner world beyond her journal, to share with others; always learning, always teaching what she knows so naturally, you hardly know you're being taught.

And J.J., the generating and sustaining spirit behind the Women's Studies Program at Sonoma State, whose endless supply of energy has become infectious to epidemic proportions; who draws out each person's unique creativity with her absolute faith and vibrant enthusiasm; whose thoughtful criticism always takes that creativity seriously; whose wit always stings in the right spot; who can comprehend madness, suicide and hope; who leads naturally by doing; and in whose presence egos fall away in the excitement of collective creation. From J.J. I am learning how the process can become the goal; how the heart can inform the mind, and how the mind can make space for the heart to be heard; how love and work and life need not be separate; how a woman can be articulate and receptive, inclusive and critical, witty and caring, in touch with darkness, alive with light.

There are so many more I could name who point a way for me to go, or rather share the road with me, for all of us are venturing together now. My heroines are not the women I can't hope to touch, but those whose hands I already feel in mine, who let me see their confusion as well as their strength. When The Joy of Cooking tells me to "Stretch out and find my own way out the door," I'm ready to listen, to catch their energy and go, because I've heard their blues; I know they've felt my pain.

Woman does not have to become the carefree adventurer man has been, turning her back on suffering, pain love —feeling, in all its forms and dimensions. Sallie Soladay, Gloria Steinem, Kay Boyle, Judy Grahn, Bernadette Devlin, Angela Davis, Susan and Joanna Griffin, the women poets and critics who read at Anaïs Nin's Celebration, my own friends are all giving me hope that it is possible to be strong, adventurous, powerful in a masculine world while remaining feminine, connected, caring.

LIFE AS VICARIOUS EXPERIENCE

I wanted to be married to an artist, rather than be one.

Anaïs Nin, 1, 82

Living through a Man

I used to think a woman
Was just made to love a man;
That a man was someone for a woman
To hold onto while she can.
Then one day my man walked out,
Oh, you know I got the blues.
I'd been livin' off him for so long,
I had nothin' of my own to lose.

The Joy of Cooking,
"Only Time Will Tell Me"

It feels as if part of the difficulty I have had in knowing who I am and what I want has been due to the notion, planted in me quite early, that I was not to find my self by exercising my talents, my intellect, my capabilities, or by following my natural curiosities and interests, but by finding a man who would do all this for me. In the first chapter of this book, I spoke of "atrophy of feeling" in men; the corresponding malady in women might be called "atrophy of identity," and it seems to come from focusing our energies on finding and keeping a man rather than, and often in direct opposition to, developing our own strengths.

Finding oneself and realizing one's potential is, at best, a long and difficult process, but it becomes almost impossible when it is not encouraged by your environment, and it can be a source of great confusion and frustration when it is simultaneously encouraged and discouraged, so that your energies are constantly being pulled in opposite directions. I have experienced this frustration, as have many other women whose families set higher expectations than "just" the role of wife and mother for their daughters, yet expect them to become wives and mothers in addition to whatever else they do. We are urged to develop our talents and abilities, to pursue professional careers, to be people in our own right, but we are also impressed with the importance of finding a man and settling down. In fact, no matter how well we do in our professional lives, we are regarded with concern, pity, and disappointment if we are not married and raising a family. It is difficult to take one's own career seriously when it is apparently of secondary importance to marriage and motherhood, and may, in fact, have to be suspended indefinitely should those possibilities present themselves.

To be sure, I never expected to be "just a housewife." My mother was a high school teacher, and did not give up her career for her children, partly because her mother lived with us. I think I must have taken it for granted that most mothers had some identity outside of the home. There is a story related to this that my parents tell about my younger sister. Alice rode to nursery school in a van which picked her up on our corner. Usually my father would wait with her, and one day the nursery school teacher, having noticed my father's brief-case, asked my sister what her daddy did for a living. Alice, not really understanding (if she had, in fact, been told) what a physicist was, said she didn't know, that he was "just a daddy." The teacher, hoping to draw her out, suggested several possible professions—a lawyer, accountant, salesman. Alice became more and more upset at her inability to answer. Finally she burst out, almost in tears, "My mommy's a *teacher,* but my daddy's just a *plain, ordinary, daddy!"* At this point, a little boy, who had been listening, said sympathetically, "Don't be afraid, Alice—my daddy's a doctor, but my mommy's just a plain, ordinary mommy." Neither of them knew, I guess, that his situation was far more usual and acceptable.

But it wasn't until I began going to school, that I discovered there were such things as plain, ordinary mommies—women who stayed home all day to cook, clean, and care for their children. I won't say that I didn't envy those children somewhat. Although I was proud of the fact that my mother was a teacher, I often wished that she could be at home more, and that she would be less tired, more available to me when she was. Also, having two mothers was often confusing, and I think I felt some wistful longing on her part to be more fully into the role of mother, more in charge of the home, less divided between domesticity, which I know she enjoys, and work. This feeling was confirmed recently in a letter she wrote to her sister and brother in which she finally made known her resentment of her favored position and the difficulty she had experienced in trying to mediate between a career, a husband, two children, and her mother, not to mention her own needs, which usually didn't get mentioned. In fact, rather than providing me with a model for an independent life in addition to a home and family, my mother actually demonstrated a tremendous capacity for self-sacrifice and accommodation to the needs of others; and it is this denial of self that I have always associated with both motherhood and womanhood, and that I have to work hard to overcome in order to be who I am.

I've also had to cope with the contradictory expectations that are placed on intelligent women in our culture. At home I was encouraged to use my mind, develop my talents, and strive for excellence in all I did. I was given piano and dance lessons, taken to the theatre and museums, read to and given books. I was expected to do well in school and was never dressed up in ruffles or bows or pastels. My father talked to me about science and politics, and although my mother never seemed quite as well-informed as he in our dinner table discussions, I don't think I got the impression that she played dumb to please him; it seemed, rather, that the smarter you were, the better you were, and the more praise and approval you were likely to get.

This changed, however, as I approached adolescence —that magic age I had looked forward to all my life. Although my intelligence and industriousness continued to be rewarded by my parents and teachers, my peers, who were more important to me now, did not react to my eloquence or high grades with affection and admiration. I began to feel out of it for listening to folk or classical music, rather than rock 'n roll, and for reading books instead of watching T.V. My teenage diaries were full of self-castigation for my failure to get with it. I would make little progress reports—"I think I like rock and roll a little more now," and "I'm trying not to talk so much in class." I had become convinced that the reason I wasn't having any dates was that my brains scared boys away. I noticed that the most popular girls were those who knew how to flirt and dress, who could be entertaining in a kind of light, intriguing way, who made boys feel important, clever, powerful. Smart girls could be popular too—especially if they were pretty—but they had to be discreet about their intelligence. As Marya Mannes says in her essay, "On the Problems of Creative Women,"

> At school the brilliant, intense girl student with dreams in her head isn't going to get the boys unless her attractions are strong enough to deceive them. In this case, she will probably get the wrong boys, for the right boys won't be ready for her.

Whereas at home, my intelligence and verbal ability had been valued, at school, where the object was to be "in" and to "get" boys, those very qualities seemed to get in my way. And the importance of "getting" boys is not to be underestimated. Although my parents never expressed disappointment in what I considered to be my retarded social development, I was sure they were secretly mortified. After all, not only did every teenage romance, every T.V. situation comedy, every popular song depict the normal teenage girl as pretty, popular, and slightly stupid, but the implication was that all this boy-chasing was simply a preparation for the man-hunt that was to follow, leading eventually to the capture of a husband and a lifetime of married bliss.

At fifteen, I felt my awkwardness and lack of popularity so acutely that I became convinced it would always be this way and that no one would ever want to marry me. Consequently, I went around telling everyone that I planned never to marry; I was going to have a career and travel and generally be independent. I'm sure many adults must have seen through my defensive posture, but all too often, instead of simply accepting my statement at face value, they would tell me I would surely change my mind when the right man came along; that I would eventually want to settle down, and have children, just as they had. The result of all this reassurance was to make me feel even more dismal—obviously, being a career woman *wasn't* an acceptable alternative to marriage in anyone's eyes. There would be no way to cover my failure as a woman.

As captain of the debating team and president of the honor society, I already felt like a failure. For far from being an early forerunner of women's lib, refusing to compromise myself to fit the popular teen image, I would have given anything to be a cheerleader, to belong to a sorority, to go to dances with handsome athletes. It was just that I couldn't, for the life of me, break into that world, nor could I completely suppress my intellect and leadership capabilities. I continued to achieve in spite of myself. I often wonder how much more I might have grown, done, accomplished, if I hadn't been fighting myself all the way; if I had been a boy, perhaps, instead of a girl.

And I don't think I am alone in this. A now famous study conducted by Dr. Matina Horner, Professor of Psychology and President of Radcliffe College, indicates that large numbers of women actually fear academic and professional success and that this fear is clearly linked to anxiety about loss of femininity and attractiveness to men. The study found that women, especially intelligent women from homes that valued high achievement, were thrown into a tailspin of anxiety at the prospect of success, and that this happened most dramatically around their junior year in college, when it became most apparent that "femininity and academic achievement are incompatible," and that if a girl is to find a husband (her parents' real reason for sending her to college), she must "reverse her appetite for human fulfillment" and not succeed too well at the academic game. Men apparently do not share this fear of success, because for them "human fulfillment and masculine fulfillment are one and the same."

Why should we have to choose between human fulfillment and feminine fulfillment? The necessity for this choice seems to be built on the assumption that in male-female relationships, the woman is to subordinate herself to the man, to accommodate herself to his needs, to be consistently available and supportive, to care for the home so that he can pursue his studies and/or career, to put the development of her own interests and career second, and, on a less tangible but no less significant level, to protect his ego by not achieving more than he does.

The easiest way to do this is to simply give up any notion of self or separate identity and put all of your energy into pleasing a man, taking care of his needs, and receiving in exchange (assuming you've found a "good" man), love, appreciation, economic security, and a vicarious identity. Not only does this stance eliminate the conflicts that would inevitably arise were you to try to fulfill *both* his needs and yours, but it also eliminates the existential dilemma of what to do with your life, and the hard work and struggle involved in trying to achieve something on your own. Moreover, the notion of vicarious identity seems to be built right into the institution of marriage; when I married, I stopped being Elizabeth Sucher and became Mrs. Robert Avakian—I had literally exchanged my identity for my husband's. The line of least resistance seems to be to give up the struggle for self-actualization, come in out of the cold, and keep the home fires burning, while your man does your living for you.

The only problem is, it doesn't work. My own is a case in point: About the time I was to graduate from college, I almost had a severe identity crisis. In all the years I had been going to school, I had never had to worry about who I was or what I was doing—I was a student, an English major, I was going to school. That was enough. Now I was faced with the prospect of graduation, a B.A. degree and not the slightest notion of what I wanted to do next. I talked vaguely of going to Europe, but I was actually frightened of travelling alone and had no money. Besides I knew that was just a stopgap; eventually I'd have to face up to the question of what I was going to do with the rest of my life. The crisis never fully materialized, however, because I immediately got married, thereby eliminating any necessity for further decision-making (or so I thought).

I returned to the English Department at the University of California (from which I had just graduated with highest honors) as a Clerk-Typist I, answering the phone, typing, and distributing mail, so that my husband could finish his B.A. and prepare himself for medical school, and eventually psychiatry. Now, I had once thought about becoming a psychiatrist myself, but had not had enough confidence in my own ability to follow through with the daydream. Also, there was that nagging feeling that somewhere along the line I'd get sidetracked by some man and give it all up anyway. But here was the perfect solution; by putting Bob through medical school, I could become a psychiatrist by proxy.

Of course, it didn't work out that way. Bob soon dropped out of college to become a full-time politico, and I naturally became resentful of having to support him by doing mindless, degrading work while he did something that was meaningful to him. Even after I began teaching high school the following year, I continued to have the feeling that he was living a life that made sense to him (working for *Ramparts* magazine as a researcher and doing political work besides), while I was struggling to keep house for the two of us and survive each day in the classroom, without really being sure that I wanted to be in either place. I vaguely thought about going back to school to become a psychotherapist of some sort, and I quite irrationally blamed the marriage for preventing me.

As Bob's politics became increasingly radical and his public manner more arrogant and uncompromising, I became more and more uncomfortable in the marriage. In exchange for giving up my own identity, I was supposed to receive love, appreciation, security, and a public image I could feel proud of. Only I wasn't feeling very secure with Bob's new revolutionary stance, I was often embarrassed or disturbed by his public pronouncements, and it was getting harder and harder to play the supportive, encouraging wife, when I really didn't agree with what he was doing. It was at this point, I think, that I realized that I did have a self that was quite separate, distinct, and different from his; a self that was finally demanding to be heard. Once I began to listen, I could no longer stay with Bob; we separated, and were eventually divorced.

Given the direction Bob's life took and the differences that developed between us, it is unlikely that our marriage could have held together in any case. But it shocks me to realize how much I had looked to him to give my life direction; how much of my own ego was at stake in whatever he did or said; how much power I gave him to succeed or fail for me, and how deadly that would be to any relationship. For not only does a woman weaken herself and stifle her own development when she tries to live through a man; she can't really let him alone to develop as he needs to either. Because I've looked to men to provide me with purpose and direction, I've had a strong tendency to try to manipulate them, to make them into the kinds of men I wanted to identify with.

I call this my "Lady Macbeth syndrome." Rather than get in touch with my own masculine strength and use it for me, I try to get my man to do what I'm afraid to do. If he succeeds, I can bask in his reflected glory (although I don't have the satisfaction that comes with knowing *I* did it). I admire him, try to please him, am constantly anxious that I will lose him. But if all my attention is focused on him, if I have no life or concerns of my own, I am likely to lose him, for a strong man has no need of a selfless woman. On the other hand, if he fails to live up to my expectations for him, I am disappointed in him, scornful, contemptuous—Lady Macbeth before the first murder. I generally get bitchy, nasty, impossible for either of us to live with, and am likely to leave him. Either way, the relationship and I are both doomed.

Trying to manipulate your man to live his life in a way that will justify your own existence is a little like trying to drive a car from the back or the "suicide" seat; in fact this image often appears in my dreams when I'm feeling the loss of control which comes with such once-removed living. To live by remote control is to give up real control over your own direction and movement, and this is indeed a kind of suicide, especially since you also give up the joy of active participation in life. Another dream image comes to mind here; the other side of Lady Macbeth—the sleepwalker. I sometimes dream of women who passively allow their lives to happen to them. I am most often a spectator in these dreams, even further removed from direct participation. One night I dreamt that we were living under a totalitarian regime, and that I was pushed into a tiny corner of my bedroom by a mob that had taken over our house. I couldn't order them to leave because I was afraid of sounding "like a bitchy schoolteacher"—I couldn't imagine a positive, feminine way of asserting myself. Finally the crowd thinned and two gangsters from the government came in looking for a young, slim, dark-haired girl who was lying on my bed, dead. As they picked her up, I asked if I could read the scroll she was holding, which I knew was her suicide note. It was a very moving poem, both political and personal, written by someone in a trance, who knows that she will be dead by nightfall. The poem and the girl reminded me of Charlotte Cordet, as she was played by the somnambulistic mental patient in *Marat/Sade*. I felt that she and I were both passive victims of a masculine dictatorship—that we had given up the right to live in order to conform to the dictates of a male world; she, by sleep-walking her way to suicide, I, by refusing to assert my right to my full living space, by failing to live out all that I am.

D. H. Lawrence writes of this suicidal dream state in *The Fox,* where March, the strong, "masculine" woman, is almost completely hypnotized into submission by "the boy."

> He wanted her to commit herself to him, and to put her independent spirit to sleep . . . He wanted to take away her consciousness, and make her just his woman. Just his woman. And she was so tired, so tired like a child that wants to go to sleep, but which fights against sleep as if sleep were death. She seemed to stretch her eyes wide in the obstinate effort and tension of keeping awake. She *would* keep awake. She *would* know . . . She *would* have the reins of her own life between her own hands. She *would* be an independent woman . . . But she was so tired . . . And there was so much rest in the boy.

Anaïs Nin says that women have had a tendency "not to merge but to *submerge* their personalities in those of their men." Often men encourage this—even demand it—and that makes it all the easier to curl up and fall asleep in them. It is like falling asleep in snow, so easy and so deadly, so deceptively temporary, and so final. But if you listen to your dreams, you may wake up in time.

Living for and through others often extends beyond the realm of man-woman relationships into the world of work. Women who pursue professional careers find themselves underpaid for working overtime at the same old job—taking care of the physical and emotional needs of others, or, in other words . . .

Being a Professional Woman

"Those who can, do; those who can't, teach."

". . . and it's such a good job for a woman."

The only professions I've ever seriously considered have been teaching or counseling. It is difficult for me to imagine doing (or being) anything else. Within those fields, I have never felt capable of becoming more than a high school teacher, a social worker, or a counselor. At one time, I vaguely considered becoming a psychiatrist, but didn't feel capable of successfully completing the scientific, not to mention medical, training required. I was urged by several of my college professors to go on for a Ph.D. in English and aim for a college teaching position, but I neither considered myself a serious enough scholar to attempt such a lengthy course of study, nor could I imagine that I would ever be able to lecture authoritatively to a college class about anything.

What caused me to limit my view of my potential this way? Although I have always done very well in school, I have neither valued my intellect very highly nor had much confidence in it. My intellect was my nemesis as an adolescent, and I wanted to have as little to do with it then as possible. Moreover, my father is both extremely bright and completely unassuming about his intelligence; since he has always been my yardstick for measuring intellectual ability, and since he never seemed convinced that he was especially smart, how could I think that I was? In addition, I've always valued the realm of feeling more highly than the thinking realm, and I think this preference was probably encouraged, because women are supposed to be more sensitive, intuitive, caring, than they are rational, objective. I've always assumed that my talents lay in relating to other people, and since that is the part of myself that I and others have valued and cultivated, my talents probably do lie mainly in that direction.

Finally, I was raised in an atmosphere of concern for the well-being of the world at large; I have always felt very personally responsible for social and political conditions and still feel strong internal pressure to pursue a socially useful career. Obviously, there are numerous ways in which one can be socially useful, but I have always seen myself as best able to help on an individual, interpersonal basis, and this assumption has been reinforced by what Margaret Adams, in an article reprinted in *Psychology Today,* calls the "compassion trap":

> that pervasive social philosophy that believes that woman's primary social function is to provide tenderness and compassion . . . the insidious notion that the needs of others should be woman's major, if not exclusive concern.

The notion was perpetuated by seeing working women only in servile or helping roles (waitress, domestic, secretary, nurse, teacher, social worker, etc.) and was reinforced by my most important female role model, my mother, a woman who always put the needs of the other members of her family first and divided her time between attending to us and ministering to her students as a teacher and speech therapist.

My limited view of my career choices was, to a large degree, culturally programmed, not just in that society views the "helping professions" as appropriate for women, but in that it insures that they will remain appropriate by encouraging women to develop those traits which lend themselves most easily to those professions. As the future protectors and nurturers of not only our own children, but the world at large, we are taught the

> virtue of subordinating individual needs to the welfare of others and the personal value and supposed reward of vicarious satisfaction from this exercise.
>
> Adams

Moreover, we have developed our intuitive capacities to a high degree, largely for their survival value, in that

> when women's satisfactions depend on the skillful manipulation of other persons' well-being, it is incumbent upon them to develop a finely calibrated skill for tuning in to the needs and moods of those individuals.

I got so good at tuning in to those moods and feelings that my therapist in Berkeley used to turn my chair so that I couldn't see him, to break me of the habit of trying to accommodate myself to his responses and get me to pay attention to my own feelings.

The "helping professions," in which women have most commonly been employed, make use of our nurturing skills—our ability to sacrifice our own needs for the needs of others, to intuit, to understand, to sympathize. They emphasize an ability to relate rather than think, to acquiesce rather than compete, and often involve not only subordinating our personal needs to the needs of our clients or students but to our male supervisors as well. Ms. Adams points out that often social workers and teachers have backed down from striking to procure higher wages or better working conditions out of concern for the immediate well-being of their clients or students, even though in the long run, all would have been better off if the women professionals had demanded that their own legitimate needs be met.

Not only are we unused to viewing our own needs as legitimate, we are almost incapable of making demands on anybody. We have been taught to be submissive and obedient, and by the time we are grown, an active, aggressive stance is foreign to us, having long ago been designated unfeminine.

This was brought home to me quite strongly when I attended a meeting of the predominantly male staff of the Sonoma State College Counseling Center with a group of women, all of whom were concerned that the center hire a full-time woman counselor for next year. (At that time, there was no full-time woman on a staff that included four full-time and several part-time men, although more women than men came to the center for counseling.) The staff had just been pressured into agreeing to hire a Chicano by a group of Chicano men who were very forceful and uncompromising in their approach. Although we were firmly convinced that the counseling center was as much (if not more) in need of a woman as it was in need of a Chicano, we presented our case very mildly and politely, sympathizing with both the difficulties faced by the staff and the needs of the Chicanos. As a result, we won the gratitude and appreciation of the male counselors, but not the assurance that they would hire a full-time woman. We were apparently not willing, as the Chicano men had been, to risk hostility or disapproval to get what we had presumably come for, and even if we had been willing to take such a risk, the reaction might have been so intensely negative as to render the approach ineffective, since it *is* so much less acceptable for women to be assertive and demanding.

Our difficulty in asserting ourselves not only limits the power we wield in our jobs; it also limits the kinds of jobs we can conceive of doing. Law, for example, would be an unlikely choice, partly because it requires an aggressive, combative style, incompatible with being a "lady."

Moreover, most women don't value their own careers or their minds enough to demand the extended periods of concentration necessary to becoming a lawyer, doctor, or college professor. In the words of Marya Mannes, herself a successful writer:

> A man at his desk in a room with a closed door is a man at work. A woman at a desk in any room is available.

Women have consistently chosen teaching over writing as their way of passing along knowledge and skills, not simply because it is more enjoyable, but because

> personal, concretely focused activities do not require the same kind of single-minded concentration that writing and other creative ventures require, and they suffer less from the interruption of external activities.

Perhaps the current burgeoning interest in crafts among women (weaving, crochet, macramé, etc.) is due partly to their adaptability as creative outlets; a woman can embroider in a room full of people, listen to another's problems at the same time, and put her embroidery down at a moment's notice to attend to a screaming child, only to pick it up again later with little or no loss of continuity in the creative process.

Writing, on the other hand, is hard intellectual work, requiring continuous periods of concentrated effort, something women usually find hard to come by. In the words of a local lady poet, Ann Greene:

> Virginia Woolf was right about that room with the padlock. . . . I know you love me and my children and I love you and your children and your friends and my Doctor but I have to lock you out you're all so distracting. . . .

Another poet friend, Lynn Sukenick, suggested to me that not only is a woman constantly being interrupted by people who feel they have a right to her attention at any time, but she frequently interrupts herself mentally, trying to keep all the strands of her life straight, all her obligations met; thinking about a short story gets cut off by thoughts of what she must remember to get at the supermarket for dinner, what time the kids have to be picked up from school, and so forth.

I have experienced enormous difficulty in writing this book, not the least of which has been my own lack of confidence that I have anything important to say or the ability to say it, a problem which I think I share with many other women. But I also find it extremely difficult to closet myself away with my writing when there are other people in the house demanding attention. The demand, of course, comes from my own notion that I should be available at all times as the sociable hostess, attentive friend, supportive helpmate, etc.

Anaïs Nin gave Henry Miller her typewriter and bought a printing press for Gonzalo, even though she wanted one to publish her own work. I often think of her when I am writing on my bed because Jeffrey is using the desk (of course, *his* writing is more important than mine because he wants to be A WRITER, while I harbor no such grandiose ideas about myself), or when I drop whatever I'm doing to listen to something he's written, while I, on the other hand, rarely make similar demands on him.

Self-effacing, blushing modesty is certainly one of the most highly cultivated feminine traits, but at this point, it clearly stands in the way of my growth. Shakespeare expressed this dilemma in dramatic terms when he had the heroines of his comedies, all of whom are far superior to their male counterparts, dress up as men to engage in some activity they couldn't perform as women. In every case, the woman has great reserves of "masculine" fortitude, courage, and wit, but is prevented from using them by social convention. Once she appears as a man, she is free to express her masculine side, and the combination of her feminine charm and sensibility and her masculine intelligence and daring prove unbeatable.

A good example is *The Merchant of Venice,* in which Portia disguises herself as a young lawyer to save the life of the man she loves, a weak individual who is nowhere near being her emotional or intellectual equal. She assumes a masculine disguise and role to plead her lover's case, trying first to move Shylock to pity with her "quality of mercy" speech. Shylock is beyond compassion, however, and she is finally forced to fight on male terms, cleverly devising the strategem of requiring Shylock to take his pound of flesh without spilling one drop of blood. Shylock runs howling with rage from the courtroom, foiled by his own insistence on the letter of the law, and Shakespeare has made a strong case against the masculine, objective ideal.

Shakespeare knew that women really are capable of more than hand-holding and dictation-taking. And he also knew that a woman in touch with her feelings and her intellect is both powerful and irresistible. This suggests to me the exciting possibility that as women enter those fields formerly dominated by men—the legal, medical, political, executive, academic—they may actually transform them, humanize them. I already see this happening in the divorce counseling center where I work, in that while helping people with the legal process of obtaining a dissolution of marriage, we also give them a place to explore their feelings about the marriage and its breakup and to work out the unfinished emotional as well as practical business that almost always accompanies a divorce. By bringing feeling into those realms that have been dominated and controlled by the insanity of logic disconnected from feeling; by getting personal about what has before been strictly business, perhaps we can realize Varda's vision of "Women Reconstructing the World." As women we can, in Anaïs' words, "put together all that is divided and give birth to all that was killed" starting with our selves.

THE MYTH OF FULFILLMENT THROUGH MOTHERHOOD

The image of woman as giver of life is an image of great power; but its counter-image, the ideal of the mother as selfless, living for and through the fruit of her womb, can be a heavy obstacle to self-realization. I want to deal with these images and their implications for myself and other women, because even though I am not a mother and have never conceived a child, the motherhood myth has so dominated my life, has influenced and shaped my behavior in so many ways, and continues to absorb so much of my thought, that I cannot leave it out.

When I thought about motherhood both in relation to myself and to the theme of self-realization, the subject seemed to fall quite naturally into two distinct parts, each with its appropriate mode of expression. First, there were my ideas about the obstacles to self-fulfillment inherent in motherhood. These I have grouped under the heading "The Jewish Mother Syndrome." The other section deals with my fantasies about motherhood, and as such is much more personal, emotional, subjective.

The Jewish Mother Syndrome

> Had a really nice rap with Phil (my supervisor in the Counseling Center) today . . . He told me I wasn't at all like his stereotype of a Jewish woman-—domineering, bitchy, and/or chicken-soupy. I told him I'd had a hard time breaking out of the chicken soup bag. We theorized on the origins of that pattern in Jewish women. I told him I thought part of it was the emphasis on learning and using the mind in Jewish homes, often with no real outlets for feminine intellectual ability—so the women use all that brain power and energy to control their kids and husbands."
>
> —from my journal, 3/21/72

It's well known that you don't have to be Jewish to be a Jewish mother. The over-protective, anxious, nosy, domineering, self-pitying "noodge," forcing you to eat more than is good for you, hurt if you don't, constantly reminding you of all the sacrifices she has cheerfully made for you, worrying herself sick if you should—God forbid—get caught in the rain, bragging about her son, the doctor, and developing ulcers over her son, the hippie, comes in all nationalities and religions. In fact, you don't even have to have children to be a Jewish mother—just mother whomever you can: your friends, your man, even your own parents can become the targets of your overwhelming solicitude. There is a book out now which tells you exactly how to do it, but most potential Jewish mothers are not in need of an instruction manual. In fact, it's the most natural fate in the world for a woman with brains and energy, the usual feminine training in other-directedness, and no creative pursuits of her own.

Although I know few women who actually fit the complete stereotype, I know many who have put most of their physical and mental energy into raising their children rather than into their own work. It is not hard to understand how this comes about. First of all, children *are* very demanding, physically and emotionally. As babies, they actually do need almost constant care and attention, and, while their physical independence increases as they grow older, they are far from self-sufficient, even as adolescents. And, of course, it is not simply a matter of attending to their needs for food, clothing, and protection from physical harm, but of responding to the less tangible, but no less real needs for attention, affection, intellectual stimulation, etc. Unless a woman sets real limits to the amount of time and energy she will spend on her children, raising them can easily constitute a full-time job, especially when added to the other housekeeping duties women are expected—and expect themselves—to perform.

Although the pattern seems to be changing a bit now, traditionally, it has been the woman's job to care for the children. The father might play a little baseball with his sons on weekends or help the kids with their math homework, but the bulk of the daily responsibility for the feeding, cleansing, chauffeuring, and protecting of the young, has been mama's. We take these roles so much for granted that it shocked me recently to read an article that suggested that men should actually perform the child-rearing functions in exchange for the time, pain, and energy women expend in pregnancy and childbirth. Certainly this argument makes at least as much sense as the old assumption that since the woman gave birth to the child, she should be the one to care for it, yet even among young and supposedly liberated couples, the old roles are dying hard, and, of course, there are many couples who don't even question them.

I think most women appreciate any help their men can give them, but there may be women who are threatened by male encroachment on their sphere of influence, possibly because it is the only area in which they *have* influence, feel competent, secure. To admit that a man could handle child-rearing just as well would be to threaten their only bastion of self-esteem. And then, of course, there are the ever-increasing numbers of divorced mothers who, for the most part, have the full responsibility for caring for their children, often in addition to being the sole financial support of the family.

Not only do we expect ourselves to take the major responsibility for our children, we are also convinced that once we have children, they should be our main priority. It is practically immoral to put yourself or your needs before those of your children. Men are also expected to sacrifice for their children, but they are not usually confronted with the children themselves on a daily basis the way women are. Also, it is much less "unnatural" for a father to turn his back on his children, either temporarily or permanently. "Your father is busy now—don't disturb him," is a familiar line in many homes, whether the man is engaged in demanding intellectual work, or simply reading the newspaper or watching T.V. Such accomodation to the mother's needs is rarely urged. And many fathers have been known to walk out on their families, not without general disapproval, to be sure, but with nothing like the condemnation levelled at women who do the same. A woman I know left her husband and baby daughter, when she could no longer tolerate the marriage, but had no way to support her child. She was deserted by many of her friends for her "unnatural" behavior, and her father still refuses to have anything to do with her, even though she was eventually awarded custody of the child and has been caring for her quite adequately ever since.

I'm sure that the last scene of Ibsen's *Doll's House* where Nora leaves her children as well as her husband, still shocks audiences, just as people are disturbed by the concept of childcare centers which take children from infancy, so their mothers can work. Such centers are common in socialist countries, which probably links them in the minds of most Americans with loss of personal dignity, individual freedom, etc. I'm not enough of an expert to know whether, in fact, placing a child in such a center at an early age does the child emotional harm. I do know that it is not good for either mother or child to be stuck with just each other day in and day out—that children need to interact with each other and that adults need the stimulation of other adults. In fact, one of the dangers of motherhood seems to me to be the loss of creative momentum after several years of baby-tending. Even if you know you've done other things in your life besides cook, clean, and change diapers, it is easy to forget what they were if you are kept in solitary confinement long enough. Being cooped up in the house all day with no one but a three-year-old to talk to could make a basket case out of the most intelligent woman in no time, unless she has developed some inner resources to keep herself alive and growing along with her child.

The pitfalls of motherhood are so many that it is truly remarkable to me that so many women overcome them. As a mother, you have a real, live person, demanding a tremendous amount of attention, love and care. You could easily let being a mother take all of your time and energy. And you could excuse yourself from any further activity by considering your child or children to be sufficient acts of creativity to last a lifetime. You would probably find plenty of encouragement for this from your husband, your own mother, art and literature, T.V., etc.

Living up to the popular image of the perfect mother would take all of anybody's energy plus. I know of few women who don't suffer paroxysms of guilt about not being good enough mothers to their children. Somehow we have been sold the misconception that the more time and energy we focus on our children, the more we sacrifice for them, the better they will be, when in fact, the opposite may be true. It has been pointed out to me by several mothers that children really *don't* need constant attention—that, in fact, they need to be given the independence of movement appropriate to their years and private time and space in which to grow and be with themselves and their peers. Secondly, if you sacrifice your own growth for your child, not only will you stagnate, but your child then becomes responsible for fulfilling your needs. Part of the Jewish mother syndrome is "trip-laying"—asking that your child become what you did not, and/or that your child affirm your way of life with hers/his. The chances are that if the child is a boy, he will carry the burden of succeeding in the active, outer world of business or the professions—the "my son, the doctor" trip. If she is a girl, the mother may want her to live out the creative, exciting life she never had, but she will probably also want her to duplicate, and thereby justify, her own way of life; hence, the emphasis on marrying and having children. In both cases, the children are not free to develop as they need to but are trapped inside the mother's unfulfilled desires.

The healthiest children I know come from homes where the parents are caring and affectionate but lead their own lives and allow their children to lead theirs. I recently heard of a woman in San Diego with four grown children, who is still actively involved in her own life. Her children are quite different from each other. One is a successful concert musician; another is a medical student; a third teaches meditation; and the fourth gets by, doing odd jobs and dealing a little grass to survive. She and her husband are not prouder of the doctor than they are of the dealer, nor do they spend much energy worrying about their children; they are too busy being born themselves. And their children are not distorting their own development by trying to "please mama." They are free to develop individual life styles, to be whoever they are.

Another remarkable woman in her sixties attends the women's group I belong to, along with her daughter, who tells the story of how, at twenty, she felt responsible, as the last child left in the home, to remain with her mother. To her surprise, her mother announced one day that Lynn would have to find another place to live because she was going to Europe! And at the age of fifty-four, knowing not a word of German, she went off to Austria for a year to study piano. She is still extremely active and energetic; gardening, giving piano lessons, going to concerts and meetings, and her relationship with her daughter is beautiful to behold in its openness and mutuality of affection. They disagree on many things and live very differently from one another, but each respects the other's judgment about what is good for her, and they have what must be the rarest of relationships between mother and child—a real friendship.

Even my own mother, who is both Jewish and incorrigibly motherly, seems to be making great strides towards asserting her own needs and exercising her talents, now that her children and her mother have finally left home. And I know many younger women who are continuing to lead their own lives despite the additional responsibility of children. All of which gives me hope that it *can* be otherwise—that the Jewish mother syndorme is not inevitable—even among Jewish mothers.

Motherhood: The Fantasy and Its Meaning for Me

For me, the fantasy of becoming a mother is so highly charged emotionally, that I have felt compelled to explore its meaning, both because I fear that to ignore it would be to give myself over to the unconscious desire to become pregnant, and because I have learned that any fantasy with that much power deserves to be listened to for whatever it can teach me about myself. This year I have had more time than previously to pay attention to my moods and fantasies, and I have come more fully in touch with the part of myself that wants to become a mother, as well as with the part that doesn't. Both sides are multi-dimensional; they speak with many different voices. I have allowed them to dialogue with each other in my journal and in gestalt group. I have talked about them in my women's group and with the man I live with. I have met them in my dreams and daydreams.

Sometimes strong feelings about having babies are brought on by seeing a young mother nursing her child or my cat with her kittens or a passage from Anaïs Nin's *Diary* or the ache in my belly during my menstrual cycle. If I allow myself to experience these feelings and express them in some way—by writing, speaking, drawing—I feel more whole, more alive, more in conscious contact with all my parts; somehow, by giving in to my feelings in this way, I feel more in control of my actions, less vulnerable to the possibility of "accidental pregnancy," and more voluntarily committed to the part of myself that takes the pill each night. It is as if each time I am overwhelmed by desire for a child, I get more in touch with what that desire symbolizes for me as well as with how much of it is actually wanting a child, and I also understand more about why I am *not* pregnant; I reaffirm the decision I have made to wait.

I have been told that there is an innate desire in women to bear children. I have also been told that while sexual desire is instinctual, the urge to procreate is not. While it may be scientifically true that I have no "maternal drive" or "instinct," that seems fairly irrelevant when pitted against the powerful archetype of woman as mother and a history of thousands of years of women whose major role in life was bearing, giving birth to, and nurturing the next generation. I can't wipe out the impact of all the mother-and-child images I've seen, of the expectation I've had all my life that I would become a mother someday, of the hollow sound of words like "childless" or "barren," or of my sense of my own body as a childbearing mechanism—of what my breasts are for, of the purpose of the monthly bloodletting which continually reminds me that I am capable of bearing new life and that I have let the chance go by again.

Kate Millett makes fun of the idea that a woman might mourn her unborn babies as she sheds her menstrual blood each month. But I'm not laughing. Yesterday, the first day of my period, I had those classic monthly blues, and I wrote:

> I am suddenly overwhelmed by my woman's body—hungering, hungering—it is not food hunger—it is baby hunger. Again and again and again it recurs. This empty, empty feeling, . . . this anguish. When will it be time? I don't want to wait any MORE! I feel I shall go mad if I do not experience it soon—the child in my belly, at my breast, *my* child.

But my rational, sensible side chimed in, critically, questioning the motives of the would-be mother, remonstrating with her, as if she were afraid the crazy lady would actually go through with it. Fat chance, the practical one having put her on the pill and all. It feels as if they want to have it out some more, so I guess I'll let them:

> (Here, I went back to my journal and wrote a dialogue, of which the following is an excerpt)
>
> *I feel empty—as if there were a huge cavity in the middle of my belly, aching to be filled. I eat, but it is not filled. I drink, but it is not filled. I lie beside my man at night and feel his warmth on my belly; he enters me but does not fill me. I am empty of life. I crave a child to fill the emptiness.*

Oh, come off it—stop being so melodramatic! You're imagining this emptiness. You can't really feel it. It's something you were taught to feel. It's just in your head and you can get rid of it.

But I don't want to. You want to, but I don't.

I want to because it would be insane for you to have a child. I'm afraid you'll feel the emptiness so strongly that you'll throw all caution away—throw me away—and fill it.

How can I, when you take that pill every night? You've made sure no slip-ups would occur.

I had to. You were beginning to get reckless. I began to fear that you would stop bothering to get up and use your diaphragm. I had to go on the pill for your own good.

My good! Is this what you call good! This barren life? How many years will you make me wait before a baby can begin to grow inside me? Soon I'll be too old to enjoy a child. I'm beginning to feel desperate.

Don't be silly. You've got lots of time. I don't want to be tied down with kids now when I'm still young enough to enjoy love and sex and travel and change. I feel like I've really just begun to enjoy my youth. I don't want to grow fat and flabby with pregnancy and after the child is born, drawn and haggard with caring for it. I don't want to lose whatever light-heartedness I have now and become completely obsessed with practicality, routine, the child's well-being. I fear what I would be like as a mother.

But I need to care for someone, to nurture someone. I have more than enough to give a man. And I want to know how it feels to carry a child within me and to give it life and care for it; to feel its little form—my very own, nourished by my milk.

That's a very romantic image, but there's more to babies than that. What about the dirty diapers, crying in the middle of the night, taking care of the child until it's grown—with no assurance of a man to share the burden with you?

> *No woman is really assured of that anymore. And I want to experience that part of it too–the day to day responsibility for another human being who really needs me.*

You want a relationship that won't dissolve like relationships with men always do. You want someone you can depend on to depend on you. But you know that's a false hope and a foolish one. Your child will certainly grow and leave you. Of all the people in the world in whom you may invest love and energy, your child is the one who is the most certain to leave you. And then where will you be? More desolate, alone, and lost than you are now.

> *No, I think it will make me more real—and make my life more whole. I feel so flighty, trivial, unproven this way.*

I feel as if you're using the idea of a baby as an escape from confronting your own life—what to do with it. You think a child would give you a purpose for living, one you haven't found yet, but you're wrong. You'll still have to deal with that problem after the child is born. And even if it were true, it would be the wrong reason to have babies. You can't and shouldn't try to live through your children. You have to want them for themselves *before I'll let you have any.*

> *Somehow, you've put me on the defensive, challenging me to prove myself a fit mother, criticizing me for copping out on my own life. What are you doing that's so all-important anyway? What alternative are you giving me?*

I guess I'm not giving you too much of an alternative, am I? Just continuing to look for a career that will be creative and keep me busy and happy and feeling productive and useful.

> *Having a child would certainly do that. At least it would give you a real, living reason to go on living yourself. You would be needed, really needed.*

I know—and that's why I'm tempted to give in to you sometimes. But I'm terribly afraid that because I don't have a sense of my own "vocation," of what I can do and will feel happy doing, I will pour all of my energy into my child and that will be unhealthy for both of us. I feel as if I need something besides children and a man—some creative work to do. And I'm afraid that if I have a child before I've found it, I'll stop looking for it.

> *That's ridiculous. If you need it, you need it. And you'll keep looking for it with or without a child to care for. Look, why don't you just relax and take a vacation. We don't really have to* decide *this. We can just wait and see what happens.*

Oh no you don't! I'm not about to leave it up to "fate." A baby is too much of a commitment. You don't just have them, nurse them, and forget about them. They're for keeps.

* * *

This dialogue brought out some feelings I had experienced before and a few new ones as well. I usually think of the part of myself that wants the child as romantic, impractical, weak, and the other part as clearheaded, rational, strong. And she is stronger; after all, she has prevailed all these years. But in this dialogue, I became aware of the escapist side of not wanting children—of my Peter Pan-like desire to remain young always, to be free of all permanent ties, to trip through life unencumbered by responsibility; and of the responsible side of my would-be mother—the desire for a real, tangible, inescapable duty to perform.

Men have often envied women for their clear and present *raison d'être;* the ability to create life and the responsibility for its nurturance excused us from any further responsibility to create, produce, search for meaningful work to do. As Hesse put it, in *Narcissus and Goldmund:*

> Perhaps women had it easier, in this respect. Nature had created them in such a way that desire bore its fruit automatically, that the bliss of love became a child. For a man, eternal longing replaced this simple fertility.

For women, the concept of alienation did not exist; there was no gap between living and working, between being and creating. But now that we are no longer needed as childbearers, and have the power for the first time in history to *choose* whether or not to become mothers, the existential dilemma is as great for us as it is for men. I often find myself envying women who have had babies in much the same way that men have envied women in the past. I am jealous of their tangible, creative achievement—a real, human life —and the very limitations it puts on their freedom of choice, for complete freedom of choice with regard to one's own life is a terrifying responsibility, one that I often wish I could cop out of with the excuse that I *can't* do this or that because of the children. I also project onto the young mothers I know, a greater depth of experience, wisdom, maturity, womanliness than I feel in myself. Compared to them I feel virginal, as if I will not truly be a woman until I have borne a child—or at least experienced pregnancy; that I am still myself a child until I have one inside me.

I am also awed by women who have chosen, finally and consciously, *not* to have children. I know a few women who have made such decisions and some who have had tubal ligations to seal their commitment. I wonder how they can turn their backs so irrevocably on the experience of motherhood. I find myself admiring their decisiveness, resolution, strength. I project onto them an inner directedness I don't feel I have, an absence of the need to be needed, which is part of my desire for motherhood and which I associate with feelings of inadequacy and insecurity.

It is difficult to be in the middle—to really stay with my ambivalence—wanting a child but feeling the difficulty of living out my fantasy in the foreseeable future.

I used to associate my desire for a child with strong and deep feelings for a man. Whenever a relationship reached a certain level of intimacy and caring, I would begin to have fantasies of bearing the man's child. These fantasies made the sexual union extremely intense. I would feel as if I were opening a deep and private part of myself; almost as if I were allowing him to impregnate me, to plant the seed of his strength within me, the seed which I would bring to life and which would give me life.

How powerful that fantasy has been for me! To consummate that closeness with a man with the creation of a life that partakes of both of us yet is completely new, unique. It is not the real, live, growing child that will be my responsibility that I envision at these times, but the child as a symbol of our union.

Now, I am beginning to get in touch with a desire for a child that is quite separate from feelings for a man, and I have begun to get clues as to what this desire is all about. One clue emerged when I read a short story in which a young girl discovers that she is pregnant. She fantasizes what her life will be like with her baby:

> I can go to Big Sur and build a house on the rocky cliffs overlooking a long sandy beach. The house will take on my shape as I shape it. I'll paint wonderful, colorful paintings on the inside walls and have a big black pot-belly stove in the center. And after my child is born and sleeping in a sheep-skin, I'll knit and paint and sell my handicrafts to the middle-aged couple at the Hand Craft Shop. They'll love me and my child who will run along that long sandy beach chasing sandpipers and collecting shells. We'll watch the sun's last golden reflections on the ocean and talk about books, and be very serious; and write plays we'll act out ourselves, and laugh. My child will be constantly curious and forever asking questions. My child will be a poet, an architect, a beach comber, a sculptor, a teacher, a painter, a philosopher.

I, too, have daydreamed in this way of the second chance that will come with a child. Every time I have had a pregnancy scare, I have felt a combination of relief and sadness at the "negative" results. I have felt a sense of emptiness, of loss—as if I had lost the hope for something better, the chance to live again through someone else.

Another clue to what having children means to me came when I read the following statement in Anaïs Nin's *Diary*, after having had a powerful dream that expressed the same perception in similar symbolic terms:

All unfulfilled desires are imprisoned children

I dreamt I heard about a woman who was delivered of several children at one time. The oldest was a girl of twelve, the youngest a tiny infant. Some were dead, having been imprisoned inside her womb too long. The cries of birth were mingled with cries of grief for the dead babies. The babies were delivered by a handsome bachelor, who agreed to take care of them for the woman; to be like a father to them.

In thinking about the dream, I felt that the children were my own unfulfilled desires; that they were the hope for fulfillment that has come with every new relationship with a man, and that I have often pictured as a child by that man. In fact, the oldest child in the dream was twelve—exactly the age she would have been had I conceived by my first boyfriend at sixteen; exactly the age she is now, if I take her to be the hopes and dreams that were born within me then. I was delighted to see that she *is* still alive, for that was a very wonderful and hopeful time of my life.

Like the woman in the dream, I have waited for a man to deliver me of my dreams; to give them life and take responsibility for their fulfillment. But I know now that I need no longer wait to give birth to the child already within me, struggling to be born, the child that is all that is new and growing in me. She is a child who needs no father to make her life legitimate, although it may take many midwives to bring her to birth; she is, for now and always, my child to nurture and encourage and sustain, no matter how many womb-children may grow from me and grow away.

MEN:
CAN WE LIVE
WITH THEM?

Conflict between my feminine self who wants to live in a man-ruled world, to live in harmony with men, and the creator in me, capable of creating a world of my own and a rhythm of my own which I can't find anyone to share.

Anaïs Nin

Living Without Them

> Above all, she must not be afraid of singleness or even loneliness, for I know of no woman, let alone man, who has any stature or worth, without knowledge of either.
>
> Marya Mannes,
> "The Problems of Creative Women"

For many a woman, the thought of being single is so disturbing, distressing, even terrifying, that she will settle for much less than she really needs from a relationship rather than risk being alone. And, as in a business transaction, where the party who has the most to lose has the least bargaining power, so it is in a relationship; the more desperate I am to keep a man, the more I will be willing to give up to please him. But if my first priority is not to be loved, but to be whole; if I am not afraid to be alone, then I can take more risks, make more demands, drive as hard a bargain as he does, and maybe even get what I want.

In the past, I have often compromised my real needs to stay with a man because I've been afraid to let go of whatever being with him did for me. There was a period of time in my early twenties when I felt that I literally couldn't live without a man. Rather than take the chance of finding out, however, I made sure never to break up with one before a replacement was fairly well assured. I remembered the awkward loneliness of my early adolescence, and it seemed to me that all of my confidence, poise, achievements, delights, had originated with my first boyfriend and would only continue so long as I had a man.

It was not just loneliness I feared, but the dissolution of my very self, as if I were a statue that could come to life only if a man believed in me and breathed life into me with his approval. What I didn't realize then was that I was actually sacrificing many parts of my self to keep that approval coming. My feelings of dependency were further intensified by the "helpless" role I easily fell into, allowing the man to become my masculine side, to take over all those functions requiring strength, guts, mechanical ability, etc. Such relationships weakened me, made me feel less capable of surviving on my own, and more likely to sell out again for male protection.

Although I now know I can survive on my own, I still haven't quite lost the sense that I'm incomplete if I'm not half a couple, that nothing I can accomplish or achieve or become really means anything "if I ain't got you, babe."

Recently, I talked to a beautiful young woman, who is a talented musician and dress designer, as well as an excellent seamstress, cook and gardener. She told me that before she met her husband, she had felt lost, empty—had, in fact, taken up music as a way of filling that emptiness. For her, having a man was what gave everything else meaning—and although she knew she could survive without him, that possibility was so disturbing that she often found herself subordinating her needs to his, so as not to threaten the relationship in any way.

Another woman I know, an extremely gifted teacher and writer, ate to fill the emptiness she felt for lack of a secure, loving relationship with a man. That this was the major reason for her "foodaholism," as she called it, became evident when, as soon as she married, she lost all her excess wieght and never gained it back.

Why this urgent, desperate need for a man, even among women, like myself, who are leading productive lives of our own and do not need a man to provide us with either a vicarious identity or economic security? Even a strong woman may find it difficult to be single in a world that often seems to be built out of couples. When I'm single, not only am I lonely for male companionship and affection, I sometimes feel cut off from other friends as well, and from social situations that would bring me in contact with other people, either because being around couples intensifies my own loneliness, or because I feel I will not be really accepted by my coupled friends if I am not part of a couple too. It is as if being attached to a man brings with it a kind of status, a legitimacy, that a single woman lacks.

Going places alone is often difficult for a woman, either because she feels awkward or because of the probability of male harassment, which is a degrading, distracting, and sometimes even dangerous daily fact of life for most unattached (or simply unaccompanied) women. The discomfort of being constantly appraised, heckled, propositioned, etc. is well-known to most women and often makes it unpleasant to travel alone or even with another woman, as a friend and I discovered on a recent trip to Mexico.

But a man is not merely a social convenience. Many women also have emotional and sexual needs that are difficult to satisfy outside of a close relationship. Women, unlike men, are not socially condoned for openly acting to fulfill our sexual needs. We have only recently begun to regard ourselves, and to be regarded, as sexual beings with legitimate desires and preferences. This makes casual sexual encounters *of our own choosing* much less viable as an alternative to sex within the context of an ongoing relationship. Moreover, we are much less used to asking, directly or indirectly, for what we want, sexually or otherwise.

Consequently, it may be more difficult for us to initiate new relationships and it may also take us longer to build up enough trust with a partner to be able to ask for what will make the sexual relationship satisfying for us.

It is also difficult to separate sexual from emotional needs. While I have sometimes been able to enjoy sex with someone I didn't feel close to on other levels, the gulf between the physical closeness we shared and the emotional distance between us left me feeling saddened and empty, more alone than before we connected. I know that many men experience this too, and it is a hopeful sign that many of them are beginning to question the macho ethic of sexual conquest, which has created the familiar "combat in the erogenous zone" that often violates the real feelings and needs of both parties.

While I think we all both need and fear intimacy, it seems to me that women are more open to and in touch with their need for emotional closeness than are men. We are raised to be sensitive, caring, feeling, loving—and we do it well—but there seem to be few men who want to do it back. I have never been involved for very long with a man who couldn't relate to me feelingly, but that is because many men have run the other way when I asked for that kind of interaction. (I've also noticed that men who are sensitive and value their ability to be vulnerable often find it difficult to share this side of themselves with male friends.) A woman's greater openness to her need for emotional intimacy makes a close relationship more crucial for her, since she will not be satisfied with the more casual, uncomplicated, and therefore, possibly multiple relationships a man may engage in, especially if he is one who fears intimacy. Many women I know have simply given up trying to share feelings with their men and look for that kind of sharing elsewhere, usually with other women. Some women become involved in gay relationships because they can't find the kind of sensitivity and closeness with a man that they can with a woman.

Lack of emotional responsiveness seems to be one of the major reasons why women leave men, although it may take a woman a long time to decide that the cause is hopeless. One explanation for this may be that her greater emotional investment makes it more difficult for her to let go of what she has with a man, even if it isn't really satisfying to her. And she may feel more acutely the separation, the loss of companionship, of the other adult she used to talk to, even if the conversation was often one-sided. This last may be particularly true of women with children, who are often more isolated from contact with other adults, at the same time as they are more burdened with responsibility and in need of stimulation and support.

Despite all of the emotional, physical, economic, and social pressures to be married, more and more women are getting in touch with their own strength and, with each other's help are finding their own ways out the door. In fact, most of the divorces that have occurred within the last several years among my acquaintances were initiated by women, as are the majority of divorce cases we handle at the divorce counseling center, and these are women who are usually ecstatic at the prospect of freedom, rather than depressed, anxious, or fearful about being single.

My own experience has been that while I dread being alone, when it actually happens, I am always surprised to rediscover all the positive aspects of being single: the wealth of time and energy suddenly available, my sense of my own strength, the friends I'd forgotten I had, the freedom to explore parts of myself I hadn't even realized I'd lost touch with, the excitement of opening myself to new people and new relationships, the feeling that the world has suddenly opened up before me, and I can head in any direction. These feelings should be a clue that I have allowed the relationship to become too constricting, that I have been trying to squeeze myself into a space that is really too small for me. Sometimes it is not the man who is really the problem, but my own failure to assert myself and to stay centered in my own life, rather than lose myself in his. Unless I learn how to take care of my own needs *within* a relationship, I will be doomed either to wander eternally in search of the non-existent "perfect" man or give up men altogether and "expect to live single all the days of my life," neither of which is an acceptable alternative to me.

Instead, I am trying to learn how to keep centered while living and sharing my life with a man. It's not easy, and often I find myself falling back into the old, familiar patterns, even though they are the ones that have proven to be dead ends in the past. I have learned a few things, however, about what I need to do for myself to keep growing while involved in a relationship, and that is what I would like to share here.

Central to all that follows is the assumption that my first priority is my own growth, not the continuance of the relationship. For me, it is often difficult to keep that priority clear, since I have always been very other-directed and very man-centered, but experience has taught me that to lose touch with my self for the sake of a relationship is too great a price to pay, and, with a little help from my friends, I'm getting better at spotting the traps before I fall into them.

Finding a Man You'd Want *to Live With*

> I want a woman smaller than I am, you love too many people, you have your work, and a crowded life. I am afraid of you.
>
> Jean Carteret to Anaïs Nin

The stronger and more self-sufficient women become, the more difficult it is to find men we can relate to. While strength, intellect, power, assertiveness are valued in men, they are definitely not so valued in women, and while it is perfectly acceptable, even common, for a man to marry a woman who is his intellectual or emotional inferior, the reverse is not true. It is difficult for men to tolerate women who are independent and secure in themselves, who will neither be dominated nor patronized, and who also demand a high degree of intimacy and emotional involvement from a relationship. While women seem to be growing intellectually and emotionally by leaps and bounds, men are having difficulty with this growth.

The woman's movement is both a cause and an effect of this phenomenon, for as we have begun to demand more of ourselves and of relationships, we have turned to each other for support, and that support has strengthened us further, making us less willing to compromise our need to be whole to be with a man. As Anaïs said at her Celebration, "We are all less lonely now, because we are giving birth to each other." Sisterhood is providing the encouragement for growing and venturing that men have not provided, and we are flourishing from each other's nurturance, while men are still, for the most part, isolated from one another, cut off from their feelings, and confused by what is happening to their women.

Traditionally, women have demanded that their men be bigger and stronger than they, in whatever way their particular social milieu defined those terms. Perhaps this is a holdover from the days when women depended on their men for physical protection; when that was the basis for the couple. Now the demand seems to be changing. As we get more in touch with our ability to make our own way in the world, we no longer need men to live out that part of our lives for us; what we do need is men who are equally well-balanced, who are in touch with their feelings and unthreatened by our growth and achievements; who will, in fact, encourage and enable that growth to take place, not only with moral but with physical support—sharing the household responsibilities equally to leave us equal time for rewarding work and relaxation.

My own concept of what I want from a man and a relationship is evolving slowly, through trial and error. I know I have a strong tendency to "mother"—a desire to be needed and to perceive myself as nurturing, giving strength. I need to be careful that this tendency is in balance; that it doesn't become the whole of the relationship, in that it not only keeps the man in a weakened, dependent position, but also drains my own energy away from other endeavors, and puts me back in the place of living *for* rather than *with* him.

I know that I need a man who has his own life and interests apart from me, who is not dependent upon me to the point where he is threatened by my relationships with other people, and who does not need me to look small so that he can look tall—who is not threatened by my brains or my achievements. But neither do I demand that he have it all together; that he be the completely self-generating person I am not. I would far rather have a man who can admit when he is feeling weak, anxious, or afraid, and who can accept help or support at those times, than one who always keeps his cool no matter what.

These are delicate balances to achieve, but for me these balances are what relationships are all about—the mutual exchange of support, understanding, appreciation, confusion, insight, resentment, joy—so that each gets to give as well as receive and neither feels inferior or impotent.

Taking Myself Seriously

In order for me to feel powerful and potent, I need to be engaged in creative work, work that calls upon my intellect as well as my sensitivity to others, that requires periods of solitude as well as time spent interacting with people. When I become deeply involved with a man, there is a danger that I will cease taking my own work seriously; that I will put so much energy into him and our relationship that I will forget to take time for myself, to nurture myself in the ways I must if I am to continue creating and giving to others.

It is easy for me to give up taking an interest in and responsibility for my own life and throw myself instead into supporting my man's work and attending to our relationship, being the amusing, entertaining, sympathetic, attentive, sexually alive woman at all times—even when I have something else I'd rather do, or should do, because accomplishing it will make me feel better about myself.

> Male adoration is a powerful deterrent to female sense, and it is extremely difficult to tear oneself away from loving arms and say, 'Sorry, darling, I've got to work.' It is so much easier to drown in current delights than gird for future daydreams.
>
> Marya Mannes

It is also easy for me to slip into the role of appreciative audience rather than demand my share of the spotlight and attention. Some men are threatened by creative women, especially if they work in the same medium, and women have often had to underplay their own creativity or suppress it completely to make their men feel powerful.

I have felt the tendency in myself to hang back from trying to write seriously or even share what I write with Jeffrey out of a fear of becoming competitive with him. My pattern has been to support, appreciate, encourage, enlarge him and his ability. Recently, as I have been involved in writing this, our roles have reversed; he has become the audience for my work, encouraging, reacting, making suggestions. I am enjoying the feeling of accomplishment that comes with writing and being listened to, and he is discovering the rewards of the listener-helper role, something he had never before experienced.

It seems to me that such reciprocity is the key to a relationship between two creative people, and that if ego conflicts do not get in the way, it should be possible for them to give energy to each other's work, rather than drain it off. Lynn Sukenick affirmed this for me when she came to Sonoma State recently to read her poetry. She is married to a writer and feels that being engaged in similar kinds of creative work enables them to understand each other better and give each other the kinds of feedback and support they both need.

What seems crucial is that each respects the importance of her/his own and the other's work. If I view my own work as important, the chances are my mate will too, but only if I make its importance real by my actions. If I take myself seriously, I will set aside time and space within my life and my home for just me—a room of my own where I can write and think and *be* without interruption.

Right now Jeffrey and I are living in one small room which serves as bedroom and study for both of us. Although the house itself is large, we often have space conflicts because we both prefer our own room and desk for reading and writing. I used to give up the desk quite easily, almost automatically, feeling that Jeffrey was the writer, while I was only scribbling in my journal, but since I have been working intensively on my writing, I've claimed the desk as mine, and Jeffrey takes his work downstairs. This is significant to me because it means that I am now valuing myself and my own writing enough to make demands for what I need to do it well.

Taking myself seriously also means distributing household chores evenly so that I don't end up doing most of them, thus robbing myself of time and energy for more rewarding efforts. Here, again, I am my own worst obstacle, in that I have to combat my compulsiveness about housework and my anxiety that we are not doing our share in a household that includes other people, rather than simply doing *my* share and letting Jeffrey take responsibility for doing or not doing his. I also have a tendency to procrastinate by puttering, and I genuinely enjoy doing routine chores when my head has been working overtime. This, plus my usual desire to avoid conflict or nagging, often prompts me to concede to Jeffrey's inertia, laziness, or male ignorance of what has to be done and how to do it. Right now, we are considering dealing with the problem by drawing up a written contract to eliminate hassles about whose turn it is or how many times a week, month, or day a particular job needs to be done.

Going in to Come Out Whole

The "room of one's own" is not just a physical space in the house where I can close the door and be alone; it is psychic space as well—the ability to shut out the distractions of relationships, roles, and duties, and be alone with myself. I am a naturally gregarious person and don't often crave solitude. Especially when I am, as now, so close to someone else, I tend to forget that I do need to spend time alone, to stay in touch with who I am, separate from him.

I have begun to view the "room" in my head as symbolic of the psychic room I have in which to grow—both the amount of private space I claim for myself in the relationship and the diversity of selves I allow myself to experience. Over the last few months I've had several dreams in which Jeffrey and I (usually at my instigation) are looking for a new place to live, one where I will have my own study. In these dreams, I seem to be expressing my need for a part of my life that doesn't include him, a place to just be me. I have begun to have fantasies about what that room would look like, what I would want to have in it. By imagining it and sketching it, I learn from the layout, the colors, the materials in the room what needs of mine are not being fulfilled, what parts of myself are craving exercise, expression. Whether or not I am able to create such an environment for myself (and I intend to try), I can begin to take care of the needs it suggests to me.

Staying in touch with all the parts of my self is more difficult when I am with a man because of my tendency to be what I feel he wants me to be, to limit myself to just those aspects of my personality I feel he will accept and love. Writing in my journal is perhaps the most important vehicle I have found for staying in touch with all of who I am. Anaïs, too, used her diary in this way, to counteract the role-playing she did so automatically and well, especially with men. The diary seems to me to be a particularly feminine literary form in its immediacy, subjectivity, involvement with the everyday details of living and feeling. Certainly diaries and letters have, until recently, been practically the whole of women's literature; we had little time or permission to do any other kind of writing. But not only is the diary appropriate to the way a woman relates to the world, it can be her main ally in keeping clear about who she is in the midst of pressures to be what others need her to be. And the experience of writing in it can be her time of communion with herself, that private space she needs to stay whole and centered.

I don't do very much formal "journal work" in my diary—dialogues, fantasies, etc. Usually I just talk to myself on paper, exploring an incident or a feeling or the hint of a feeling until I understand its meaning for me more fully. But sometimes when two voices emerge very clearly out of the chaos of feeling, I stand aside and let them speak to each other, and in this way I may discover a part of myself I haven't been listening to.

I had a powerful experience with this kind of internal dialogue when I was travelling in Mexico with Jeffrey, just after we met. I had been spending almost all my time with him and very little alone or with the friend with whom I had started the trip. I had been feeling somewhat guilty about having deserted my friend for a man, and the day after she left to go back to the U.S., I was feeling particularly bad about it, although she hadn't seemed resentful or angry about the way things had worked out. Jeffrey and I had decided to spend the afternoon apart, and in the time I spent alone, I began to feel a tremendous stirring of energy and excitement. As I wrote about these feelings in my long-neglected journal, a voice began to emerge, that was clearly not the voice of the person who had begun to write. She seemed to be my inner self, someone I thought I had left behind in Sonoma County, but who was apparently still with me, trying to get through to me. As I dialogued with her in my journal, I discovered that the woman I had deserted for my man was not only my friend but myself.

Dreams are another way of getting in touch with my inner world, if I will take the time to allow them to speak to me. Often Jeffrey and I tell each other our dreams when we awaken, and sometimes we help each other work with them, taking the roles of various people and objects in the dream, or just associating to the parts of the dream that are particularly powerful. My dream group at school has contributed enormously to my ability to work with dreams; in fact, before this year I rarely paid attention to them because I had no way to get inside them and no one to share them with. Having the dream group is an incentive to remember my dreams and write them down, and the more I work with them, the more they reward me with insights into the parts of myself I have been neglecting or ignoring.

I've also learned to use the *I Ching* as I might a dream. When I am in a situation of crisis or indecision or when I need clarification of my emotional state, I often throw the *I Ching* and allow the hexagrams to speak to me as if all the figures mentioned were parts of my self. Although I have a deep-seated rationalist's resistance to things mystical, I have been amazed at the number of times the hexagrams I have thrown seem to speak directly to whatever problem I'm considering. I use my journal for this too—to write my own commentary on whatever hexagram I've thrown that day and play with the possibilities it suggests to me.

One of the parts of myself that tends to get easily lost when I am with a man is my own masculine side—the part of me that takes care of business in the world, fixes things when they break, reasons and analyzes, creates and accomplishes. It is this giving over of all my masculine power to my man that weakens me, makes me dependent and fearful of being on my own again. One way in which I am trying to counteract this tendency is by staying involved in the projects I have undertaken before Jeffrey came to live with me —the classes, groups, counseling work, etc.—and taking on new ones, like the divorce counseling I'm now doing. I've also been participating in "masculine" tasks that I might otherwise have hired someone to do for me; for example, when my car broke down recently, Jeffrey wanted us to try to fix it ourselves. In the past, I would have taken it to a mechanic, but since he seemed confident that we could do it, and anxious to try, I agreed. Although he did almost all the mechanical work, I watched most of the process, fetched tools, and read him the directions, and now I feel a much closer bond with my car, and an appreciation of how the engine works, something I never thought I'd be able to understand.

Another way I've lost touch with myself in the past has been by keeping back feelings I thought would be disapproved of or cause friction. I've been especially afraid to show anger or stay with it for any length of time for fear of permanently alienating my man. I find I'm better now at expressing angry feelings *when* I'm feeling them without waiting until it's safe or until I have plenty of good reasons to back them up. Usually when I express the anger right away, it doesn't last very long because it hasn't had time to really build up, and then it isn't so scary. Of course, it helps to be with a man who isn't afraid of feelings and encourages me to express them. But then, at this point, I don't think I could live with any other kind.

For me, negative feelings are much harder to express than positive ones, and often I will repress them until several get mixed up together and I'm not sure what it is I'm upset about. I find that once I begin talking about the dis-ease I feel, if I am attentive, patient, and honest with myself, I generally find my way back to its source. Something like this happened when Jeffrey told me he'd invited a girl with whom he's been corresponding to come and see us when she visits California. I felt uncomfortable about meeting her, but worse at the thought of Jeffrey spending time with her alone. I didn't understand where my jealous feelings were coming from until, as I talked about them, I became aware that what I resented about their relationship was Jeffrey's romantic image of her which allowed him to share the romantic side of himself. I realized that I, too, have a romantic, poetic side which rarely gets expressed in our relationship. This part of me felt left out, resentful at being overlooked by both of us. Once I expressed my need for "poetry," the feelings of tension and jealousy went away—I felt closer to Jeffrey and to myself.

It takes time and energy to stay in touch with all my parts and with someone else as well, but for me, at least, the two seem to nourish each other, as long as I feel free to *be* all the different people I discover I am.

Reaching Out

In a relationship where there is a high degree of sharing and intimacy, there is a danger that it can become exclusive, leaving no room for others, and may eventually die of suffocation. Such complete absorption in one another seems natural, especially at the beginning when there is so much that is new to discover, to share, to explore together. For the first couple of months that Jeffrey and I were together, I really didn't have much time or energy left over for relating to anyone else—nor did I feel the need for other people at that point.

Now, although I still feel closest to Jeffrey, I also need others, and I have been rediscovering my old friends and making some new ones as well. Different people bring out different aspects of me, and often I will not know that a certain part of me exists or has gotten lost until someone else calls it out of me. Then I feel richer and stronger, more whole, more like myself.

I know that one relationship cannot satisfy all of anyone's needs for companionship or stimulation, but I think that often we hope that a relationship with a man will do that and are disappointed when it fails. I feel particularly strongly that I need friendships with other women for the support, understanding, inspiration, encouragement, and perspective we can give each other. When I talk with other women now, I feel a new and special bond between us, and I experience my struggle as one that is shared by many. We exchange ideas for coping with our common difficulties and we celebrate our triumphs and achievements together. My small women's group, which exists specifically for this purpose, is becoming more and more important to me as a source of energy and support.

I've also discovered letter-writing as a way of making contact with other women, not only friends who are far away, but friends I have only heard of from others or met through their writing. Each time I have reached out to another woman by writing to her, I have been rewarded by a warm and personal response and the sense that I need no longer fear to be alone, that I have sisters everywhere. I am learning to trust that impulse to reach out and to follow through by writing the letter, saying the words which at some other time I might have left unsaid out of shyness or neglect or fear of being misunderstood.

Writing this has been part of the process of reaching out. There have been many times when I have wondered to whom I was writing and whether anyone would be interested in what I have to say about my life and the lives of women as I perceive them. I have doubted that my life, my feelings, my perceptions could be useful to anyone else and have questioned writing this at all. Two thoughts have kept me going, pushing me past the doubts and self-deprecations: One was the awareness that by writing, I was coming to a new understanding of myself; I can see more clearly now the route I've taken to get to where I am, the person I've become and am becoming. And the other was my own hunger for personal, thoughtful writing by contemporary women. I knew that if I wanted to read this kind of woman's writing, I would have to be willing to attempt it myself. Until now, I didn't really know for whom I was writing besides myself, but as I wrote that last paragraph, I realized that in the back of my mind all along was the hope that another woman would read this and respond to it; that maybe she would even give me her response directly; and that perhaps she too would write her story for all of us to read.

EVERYWOMAN'S GUIDE TO COLLEGE
Eileen Gray

The emotional, financial and academic realities of the returning woman student of any age. 903-6, paper, $3.95

TO DELIVER ME OF MY DREAMS
Elizabeth Avakian

A present-day journal of the pain and joy of being female.
906-0, paper, $3.95

THE SAME OLD GRIND
Judy Roe

A tragicomic novel about 36 hours in the lives of a bunch of losers in a sleazy burlesque house. 900-1, paper, $4.95

MEANWHILE FARM
Margaret Cheney

A chronicle of the struggles and joys of woman's return to the land.
905-2, paper, $4.95

STAYING MARRIED
Margaret Frings Keyes

A long-overdue examination of *what's right with marriage* by a counselor and therapist. 902-8, paper, $4.95

THE WORLD OF EMILY HOWLAND: ODYSSEY OF A HUMANITARIAN
Judith Colucci Breault

One of the nineteenth century's foremost but forgotten activists in human rights. (biography) 904-4, paper, $5.95

RUTH KRAMER
Publisher

Not My Mother's Son

Things Aren't Always What They Seem

A Novel

by

R. K. Avery

Published by
Brighton Publishing LLC
501 W. Ray Road
Suite 4
Chandler, AZ 85225

Not My Mother's Son

Things Aren't Always What They Seem

A Novel

by

R. K. Avery

Published by
Brighton Publishing LLC
501 W. Ray Road
Suite 4
Chandler, AZ 85225
www.BrightonPublishing.com

Printed in the United States of America

ISBN 13: 978-1-621830-09-2
ISBN 10: 1-621-83009-8

FIRST EDITION

Cover Design By: Patricia McNaught Foster

Dedication

To Sue, the most wonderful friend a person can have.
In another time, I am certain we were sisters.

To Kim, even though I met you later in life, we immediately had a special connection. I will always have your back.

Prologue

The aroma and feel of the air was that of autumn. The once-green leaves, now transforming into beautiful hues of red, orange, and gold, were starting to fall and catch in the wind gusts, causing them to scurry across yards, parking lots, and streets like field mice darting in fear from an irate person with a broom. Fall was always a pleasant time of the year, as it reminded David of Halloweens-past when he, Joshua, and John dressed up in funny costumes and went door-to-door begging for candy from all the strange neighbors in the trailer park. David had been amazed at how the rule of "never take candy from strangers" was tossed out the window for the sake of a few hours of fun.

Halloween was one of the few holidays Bea allowed them to celebrate and that was only early on—the first few years they lived in Bunting Valley. Of course, when they returned home with their worn-out pillowcases full of tasty, sugary treats, Bea hid them. She told David and his brothers they were allowed to have a piece or two of candy per day, if—and only if—they were really good and deserved it. The problem was that David didn't ever remember seeing the candy again. Once it left his grasp it was all over and he knew it. Obviously, in Bea's opinion, he and his brothers were never good enough.

Beatrice Miller was being held in prison at the federal building. In July, she'd been arrested on two counts of kidnapping. During the search for evidence and witnesses, it was discovered she had kidnapped two additional children, who had since been returned to their families—one in New Orleans, the other near Seattle. Bea claimed she had a reason for kidnapping each and every one, although she refused to call it kidnapping. She simply referred to it as "removing them from an unpleasant situation." The question was whether the jury would empathize with her or find her guilty and recommend the maximum sentence.

David Miller, now twenty years old, was forced to grow up way before his time. The only biological child of Beatrice and Henry Miller, his life and upbringing would be described as nothing less than fiction; the sad truth was that it wasn't fiction at all. He had lived through it and sometimes wondered how he had not only survived, but also came out at the other end older and wiser than his years. Tall, with eyes the color of creamy milk chocolate, his once-dyed, jet-black hair was now back to its natural shade of light brown with golden highlights, cut and styled in the latest fashion. He was a very attractive young man. He was told more than once he looked like his late father. Growing up, he thought the day when he grew taller than his mother would be when their relationship would change, but it hadn't. She still found ways to push him around, manipulate him into doing her dirty work, and clean up her messes.

Benita Adams, David's great aunt, had been contacted to appear as a witness for the prosecution. Aunt Benita was the picture of glamour, and everyday life was her runway. No matter where she went she dressed to the nines, and her visit to Bunting Valley was no exception. She had wedge-cut silver hair, the soft layers framing her face, and laugh lines around her eyes and mouth. Prior to her visit, David wasn't even aware he had a great-aunt. Bea made it a point never to talk about family—except Henry, who'd passed away in a freak accident the year David turned seven. David tried many times to remember his father, but he wasn't sure if he remembered things about him, or if they were things Bea had told him. She always managed to paint a picture with only happy times and joyful memories, using only the bright and cheerful colors in her palette. As dysfunctional as the family was, David doubted things had ever been quite so utopian.

Despite Aunt Benita's upturned nose and her initial reaction to David and the trailer park he lived in, she'd been back to visit a few times while waiting for the trial. After much persuasion, Benita took David shopping, and he finally relented and allowed her to buy him a new three-piece, charcoal-gray suit, along with a few other articles of clothing. She told him he needed something professional-looking for the trial. Oh yes, the trial; David was not looking forward to seeing his mother again, but knowing he'd get to dress up in his brand-new suit made that bitter pill a little easier to swallow.

On the day of the trial, Benita sent a limousine to pick him up. Unable to sleep, he was up early and dressed, looking out the small, dirty, rectangular window in the door when the shiny black limo with tinted windows pulled into the dirt-covered driveway of the single-wide trailer on Crimson Lane. He'd lived in the house trailer for most of his life—most of the years he could remember, at least. When Benita said she'd send a driver, David thought it would be a taxi—but a limousine? It was times like these when he missed his brothers. He could only imagine the joy they'd get from riding in a stretch limo. The more he thought about it, the angrier he became. Bea had kidnapped those boys and led David to believe they were his brothers; he'd bonded with them as they grew up together. Now he suddenly found out he was an only child. *Damn you, Bea. Not only did you destroy their lives, but you did a pretty good job on mine, too.*

On the drive to the federal building, David played with controls and pushed buttons, trying not to think about the day ahead. He closed the partition between the front and back seats more than once. The driver, dressed in a black suit and white-collared dress shirt, rolled his eyes as he watched his jubilant rider in the rearview mirror. David imagined he'd probably seen his share of elated passengers, and not wanting to waste the experience, decided to make the most of it.

David was shocked to see all the news media gathered outside the federal building, an old historic landmark in downtown Jamestown. Something like this didn't happen very often in North Dakota, especially a sleepy little town like Bunting Valley. Every local news station and national news affiliates had representatives camped out on the sidewalk, waiting to hear details of what they were calling "the trial of the century." When the limo rounded the corner, several camera men came running toward them, thinking David was someone important. Unsure of who they thought he was, he sat back and smiled through the tinted windows. *I am someone; you just don't know it yet.*

David and the other witnesses were corralled together into a large conference room off the main hallway, the same hallway that led to the courtroom where he would face his mother. Aunt Benita was there, as was Mrs. Edna Brown, David's elderly next door neighbor; Officer Butler, who was the arresting police officer in the kidnapping of Maggie Taylor; and a couple other people he didn't know or recognize. David looked very nervous as he took a seat beside Aunt Benita. "You look so handsome," she said, reaching for his hand.

"Thank you, and thank you again for the suit. I've never had anything this nice before. As I told you, Mom did most of our shopping at Second Hand Sam. The only time we got anything new was when someone gave it to us…and that wasn't very often."

"I'm so sorry, David. I wish I'd known. I would have done something to help." She squeezed his hand a little tighter.

"You don't need to be sorry. It's none of your doing, and I didn't know any different. And the limo! Oh my gosh, Aunt Benita. It was unbelievable."

Prosecutor Gregory Hildebrand, a young attorney handling his first high-profile case, burst into the room, full of energy, a whirlwind followed by a blur. Wearing a very nice navy blue suit and matching tie, he'd come by to say a few words before the trial began, to let them know what was going to happen, and the order in which they'd be called to testify. David was told he would be the second witness, after Aunt Benita.

Unbeknownst to David, Benita Adams had met with the prosecutor for several hours the day before. They discussed the time she'd lived with Edward Noslen, her brother, and her niece Beatrice, the accused. Even though it had only been six years, they were six formative years in Beatrice Miller's life, and explained a lot about the way she lived. Benita told of how she'd bumped into Beatrice, years later, on a street corner in Dallas. Beatrice, sitting in a wheelchair, held a sign that read "Homeless and penniless. Please help." Hildebrand said that con artists and swindlers often did such things to garner sympathy, and asked Benita if she thought this was the case. She hesitated, and then nodded. He needed to be sure she was one hundred percent certain it had been Beatrice Miller on that street corner, and Benita Adams confirmed there had been no mistake. Even though Beatrice was several years older, she would never forget those eyes; and even though the baby teeth had been replaced by adult teeth, the smile was the same. The sad, hollow look on her face was enough to keep Benita awake at night, wondering what went wrong. Now she knew. But she wanted to make sure the court knew she didn't fault Beatrice and was convinced the whole scam was Edward's idea. She'd made the trip to help Beatrice, not hurt her.

While David waited for his turn, he paced back and forth in the conference room, carpeted with commercial-grade gunmetal gray carpet. A large, rectangular, dark oak table sat in the center of the room, with twelve or more chairs spaced around it. Its edge was slightly worn from arms and sleeves that had inadvertently polished it over many years. On the wall hung elaborately framed photos of President Barack Obama and the current governor, John Hoeven, next to a copy of the Declaration of Independence in an ornate, vintage-looking frame. David had been required to memorize portions of it for his freshman social studies class, but as he stood reading it, none of it seemed familiar. A window with a faux wood-grain blind let some natural light into the room, but a bank of overhead fluorescent lights overtook the space. Some armless chairs, matching those pushed under the table, lined the walls. Most of the people sat in them, awaiting their turn. On a taller table, pushed up against a wall, was a clear plastic pitcher of ice water and several Styrofoam cups.

Officer Rich Butler, one of Bunting Valley's finest, had befriended David in the midst of all that was going on. He was the first officer to arrive at Lake Gerber on July 17, 2010, the day Maggie Taylor was abducted. Never having been involved in a kidnapping case from beginning to end, and after talking with the Chief of Police, he had adopted the role of lead investigator, a position he did not take lightly.

On the morning of the arrest, Officer Butler had visited the Miller trailer and spoken to Bea Miller and one of her sons, although David was nowhere to be seen. A few hours later, Officer Butler was also present when the arrest was made in an abandoned parking lot at the end of Crimson Lane, and both Bea and David were handcuffed and taken away. Having seen David change so much since the initial arrest, Officer Butler knew there were great things in store for him now that he was free from his mother's influence. He could sense David's uneasiness, and came over more than once to tell him everything was going to be okay.

David wasn't really worried about testifying; he was more worried about seeing his mother. He'd avoided it to this point. She'd sent messages through her attorney's office more than once, saying how much it would mean to her if David came to visit. He even got a couple of letters in the mail, which he did not open. He didn't have it in him to forgive her yet. And he didn't want to hear her side of the twisted, demented story until after the trial. David didn't want anything to change his opinion, which might ultimately change his testimony.

Growing up, he'd never tried to defy her, knowing he'd somehow pay for it in one way or another. To think he was about to go before a judge and jury and tell the truth without repercussions was beyond his wildest dreams. It was daunting, and even though it was the right thing to do, he still worried Bea would find a way to punish him. If he had a dollar for every time she'd threatened to cut out his tongue if he told anyone what was going on—well, he'd have enough money to buy more than a hamburger from the dollar menu. David snickered at the thought.

Aunt Benita seemed to be gone for a long time, but when she came back she told David she thought it went well. "How did she look?" he asked, not really sure he wanted to hear what she had to say.

"She looked like an older version of Beatrice, the little girl I still love with all my heart." Benita, a little flushed, tapped her chest over her heart with her hand as she continued, "She looks a little tired, but beautiful. Honestly, the whole setup is exactly like those crime shows on TV. You know, like Law & Order."

"I've never watched TV." David hung his head. "She refused to let us have one."

Benita's brow furrowed. "Really? I thought everyone watched TV. I can't imagine." She looked deep in thought. "So how do you keep up with the Kardashians?"

"The Kar-who?" David asked, as if she were speaking a foreign language.

Benita shook her head. "Well, anyway. Beatrice is sitting at a table next to her attorney…I think his name is James Monroe…facing the judge's bench. There's another table just like it where Mr.

Hildebrand is sitting, if you can call it sitting. That man looks like a professional shopper on Black Friday…never in one place very long. The courtroom is pretty full. I guess everyone is curious."

"What did they ask you?"

"Just stuff about when Beatrice was a little girl and how your Grandpa Edward treated her."

"Was that it?" David was hoping for more. He wanted to know what to expect when it was his turn.

"More or less," Benita said with a strained smile.

"David Miller, you're up next," a middle-aged woman announced, holding the door open for him. David took a deep breath and followed her to the heavy wooden double doors at the back of the courtroom.

David entered slowly, feeling uneasy, as if he were walking the plank. Officer Butler had somehow managed to escape the conference room and was seated near the back. David spotted him, comforted to see a friendly face in the crowd. He tried to avoid looking at Bea as he glanced around at everything except the table where the woman—whose DNA confirmed she was his mother—sat. Everything was wood; wooden doors, tables, benches, floors, even the blades on the ceiling fans. After he was sworn in, he repeated his name and his relationship to the accused, and took a seat in the witness box.

The prosecutor got right down to business, asking David to tell the jury what happened the day Charlie, also known as Mikey, was abducted from the Stop-N-Save grocery store in Greenfield, North Dakota. Mikey was one of the two children Beatrice Miller was on trial for kidnapping. David had repeated the story so many times he had it memorized. He even knew when to give a pregnant pause, to allow the best reaction from the jury and audience.

David had seen a few movies, when they had the money and Bea allowed him out of the house. As he sat there on the witness stand, he felt like a character in a film. The attorneys were so articulate David swore they were reading from a script.

He sat straighter in the witness box, trying to ignore the wooden spindles poking him in the back, and told how Bea went to the Stop-N-Save in Greenfield in search of a little girl. When she first saw the baby, dressed in a yellow snowsuit and wrapped loosely in a Winnie-the-Pooh blanket, she thought it was a girl. When she got the baby home and found it was a boy, she panicked and asked David to get rid of it. David smiled as the audience gasped, right on cue. Then he explained that when he told Bea he would do no such thing, she threatened to cut off his penis and dress him like a girl. Again, a major reaction from the crowd, and David loved it. The whole experience was surreal, something he would remember for the rest of his life.

When the prosecutor asked who the child was, David looked straight at his mother for the first time and stated the truth. "I've been told his real name is Charlie Novak. We called him Mikey."

Mr. Monroe stood and walked over to the witness box. He walked back and forth, boot heels clicking on the wood floor, repeating one word—"David"—over and over while tapping his lips with his perfectly manicured index finger. David disliked him from the start. Balding, with a bad comb-over, he reminded David of a used car salesman—seedy and dishonest. "You stated your mom took a child from the Stop-N-Save in the fall of 2003. Is that correct?"

David rolled his eyes, knowing Monroe was trying to catch him in a lie. *For once I'm not lying, and this jackass has the nerve to give me a hard time.* "No, I stated Bea took a baby boy from the Stop-N-Save in the fall of 2003."

Mr. Monroe found something humorous in David's response and softly chuckled. He turned to look at David again. "How old were you when this happened?"

"I was twelve."

Monroe continued to pace. David could tell he was trying to find fault with his answer. With his finger still tapping his lips, Monroe abruptly asked, "And as a twelve-year-old-boy, did you not think about calling the police?"

"I threatened to call them if she hurt Mikey." *Your questions are going to take her down, and you're not taking me down with her.*

"But not because she kidnapped a baby?"

"No. She told me his mom had left him unattended in the shopping cart. She thought Mikey was better off with us."

Monroe stopped and leaned in, his face inches from David's. "And was he?"

It smelled like Monroe had eaten an onion and garlic sandwich for breakfast, and David quickly turned his face. "It's impossible for me to answer that question, not knowing his background," he shrugged.

"No further questions, Your Honor."

David felt as if he'd been punched in the gut. Bea had kidnapped Mikey in broad daylight from a shopping cart at the grocery store, and Monroe was trying to make it look like he was just as guilty because he didn't call the police. If Monroe had any idea what it was like to grow up with Bea Miller as your mother, he would understand that calling the police was not an option. As he stepped down from the witness stand, he glanced in the direction of his mother for the second time. She smiled at David, and as he read her lips, he felt sick to his stomach. "I forgive you, David." He was then led back to the conference room to wait with the others to learn her fate.

Shortly after he returned, Officer Butler came in and told him what a fine job he did. "If you stick to the truth and give the facts as you remember them, you'll always win out in the end."

"I couldn't believe Monroe! What a slimy bastard."

"He's not that bad. Remember, he was hired to defend your mother and show that she isn't as horrible as everyone thinks she is. Don't take it personally. He cross-examines everyone that way."

"Well, maybe he does, but I don't like him. How can he sleep at night knowing he's in there protecting her? What she did was wrong, and she deserves to be punished. I'd give anything not to be her son."

Officer Butler patted David on the back. "It's times like these we hope the justice system works the way it should."

"I guess, but it still makes me mad."

"I understand completely. They're taking a fifteen-minute recess, and then I'm going back in. Do you want to come with me? We could sit near the back."

"I don't know if I want to hear what's going on."

"It might help you realize Monroe isn't out to get you."

David thought for a moment and nodded. "Do you mind if Aunt Benita comes with us?" he asked.

"Not at all." Officer Butler, being a little taller than David, glanced over to see if Benita was still sitting where they left her.

After asking her, Benita said she was tired and would rather sit in the conference room and wait. As it was, she knew more than she cared to. Her memories of Beatrice were still innocent and untainted and she wanted to keep them that way. Benita remembered the promise she'd made Beatrice when she was only a year old—to protect her, love her, and make sure Edward never hurt her. Tears welled in her eyes when she realized how miserably she had failed.

As David and Officer Butler sat at the back of the courtroom waiting for the trial to recommence, Officer Butler told David the next witness was Detective Kenneth McClure from the Greenfield Police Department. He'd been the first on the scene when Charlie Novak was kidnapped in 2003. Hildebrand had him walk everyone through the events of that fateful day. When Detective McClure finished his story, he stated that DNA testing had confirmed Charlie Novak and Mikey Miller was the same person. Monroe declined the opportunity to cross-examine the detective. *Coward.*

Next on the stand was Mrs. Nancy Novak, Charlie's biological mother. She was very pretty, with big blue eyes, and flawless, snow-white skin, exactly like Mikey's. David was torn apart listening to Mikey's mother tell how horribly he was adjusting to his new life.

"When I think back on all the things I missed…his first tooth; his first step; his first word; his first day of school; the first time he said Mama, which he said to her," she said as she pointed at Bea, "and not me; the pain is unbearable." David was close to tears when Mrs. Novak broke down on the witness stand. Bea remained unmoved.

Monroe smiled and seemed pleased with the way things were going thus far. This was very confusing to David because, at times, it was difficult to tell which side Monroe was on. But one thing for sure: if David thought Monroe had been hard on him, it was nothing compared to what he did to Mrs. Novak. By the time she stumbled timidly from the witness stand, Monroe had painted her as an unfit mother who abandoned her baby boy at a grocery store and who should be grateful Beatrice Miller was there to rescue him.

After a break for lunch, Mrs. Brown, David's next-door neighbor, was on the stand. She'd moved into the trailer park a couple of years after the Millers. She had powdery white hair and extra skin stretching downward from her chin. When she turned her head quickly, it wiggled like a turkey's wattle.

Although never close with the Millers, when she was asked about how Mikey came to join the Miller family, she smiled and said it was such a good story. Officer Butler remembered the day he was sitting in her living room and she began telling him the story in the exact same manner.

"Elizabeth, Bea's sister, and Bea were about five years apart in age. Elizabeth was always mature, and she seemed mostly grown when Bea came along, so Bea felt as if she were an only child. Elizabeth was very intelligent and graduated from high school early, when she was just sixteen years old. She went off to Europe and never came back. Then one day, out of the blue, she contacted Bea and told her she had started the adoption process to adopt a baby and was hoping for a boy. Since both of *their* parents were dead, Elizabeth wanted her adopted child to know his only living relative, as well as his cousins. It took four long years, but when Mikey came into her life, she decided it had all been worth it. Elizabeth spoiled him rotten. Shortly after Elizabeth adopted him, she tragically found out that she had stage IV terminal breast cancer. She went downhill extremely fast, and when she died, her Last Will and Testament stated that Bea was to get sole custody of Mikey."

Hildebrand paced back and forth. "Mrs. Brown, where did you hear that story?"

"Bea Miller told it to me. She was sitting in my living room and told me every word."

"Mrs. Brown, are you aware that Mikey was kidnapped?" Hildebrand asked.

"Well, yes, I know that now, but back then, I thought Bea told me the truth. She seemed so sincere when she said it. I had no reason to doubt her."

David was amazed at how easily believable stories came out of his mother. She could rattle one off at the drop of a hat and leave no questions unanswered.

Thinking there wasn't much left to shock him, David almost passed out when he learned Mrs. Brown had dated his grandfather Edward, and Bea had shot and killed him in their trailer. His mouth flew wide open, joining the gasps from the crowd. Obviously, it was something Monroe didn't want discussed, because he jumped up from his seat and ran to the judge so quickly that David wasn't sure his boots even touched the floor. When the trial started again, they were no longer talking about David's grandpa, and Mrs. Brown was excused from the witness box.

A gentleman David didn't know was up next. His name was Tim Taylor, and he was the biological father of Maggie, the cute little three-year-old girl Bea decided she just had to have from the beach at Lake Gerber. He seemed like a nice man, tall and fit, and very charming. David thought he remembered Bea describing Maggie's parents as Barbie and Ken, and the portrayal was right on. However, when "Ken" started talking, David was sorry for ever having agreed to be an accomplice to Bea's scheme. Before today, David never realized there were other people Bea's bad choices and actions had affected; other lives she had ruined, or come close to ruining. He could only shake his head in disbelief as Bea sat and listened, as if someone was telling her a beautiful fairytale. Again, Monroe made Mr. Taylor look like the bad guy and, even though he didn't say it outright, accused him of leaving Maggie, who could not swim, all alone on the beach, at risk of drowning.

A short while later Bea took the stand in her own defense. Looking pale, she placed her hand on the Bible and took the oath. She then turned and smiled at the judge, displaying bright red lipstick smudges on her two front teeth. Her hair was pulled back into a ponytail and the roots, looking like spilled coffee, overpowered her head.

Bea stuck to her story—that she'd rescued those children from unpleasant situations—never faltering. She fiddled with the buttons on the cuff of her suit jacket as she spoke, seeming nervous, which was a side of her David had never seen before. She did not apologize or show any sign of remorse. She'd wrapped her twisted mind around the situation as if she'd done a good thing, and she was almost believable. *No, no, no. It wasn't a good thing!* David wanted to scream as he looked at the jurors to see if they were buying any of it, but he couldn't tell.

When Bea left the stand, Hildebrand and Monroe gave their closing arguments. Again, David tried to read the faces and body language of the jurors, but they didn't reveal much. He did think he saw, more than once, some of them nodding in agreement as Hildebrand spoke. He took that as a good sign until the same people nodded in agreement when Monroe spoke. The jury was given instructions and led into another room, where David assumed they would determine her guilt or innocence.

He turned to Officer Butler. "Now what?"

"We wait."

"How long?" David asked, looking at the closed door of the jury room.

"I don't think it will take long. Either they believe her, or they don't. I'm going to stretch my legs. Do you want to come?"

"Sure. I should probably check on Aunt Benita anyway. I wonder if she knows Mom killed her brother."

"I have no idea," Officer Butler shrugged, leading the way.

They walked through the crowded hallway to the conference room. Aunt Benita was seated exactly where they left her. She didn't look good; her face was pale and her eyes distant. David startled her when he put his hand on her shoulder.

"Aunt Benita, are you okay?"

"I'm fine, David." She reached up and patted his hand.

"You don't look so good. Can I get you something to drink?"

"Yes. Some ice water would be divine. I was just thinking about Edward. I know Beatrice shot and killed him."

David exchanged glances with Officer Butler. "Yes, that's what they said. I'm so sorry."

"Now it's my turn to say 'don't be sorry.' You didn't know. Given the way he treated her when she was a little girl I can't say I blame her. But the Edward I knew was my best friend as well as my brother. When our mother and father died, all we had was each other. He was a couple of years older than me and always protective. When I was a senior in high school, Edward knew our parents couldn't afford much, so he worked and saved his money to buy me a dress so I could go to the prom like the rest of my classmates. It was one of the nicest things he ever did for me. It's those times I remember, not the bad times when he lost his temper. He was a hothead, but so was our father. It was something he was destined to be and couldn't deny or escape."

Officer Butler said, "David, stay here with your aunt. I'll get the water."

The pitcher in the conference room was empty, so he went in search of a drink for Aunt Benita. When he returned, he announced that the jury had reached a verdict. It was quick, but given all the publicity the case had gotten over the last few months, many of the jurors probably had their minds made up before the first witness took the stand. Courts and lawyers normally try to weed such potentials out, but unless they'd brought in people from a third-world country, the chance of finding someone who had not heard about Beatrice Miller were slim to none. Everyone piled out of the conference room and stood at the back of the courtroom. Even with such a crowd, it was so quiet David could hear the hum of the wooden fan blades overhead.

A male juror rose to read the verdict. "We, the jury, find Beatrice G. Miller guilty of two counts of kidnapping. First, a baby boy by the name of Charlie Novak from the Stop-N-Save on October 18, 2003; and second, a girl named Maggie Taylor from Lake Gerber on July 17, 2010."

The whoops and hollers were thunderous. Officer Butler ran over to congratulate Detective Randy Baker, the man he'd worked behind the scenes with for many hours to assure a guilty verdict. No one seemed more pleased with the announcement than Gregory Hildebrand, who finally won his first case as the lead prosecutor. Prior to the trial no one knew who Gregory Hildebrand was. Now, as he pushed on the heavy doors at the rear of the courtroom, television crews were already rushing at him, leaving him little, if any, room to walk. The verdict had turned Gregory Hildebrand into an instant celebrity for all the wrong reasons.

Beatrice Miller collapsed in her seat after the verdict was read. She was eerily smiling with an odd expression on her face. It reminded David of a look of blamelessness; that of a child who had done something wrong but didn't understand the full ramifications of their actions. A moment later, she was handcuffed and led away to await sentencing. David hoped she'd get the maximum, which he'd been told was twenty years for each of the kidnappings, plus a ten-thousand dollar fine. Either way, he didn't have to worry about his mother knocking on his door anytime soon.

A few hours after the trial ended, Aunt Benita seemed in a hurry to catch a plane back to Phoenix. David was sad to see her go. He loved talking to her about his mother and things that happened when Bea was a little girl. The more Benita shared, the more the layers of ice started melting away from his heart, and he began to see his mother in a different light. She, too, may have been a victim.

It takes years to build up trust, and only seconds to destroy it.

~ Anonymous

Chapter One

It was early November. David finished his part-time shift at Music Mart and took the bus home. With winter right around the corner the air had turned blustery, and he pulled up the collar of his fleece jacket to ward off the cold, shivering as he stepped off the bus. David had been working at Music Mart for almost two months, and he really enjoyed it. It was the first time he felt he had something in common with kids his age. While in school, he was always considered weird and different. The few times he did make a friend, when they came to his house to hang out, when they saw where and how he lived, they never returned. He remembered more than once watching a classmate's mom forcefully grab the child and jerk them out of the trailer and into a waiting car as fast as possible. He attributed it to the atrocious smell—the smell he felt he'd finally pinpointed.

Opening the rusty mailbox that stood at the edge of the driveway, he found a letter from Aunt Benita. She apologized for the old-fashioned handwritten letter, but claimed she'd never owned a computer and wouldn't know the first thing about how to use one. David didn't think it looked like old-fashioned handwriting; it looked more like a work of art, with beautifully shaped letters and curlicues everywhere. She told him she was back in Phoenix, and her health had taken a turn for the worse. She confided that she'd been diagnosed with pancreatic cancer four years ago, and her doctor said she was now in the final stages. She was grateful she got to meet and spend time with him, even though it wasn't under the best of circumstances. She was also glad she got to see Beatrice one last time. Since David was her only living relative she was aware of, she'd changed her will, leaving everything to him, and it would mean the world to her if he would move to Phoenix and live in her house. She hated to leave it empty and couldn't imagine turning it into a rental property. As soon as he received the letter, he phoned her and promised that when the time came he would fulfill her request.

Three days after the first letter, a second arrived via overnight mail from Aunt Benita's attorney. In it was a check for fifty thousand dollars to cover moving expenses, a copy of Benita Adam's will, and her death certificate. She'd died on November eighth. David sat down and cried. Not long ago his dysfunctional family was happily surviving on Crimson Lane, where he sadly existed as a son and an older brother. Then in a matter of what seemed like a split second, he found out he was an only child. It gave David some solace knowing he had a true blood relative in Aunt Benita. Now she, too, was gone and he never felt so all alone.

David decided to use a portion of the money to buy a used maroon Ford Escape; one that had been turned in after a two-year lease with just over 34,000 miles on it. It wasn't a color he'd have chosen, but he needed reliable transportation and the small SUV would allow him to get the most for his money. Never having had much disposable income, David was very frugal and analyzed every situation, every decision, to make sure it was the right and the most economical thing to do. After the trial ended, the state of North Dakota offered to return Bea's conversion van, but he declined. He wanted to forget the life he'd known and start fresh, away from Bunting Valley, away from the memories of his serial-kidnapper mother, and away from the blood stain on the carpet that reminded him of how brutally his Grandpa's life had ended.

David rented a U-Haul cargo trailer, had it hooked to his Escape, and was loading it up when he heard someone pulling into the driveway. When he turned, he was alarmed to see a police car, but surprised and pleased to recognize Officer Butler in the driver's seat.

"David, where are you headed?"

Butler climbed out of his patrol car, in uniform, and stood beside David at the rear of the trailer. Now back in command of the K9 Unit, he had his German Shepherd canine partner, Max, in the back seat.

David was wearing a navy-blue, goose-down winter parka, striped stocking cap, and fingerless gloves; he was holding a small, tan box which was held together with packing tape. He turned to look at Officer Butler.

"I received word that Aunt Benita passed away. Since it came out in the trial that Mom killed her brother, my grandpa, I'm her only living relative who's not in prison. She changed her will and left everything to me. I spoke with her a couple of days before she died, and she made me promise to move to Phoenix and live in her house." David set the box inside the open trailer.

"I'm sorry to hear about her passing. She was quite a character, wasn't she?" Officer Butler asked.

"Yes. That she was," David nodded in agreement.

"Wow, Phoenix. That's a long way from here...and a big change."

Officer Butler's uniform was pressed into clean and crisp creases, and David guessed he probably weighed no more than two-hundred pounds, if that. He was wearing mirrored sunglasses, but removed them to reveal a familiar pair of mystical, blue-green eyes.

"Yes, it is. I'm excited about moving, but a little apprehensive about the unknown. One thing's for sure, I won't be sad to get away from this," David smiled, tugging at his parka. "I'm completely shocked at how wealthy Aunt Benita was, though. Her late husband Patrick was a bigwig with some oil company. I plan to use a large portion of the money to start a foundation to help kidnap victims and their families, and call it 'Never Give Up.' You know, Bea kidnapped those kids years ago, and eventually everyone stopped looking for them. If they hadn't given up, they might have found them sooner and stopped the vicious cycle that consumed my mother. She lived her life as if she were above the law." David turned to shuffle some of the boxes around inside the U-Haul.

"Are you going to see her before you leave town?" Officer Butler asked, reaching up to rub what would be razor stubble on his chin, if it had been there. Actually, the more David looked at Officer Butler, the more he realized what a baby face he had. Not knowing how old he was, David was sure he could easily pass for someone in his late twenties.

"I've been thinking about it. At the very least, I should let her know Aunt Benita passed away and I'm moving to Phoenix." David hesitated, deep in thought about what it would be like to see his mother again. "Would you like to come in for a minute? I'd like to take a break, warm up, and get something to drink."

"No, no, no. I showed up uninvited and I've taken up too much of your time as it is. I don't want to keep you from packing."

"Don't worry about it. I have all the time in the world," David said as he started walking toward the trailer, rubbing his hands together and blowing on them for warmth.

Officer Butler followed close behind. "If you're sure you don't mind." He turned and glanced back at Max, who was panting heavily. "Just let me crack the back window a bit so Max can get some air." When the weather turned cold, Officer Butler didn't wear a coat, and usually kept the temperature in the cruiser around seventy-eight degrees. As he rolled the window down, Max stuck out his long snout to breathe in the fresh air.

When they entered, David pulled off his coat and tossed it on the old sofa, still covered with a stained slipcover. He turned to Officer Butler.

"I think I finally figured out what the stench is. It's bothered me for a while, and I could never put my finger on it. Usually it hits you as soon as you walk in the door. After being inside for a while, you get used to it."

"Yeah, I remember it. What is it from?"

David walked over and, grabbing the fringe on a braided throw rug, flipped it back to expose the large crimson stain on the worn carpet. "I'm assuming it's from Grandpa."

"Oh, David, I'm so sorry you had to find that." Officer Butler shook his head in disbelief as David released his hold on the rug and it fell back into place. "But honestly, I've seen a lot of blood stains, and they typically don't have an odor…at least not one that lingers that long. Has it always smelled like this?"

"I don't think so. I was pretty young when we moved here, but I don't remember it back then. It seemed worse this summer, when it got really hot. Right now, it's pretty mild. I thought maybe some of the blood seeped through the floor and collected under the trailer." David frowned.

"Do you have any idea where Bea is? I mean, I know she's in prison, but I'm not sure where exactly," he asked, walking towards the kitchen.

"Yes," Officer Butler said, as he followed David into the kitchen. "Since she's not considered a dangerous felon, she's being held at the minimum security women's prison in Hill Valley. It's about an hour drive from here, mostly highway. I'll go with you if you like."

"Thanks, but I think this is something I need to do on my own," David said as he opened the cupboard, grabbed two mugs, and busied himself filling the tea kettle.

While they waited for the whistle, Officer Butler told David about a few things going on at the station and David talked a little bit more about the foundation and how excited he was at the prospect of doing something charitable. Officer Butler seemed pleased at how enthusiastic David was.

It was hard to believe Thanksgiving was just around the corner. Officer Butler indicated he would be spending it with his mom and dad, as he always did. Holidays were a sad time for David, as he didn't have good memories of them.

The kettle whistled, and he poured steaming hot water into big, chunky, mismatched mugs, making each of them a cup of hot cocoa. Officer Butler blew on his and carefully sipped it while telling David how proud he was of him and how he knew David would be the one to break the cycle and make a difference.

When the cocoa was gone, they walked back outside. Officer Butler told David how happy he was to have Max back, and how much he'd missed him while one of his colleagues was running the K9 unit. They talked a little about school, and David said he was planning to major in criminal law at the university near where Aunt Benita had lived.

"I'd like to be on the other side of the law for the next part of my life," he smiled. "You know, that slimy lawyer Monroe made me so angry at the trial, I think I'd like to be a prosecutor. Then I can tear people like him apart."

"Well, whatever you decide to do, I'm sure you'll be good at it. Oh, before I forget, I have something for you. Your mom wanted you to have this." Officer Butler opened his door pulled out the journal Bea had been writing in for over thirty-five years. "I know it's difficult, but someday you should read it. I think it'll help you see things differently," he said, handing it to David, who'd forgotten to put on his coat and was busy rubbing his arms for warmth.

He took the old, tattered book knowing it would take some time, but eventually he would read it and forgive her. He had to. She was all he had left.

"Give me a call once you get to Phoenix and get settled. It would mean a lot to me if we could keep in touch. I'd like to hear how things are going," Officer Butler said, handing him a business card. David glanced at it and saw Officer Butler's home and cell numbers on the back. He smiled as Officer Butler scratched Max on the top of his head before climbing in his patrol car.

As he backed out, David waved, and then turned to go back into the trailer and get his coat. He stood for a moment looking at the journal, thinking about his mom and wondering how things had gotten so far off course. He gently placed it in an open box, and then started carrying his few belongings out to the U-Haul again. He didn't have much, and he wasn't sure what he wanted to take with him of what he did have. He'd phoned their old landlord, the person whom Bea had purchased the trailer from years earlier, to see if he was interested in buying it back. After a short conversation, David agreed to sell it for $5,000. He'd hoped for $10,000, but it was over thirty years old and needed a lot of work.

David heard a door slam and saw Mrs. Brown, dressed in flowered flannel pajamas and a hot pink housecoat with matching furry slippers, come out of her trailer; she was headed toward the mailbox. From what little Bea had shared with him, he remembered that Mrs. Brown's husband had died some time ago, which would explain why she liked to butt into everyone else's business. It was Sunday, and David knew she was making up an excuse to come over and talk to him. She probably wanted to know why the police were there.

"Hello, David," she said. "I don't know where my mind is. Today is Sunday, so there's no mail."

David, didn't turn around; he just smiled to himself and responded, "Hello, Mrs. Brown."

"It looks like you're moving."

Duh, David thought to himself as he rolled his eyes. "Yes, I'm heading to Phoenix. I plan to enroll in college there."

"Phoenix? Why Phoenix?" Mrs. Brown asked.

Even though she was a nice old lady, David didn't want to give her any information she could use after he'd left. Lord only knows what she'd already said. "I have family there," he said, which wasn't technically a lie since Aunt Benita had been cremated and the ashes were there waiting for him.

"Really? What family?"

"Just some distant relatives on my mom's side. No one you would know."

"I'm curious if you've seen your mother since the trial; how she is doing?"

"No, Mrs. Brown, I haven't. I've been busy working and packing. I just bought the SUV, and before that, I had to take public transportation everywhere. I really didn't want to take the bus all the way out to the prison to see her."

"Yes, I saw the *new* car. Did you win the lottery or something?"

David couldn't believe her. "It's not a *new* car and, yes, something like that."

"Which prison is she in?" Mrs. Brown just wouldn't give up.

"Officer Butler just told me it's the one over in Hill Valley."

"Oh. I wondered what he was doing here. I've heard the prison in Hill Valley is one of the nicer ones," she said, cinching the belt on her robe a little tighter.

"I don't know anything about it, but I really don't think any prison is nice."

"I suppose. Tell me, did you know Bea killed your grandfather?"

Ahh, she finally got to the point. "No. Not until the trial."

David had his back turned to her and was doing his best to hint that he wanted her to leave. He continued rearranging and stacking boxes in the U-Haul.

"Did you know Edward and I knew each other?" Mrs. Brown kicked the dirt with the toe of her furry slipper. The dirt was pretty much frozen, so it was a futile gesture.

In his peripheral vision, David could see her tilt her head. "No, I didn't." He turned to face her. "I never met him."

"Really? I find that very odd considering he lived here in Bunting Valley for quite a while. You mean to tell me he never came for a visit?"

"Not that I'm aware of. At least not when I was home."

"Oh. Are you going to sell the trailer?" She stood before him with her hands shoved in the pockets of her housecoat. David knew she had to be freezing.

"I already have. Mrs. Brown, I don't mean to be rude, but if you'll excuse me, I need to get back to packing."

As if she hadn't heard David speak, she continued, "If I can ask, who bought the trailer? I'd like to be prepared for new neighbors."

"I sold it back to our old landlord. He's going to rent it."

"Oh, I see. Well, I hope the next family takes better care of the yard." She turned and walked away.

David shook his head. Bea always complained about Mrs. Brown, whom she referred to as the "old biddy next door." He never thought she was that bad, but now he saw her differently, and it made him all the more glad to be moving.

Later that evening, David phoned the women's prison to make sure the inmates were allowed visitors. He planned to see Bea the next day, before he drove to Phoenix.

~

Looking around the inside of the trailer, trying to remember the day they moved in, David made one last visual sweep of each room to make sure he hadn't left anything of value behind. It was pretty dilapidated: paint chipped, curtains faded, holes knocked in the walls, cupboard and closet doors hanging cockeyed, some missing knobs, threadbare carpet, windows broken and held together with tape. They moved in shortly after his father had been killed in a horrific car accident. His mom packed up Joshua, John, and him, and left their home in Seattle, driving most of the night. He didn't remember much, but he did remember how lost his mom seemed, unsure where to go or what to do.

Early on, his childhood seemed pretty normal: a mom, a dad, and a brother. Even after his dad passed away and John was born, they moved to Bunting Valley and things weren't that bad. Bea had a job and they enjoyed life and had fun together, at least from what he could remember. When did everything change? David shook his head, trying to put his past behind him and think about the future.

He decided to leave all the furniture; it came with the trailer, and he didn't need it. Lord knows it had seen better days. He decided to take a few dishes, glasses, and utensils; towels, washcloths and bed linens; pillows and blankets; and some toiletries. He wasn't sure what Aunt Benita had in her house, and he wanted to be prepared.

It struck David odd, but when he was going through the dishes to pick the nicest ones, he found money stashed in bowls and cups. Not a lot of money—mostly dollar bills—but he was curious where it came from and why it was hidden.

He remembered how hurriedly they'd packed the day both he and Bea were arrested. They managed to grab a lot of things, even though they were under duress. He recalled how his mother gave Mikey such a hard time about bringing his worn-out blanket with him, the one he'd been wrapped in when Bea kidnapped him. Over the years, Mikey had grown extremely attached to it; it was one of the few things that could calm him down after a nightmare. David shook his head, remembering how Mikey started crying when Bea told him they didn't have room in the van and he had to leave it behind. "Michael, stop crying this instant, or I'll give you something to cry about," she'd said. Bea called him Michael when she was mad, and Mikey knew not to push her.

Thinking back on the trial, the way Nancy Novak described him, and the difficulty he was having adjusting to his life as Charlie Novak, David felt awful. *Why didn't I call the police that day?* David picked up the blanket and held it to his face, inhaling what remained of the scent left of Mikey; then he draped it over his arm, took one last look around, and left the shattered pieces of his dysfunctional childhood behind.

~

A little over an hour later, just after six o'clock, David pulled into to the parking lot at the Hill Valley Female Correctional Institute, the place his mother called home, and probably would for the next several years. The prison was less than ten years old, an expansive white brick building covering several thousand square feet, two stories high and surrounded by a chain link fence topped off with barbed wire. It was a little overwhelming, but by the time he went inside, his nerves had calmed a bit.

When David phoned the prison the evening before, he found out visiting hours were from six-thirty to eight-thirty p.m. He could only visit with Bea in the secure visiting area, because his name was not on her list of approved visitors. A visitor application had been mailed to him on three different occasions, but had never been completed and returned. David vaguely remembered getting mail from the prison, but assumed they were letters from his mom and, still angry with her, threw them away unopened. He was fine with seeing her in the secure area; never having visited anyone in prison before, he was sure he wouldn't know the difference.

As he entered the double glass doors, David noticed the dull, depressing colors of the paint: muted grays, blacks, and greens. After seeing the long faces of the attendants on duty, he wondered who'd died. They checked his identification, had him complete a visiting card, and directed him to the visiting area.

What a contrast to the lobby! The stark white cinder-block room had no windows, but the big banks of fluorescent lights overhead made him squint and wish he'd brought his sunglasses. The confetti-flecked tile floor looked like it belonged in a hospital. A table against one wall held board games and a few decks of cards. Three square black vinyl couches, without pillows or armrests, were pushed up against the walls, and a faux-wood dinette table with four chairs sat in the middle of the room. David sat on one of the couches, then reconsidered and moved to the table.

When Bea finally arrived, she seemed both elated and surprised to see him. The security guard, an overweight bald man, sat on one of the couches to keep an eye on things and to be sure David had not brought her any contraband. When he arrived, they asked him if he had any contraband items, and since he didn't know what "contraband items" were, he shook his head. The three were the only people in the room.

"Hello, David," she said, smiling, showing her tiny teeth and big gums. All things considered, she looked good. Her dark roots had grown out substantially and reached almost halfway down her head. The tips were still bleached blonde, which David never thought suited her. She was wearing no jewelry or make-up, prompting David to try to remember the last time he saw her without bright red lipstick. The only thing really different was a pair of glasses, silver wire-rims with an obvious bifocal line.

"Hello," he said. Having wrestled with what he should call her the entire drive, he blurted, "Mom."

"How are things at home?" she asked, taking a seat next to David at the table. She looked around nervously, as if she was afraid that someone had followed her.

"I guess everything is all right, but that's partly why I'm here." David scooted his chair closer to her and rested his elbows on the table.

"What? Did something happen? Are the kids okay?" Bea looked concerned.

"What kids?" David was confused.

"Josh, John, Mikey, and Maggie. What kids did you think I was talking about?" Bea giggled. "Sometimes you're so silly."

David shook his head and ignored her question. "I need to tell you something, and I'm not sure how you're going to take it."

"It's better to just spit it out. It's like pulling a Band-Aid off a sore…just get it over with quick."

"Okay, here goes. Aunt Benita passed away."

Bea's reaction was totally unexpected. Bea placed her hand over her mouth. "Oh, no. What happened? Did Papa kill her?"

David frowned. "What are you talking about?"

"Papa was always so abusive. I knew one day he would kill someone." Bea moved closer and cupped her hand in front of her mouth. "Just between you and me, I'm glad it was her and not me."

The security guard rose to his feet. "No whispering."

David looked at the guard and then said, loud and clear, "She died of pancreatic cancer, Mom."

"Are you sure? Papa was always good at making things look like an accident."

"Yes, I'm sure. I don't think Grandpa could forge her medical records. What's wrong with you? Are you on medication?"

"Nothing's wrong with me. I'm fine. That's enough talk about depressing things. Tell me, how are the kids?"

"I don't know. I haven't seen much of them since the arrest."

"The arrest? What arrest? Were you arrested?" Bea looked so sincere.

David shook his head. "I'd rather not talk about it. Tell me how things are going with you."

Bea replied, "Well, this hotel is okay. I've seen better, but then again, I've seen worse. In my spare time, I've been working on my GED. I'd like to get my high school diploma, and then maybe take some college courses. I need to set a better example for you and the rest of the children."

David didn't know if he should tell her about Phoenix or not. She was talking crazy. Finally, he just said, "I sold the trailer, and I'm moving to Phoenix."

"Phoenix? You can't go to Phoenix and leave me here."

"I'm sure they'll take good care of you."

"I don't know, David," Bea leaned in to whisper. "I think some of these people are crazy."

The guard, on his feet again, had a deep, intimidating voice. "What did I tell you about whispering?"

"Okay, Sir," David said. Then, not wanting to upset her, he changed the subject. "When did you get glasses?"

Bea reached up to touch them. He could tell she still wasn't used to them. "I had a physical and eye exam when I first got here, and they determined I'm legally blind. Can you believe that? All those years I was driving around, not realizing I couldn't see. So I picked out some frames and they made me a pair of glasses. When I first put them on, the whole world came into focus. Colors are so vivid and bright! And faces across the room are so crisp and real! It's amazing."

"I can imagine. Legally blind, you say?"

"Yes. It sounds worse than it is. It just means I can't drive without them. The bottom part is for reading. Now I don't have to hold everything at arm's length for it to come into focus. There weren't that many different styles to choose from. How do you like them?" Bea turned her head from side-to-side so David could get a good look.

"They look nice. They suit you. Make you look smart and sophisticated."

"Thank you, David. That means a lot." Not used to compliments, Bea seemed uneasy and started picking imaginary lint from her uniform.

"So, what else can you tell me about life here in this, um, this hotel?" David gestured to their surroundings.

"Well, the food isn't great, but at least I don't have to cook it. Everyone has to pitch in and help with housekeeping. I'm working in the cut-and-sew program. We make hospital gowns and scrubs. I'm not really sure why a hotel needs those," Bea shrugged. "I haven't sewn anything since I made those kitchen curtains out of a sheet. Do you remember that, David? Or were you too little at the time? I have a hard time remembering things lately."

"No, I don't remember you making them, but I do remember the curtains in the kitchen. It sounds like you enjoy sewing."

"I do. I do. It's calming in a way I can't explain."

"Have you made any friends?"

"I don't know if I'd call them friends. Some of the other guests pretend to be my friends, but then they talk behind my back. That's too much drama for me. One thing we do every night is get together in the gathering room and stare at a box. There's one right there." Bea pointed to the corner of the room.

"A television set?"

"No. It's called a TV," Bea whispered, as if sharing a national secret.

The security guard rose again and stated, "One more time and this visit is over."

David giggled, thinking the security guard was getting his dander up over talk about a TV. "Sorry, Sir, it won't happen again. Yes, Mom, I've heard of those. What do you see when you look at the TV?"

"Every night is something different. Last night we watched someone trying to win a million dollars by answering some questions. There's another show where everyone is trying to be the biggest loser. I thought being a loser was a bad thing." Bea looked at David as if waiting for him to reassure her that she was not misguided. "And there's a channel that tries to sell you stuff. All you have to do is call them, and you can buy things without ever leaving your chair. It's magical."

After a while longer, Bea made David promise to give his brothers and sister a kiss for her. He told her what a wonderful woman Aunt Benita was and he wished he could have gotten to know her better.

"Things aren't always what they seem, David. Remember that," Bea said.

"What does that mean?"

"I'm just saying," Bea replied as she shrugged.

He wished her a happy Thanksgiving, and Bea, in her orange-cotton prison jumpsuit, was ushered back out the door through which she'd entered. When she was out of sight, David, concerned that she was losing it, asked to talk to someone in charge.

They confirmed that Bea's short-term memory was failing, and she seemed to have no recollection of what had happened and why she was there. They had her on some pretty strong antidepressants, but aside from that, she was adjusting well. Everyone liked her, and she never caused any trouble. David informed them he was moving to Phoenix, and wrote down his new address and phone number, just in case they needed to contact him.

Before he left, they gave him Bea's jewelry—a wedding band and her cherished charm bracelet. David had never paid much attention to her jewelry, but he looked closely at it now. The wedding band was gold, with small leaves delicately etched all the way around. He held the charm bracelet and remembered the first time Bea showed it to him, which was shortly after his father passed away and they left Seattle. He thought back to the day at Lake Gerber when Bea thought she'd lost it and how upset she was. The charm that held his name, a silver football with his name engraved in capital letters, was smooth to the touch and beginning to wear in some spots. He stopped a moment, and realized that three of the charms bore the names of someone else's children.

Don't be discouraged.
It's often the last key in the bunch that opens the lock.
~ Unknown

Chapter Two

Around midnight, David spotted a blinking, illuminated vacancy sign at a small motel directly off the highway. He was hoping to get more distance between himself and Bunting Valley, but he was so exhausted he decided to stop. It wasn't as if anyone was waiting for him in Phoenix. Greeted by an unfriendly attendant missing her front teeth, David checked in with only a small overnight bag. He made sure to set the alarm to seven a.m. so he could shower and get back on the road no later than eight. He was sound asleep as soon as his head hit the pillow.

Rising early, eager to get back on the road, David pulled in to a truck stop for breakfast and to fill up the SUV. As he drove, mile after mile he thought of his mother and how weird their visit had been. Some of things she said really threw him for a loop—even for Bea, strange as she'd always been. He was beginning to think she was crazy.

Shortly after seven that evening, hungry and tired, David decided to get another room. Tonight he took his time and found one that was part of a well-known chain. He'd hoped to make the twenty-hour drive in a day and a half, but it was more taxing than he'd anticipated. It would have helped if he had a passenger, but there was no one. It would have been nice just to have someone to talk to, because the songs on the radio were putting him to sleep instead of keeping him alert and awake.

Just after three p.m. the next day, David saw a gigantic sign that read, "Welcome to Phoenix. Mayor Phil Gordon Welcomes You!" He was overjoyed. His first stop was at the offices of Cooper and Boyd, Aunt Benita's attorneys. Located in a suburb just outside the city, it was a modern office building with six floors, lots of mirrored windows, and a beautiful shiny silver sculpture in the front courtyard.

David walked inside and found Louis Cooper, Esquire, on the directory mounted on the wall directly inside the front entrance. He took the elevator to the fifth floor, and after giving the receptionist his name he was ushered right in.

Mr. Cooper's office was contemporary, with an oversized, executive cherry desk and matching credenza, which was centered under a big window. A matching cherry shelf with glass doors, which reminded David of a liquor cabinet, stood against another wall. When David entered, Mr. Cooper, an older gentleman with wavy silver hair and glasses, stood up from his high-backed burgundy chair and came around to shake David's hand. The diamonds in Mr. Cooper's big, chunky ring caught the sunlight, producing reflections on the ceiling during their handshake. Then he handed over a very thick, black three-ring binder.

David, caught off guard, said, "What's this?"

"It's a manual Benita made. It shows how to work things at the house, like the security system, front gate, air conditioner, pool filter, gas fireplace, and sprinkler system, among others. Her house was pretty high tech, so she thought it would be best to compile all the information in one place so you wouldn't have to hunt for the instruction manuals."

David remembered how Aunt Benita had apologized for the handwritten letter and softly chuckled. "What kind of house is it?"

"Don't you know?" Mr. Cooper asked, standing with his arms folded in front of him.

"I have no idea." David shook his head. "We never discussed it. She just asked me to move in when she passed away because she didn't want it empty and she didn't want to rent it."

"David, you're in for a real surprise," Mr. Cooper smiled. "Oh my goodness, where are my manners? Would you like to sit? Something to drink?" Mr. Cooper pointed at a guest chair that sat directly in front of his desk.

"No thanks, Mr. Cooper. I've been riding in a car for two days, so I'd rather stand. What do you mean I'm in for a surprise?"

"Please call me Lou. Mr. Cooper makes me feel so much older than I am. Anyway, the house is rather large: almost six thousand square feet, with seven bedrooms and seven-and-a-half bathrooms. It sits on two-and-a-half acres of lush, green land, and has a pool with incredible mountain views. At today's prices, I'm sure it would sell for well over two million dollars."

David's eyes were huge, and he was having a hard time speaking. Finally, he gulped loudly and found his voice. "You've got to be kidding me!"

"No. Benita and her late husband invested in real estate. Besides the one in Phoenix, they had homes in the Bahamas, Fiji, and Honolulu. She sold those shortly after Mr. Adams died. She said they just weren't the same without him."

"Oh, my gosh!" David's mind was racing. *I think the house trailer in Bunting Valley was about six hundred square feet, if that.* "What am I going to do with all that space?"

"I have no idea." Lou seemed to be taking pleasure in David's reaction. "I guess enjoy it. That's what Benita would have wanted."

"Why didn't she just sell it?"

"I asked her that, and she said you needed a better place to live."

David, remembering how Aunt Benita had grimaced the first time she saw the trailer right before the trial, was overwhelmed by her generosity. "Now I feel silly. I wondered if she'd have any dishes or bath towels, so I brought my own."

Lou laughed. "Yes, the house is fully stocked. At one point it had a maid, cook, gardener, and chauffeur. When Benita got older, she suffered from night blindness, so she hired a driver to take her wherever she needed to go. I think she hired the rest of the staff so she didn't have to be alone. She was a people person through-and-through."

"Are they there now?"

"No. When Benita died, I told them their services were no longer needed. If you decide you'd like to hire them back, just let me know; I have their contact information. Assuming they haven't secured other employment, I'm sure they'd be thrilled to work for you…the nephew of Benita Adams."

David didn't know what to say. Never in his wildest dreams did he ever think something like this would happen to him. He wondered if this is how it felt to win the lottery. "How close is the house to the university?"

"Not far. In fact, in the manual is a street map of Phoenix and a couple of the surrounding suburbs. I think Benita marked where the university is so you could find it."

David flipped through the thick manual. "It looks like she thought of everything."

"Yes, she did. Benita was a planner. She planned her funeral, right down to the flowers, the casket, the music, and even the scent of the candles she wanted burning. Anything she thought you might need, she had made and put in the binder. There should be operating manuals in there for everything in the house that has a button, dial, cord, lever, or key. She also provided you with all her bank account numbers."

"Numbers? How many bank accounts did she have?"

"Oh, there were many, but she closed some recently. When she passed away, there were five or six."

"Why so many?"

"She had a reason for each, and I'm sure it's explained in the manual. I know one was a payroll account and another was for the charities she supported." Lou and David stood looking at each other. "Well, if there's nothing else, I'll turn everything over to you." Lou turned to grab a medium-sized decorated box from the top of his desk. "This contains keys to the house. There are some other things as well; business cards, legal documents, and such. You should probably take a look as soon as you get a chance. The directions on how to get to the house are in the manual; I believe I saw them in the very front."

He handed the box to David. Still sitting on the corner of the desk was the manual and a paisley vase, which David assumed was Aunt Benita's urn filled with her ashes.

"Actually, there is something else. Since Aunt Benita trusted you and you were her attorney, I may need your help with something."

Lou leaned against his desk, folded his arms, and let out a huge sigh. "You aren't in trouble, are you?"

"No, no, nothing like that. I want to start a non-profit foundation to help find missing children."

"Okay, then." Lou, relieved, slapped his hands together. "That's something I can help with. You said non-profit?"

"Yes. I'll open it using Aunt Benita's money, but I hope to operate it solely on donations."

"Do you know anything about running a charitable foundation?"

"Absolutely nothing. I'm hoping to hire good people who can teach me. I'm also going to take some business courses at the university."

"Well, it sounds like you're on the right track. Why have you decided to do this?"

"I don't know how much Aunt Benita told you, but my mom did some pretty terrible things. Having grown up in the environment I did, I think I may have more insight than other people. Everything that's happened in my life has happened for a reason, and I think I should use some of Aunt Benita's money to do something good. This is something I feel I have to do."

"I understand. I can probably recommend a few people for that type of endeavor. I'll start working on it right away." Lou stuck out his hand, and they shook a second time. "Benita told me what a wonderful young man you are. I'm embarrassed to say that when I heard you were only twenty years old, I was a bit skeptical. But she was right. You're eloquent and well spoken. She would be proud if she knew what you intended to do with some of her money."

David smiled as he looked at the beautifully decorated box. It had Aunt Benita's charm written all over it. Lou grabbed the tall urn and manual and offered to help him carry things out to his car. David reflected that she'd left instructions for him to dispose of the ashes as he saw fit; however, not knowing much about her, he had no idea what to do with them. He knew she liked to shop, but he didn't know how he could work shopping into scattering Aunt Benita's ashes.

~

When David arrived at the gated community, he gave his name to the guard and was admitted to Pembrooke Gardens. The map showed Benita's house situated on a cul-de-sac just off the main road that provided access to the entire development. The address was 957 Rambling Brook Way. When he arrived, he had to pull out the manual to figure out how to open the front gate. The massive wrought-iron fence stretched the entire length of the property, and had a huge privacy hedge directly behind it. When David reached the house, he was unprepared for what he saw. Lou had tried to warn him, but the image he'd conjured up in his mind didn't do it justice.

The outside was ivory stucco, with huge white pillars and a red tile roof, and an adjacent four-car garage. David rolled down his window to admire the beautiful landscaping; palm trees with broad grayish trunks and greenish-blue leaves formed bushy, lush canopies that shaded the luxuriant, exotic flower beds, which produced fragrances like nothing he'd ever encountered. There were rock gardens, winding concrete sidewalks, hanging planters overflowing with beautiful flowers, and a fountain spurting crystal-clear water into the air. David had to blink a few times to ensure he wasn't dreaming, as he had never seen anything like it.

Again, he had to refer to the manual to open the garage door. When he found the instructions, it stated, "Use the garage door opener in the box." David opened the box and found a small garage door opener, some keys, photos, and a small Rolodex filled with business cards. He grabbed the opener, and when he pushed one of the three buttons, the huge double door on the left swung out and slid back against the roof of the garage in one piece. When it was completely open, he parked inside on a floor made of tiny tan, brown, and black rocks. Sharing the space was a beautiful silver four-door car with a hood ornament that looked almost like a peace sign. *I bet that's what the chauffeur used. My SUV looks so out of place.*

After more searching in the manual, David figured out how to disarm the security system, and he stepped inside his new home. *Oh, my gosh. This cannot be happening.* He walked into the kitchen and ran his finger across the smooth, midnight-blue granite countertop. It was the most beautiful thing he'd had ever seen—deep blue with small flecks of gold that looked almost three dimensional. He opened the professional-sized stainless steel refrigerator to find it almost empty, except for some condiments. *I guess I need to go grocery shopping.*

Directly off the kitchen were French doors leading to a covered patio, which overlooked a swimming pool and hot tub. *Someone pinch me!* Both had been drained, but it would be easy enough to fill them up again. The paved area around the pool included a grill and seating. After looking around outside, David spotted a small building, which he assumed was a shed, just past the pool. When he tried to enter it, he found he needed a key, which he hadn't brought with him. He cupped his hands around his eyes and peeked through the front window to see a small sitting area with couch and television. To the right was a doorway that led into another room. *Um, this doesn't look like a shed.*

Going back into the house, David found a door off the kitchen that opened into a pantry, stocked from ceiling to floor. *This room is bigger than our living room on Crimson Lane.* He walked inside and looked around. He had never seen so many bags, cans, and boxes of food, except at the grocery store. Further inside the room was another refrigerator. *Another refrigerator? What for?* He opened the door and found it was a fully stocked wine cooler, which held some soda, too. Bea had never allowed them to drink soda, saying it would make them hyper and lead to other indulgences, such as alcohol. Once again he thought of his brothers. *All this stuff would mean so much more if I had someone to share it with.*

He left the room to continue his tour and found each room larger and more elaborate than the last. The furniture was museum-like. David wasn't sure if he was supposed to sit on it or just look at it. Lou had said there were three fireplaces; however, he'd only seen two. The first was in the living room, which was decorated with sparkling crystal, deep, rich leather, and silky smooth satin. The second fireplace was in what he assumed was the master bedroom. Located on the first floor, away from the hustle and bustle of the rest of the house, it was enormous. As he finished his self-guided tour, the phone began to ring, or what he thought was the phone. He had a hard time finding it because the ring wasn't like anything he'd ever heard before, and the phone looked like none he'd ever seen. There was no cord.

"Hello."

"David? Is that you?"

"Yes, this is David." *Who would be calling me at this number?*

"This is Lou Cooper. I just wanted to make sure you found the house and were able to get in. I called ahead to tell the security guard you were coming. I hope he didn't give you a hard time."

"Yes, I found it. The guard was very cordial and let me in, no questions asked. Oh, Mr. Cooper...Lou...I've never seen anything like this in my entire life."

"I told you it was nice. I hope it has everything you need."

"I haven't had a chance to check that out yet, but I did notice that I need to do a little grocery shopping. The refrigerator is almost empty."

"Yes. I instructed the staff to clean everything out of the refrigerator that had an expiration date since we didn't know when you would be coming. The only things remaining should be Benita's collection of rare wines in the wine cooler in the pantry. I don't know how much you know about wine, but some of those bottles are expensive and extraordinary. Whatever you do, just make sure you keep them in the wine cooler on their side."

"I don't know anything about wine, and I'm not even twenty-one, so they'll stay where they are," David replied.

"Benita arranged for a tab at the grocery store, which is tied to one of her bank accounts. She has it set up so all you have to do is show your identification, and you can purchase anything you need. Heck, you don't even have to go to the grocery store if you don't want. They deliver, or at least they did for Benita Adams. You'll find, as you meet people, that your aunt was extremely well known in Phoenix. She was generous to a fault, and I never met anyone who didn't like her. She may have been one of the wealthiest women in the city, yet she didn't flaunt it. Don't get me wrong...she enjoyed her designer labels and vacations...but she would give you the clothes off her back if she thought you needed them. Her funeral was attended by over a thousand people."

"I can believe that," David said, staring at the phone cradle. There were so many buttons—mute, redial, gate, alarm, intercom, music, conference, speaker, record, erase, ringer, menu, clock, transfer, volume, directory. *Holy crap!*

"Did you see the basement?"

"Basement? There's a basement?"

"Yes. The entry is through the garage. I thought it would be the perfect spot to set up your foundation. It's plenty big enough, and it already has a bathroom; just add a couple of walls and it would work nicely. The staff could come and go through the garage, so you wouldn't have to be home or worry about them traipsing through your house. I contacted the city to see if the area is zoned to run a business out of your home, but since it will be non-profit, you don't have to follow the for-profit regulations. It might be a good idea to get Benita's accountant involved now, just so we make the right decisions and do everything on the up-and-up. He's a pretty good friend of mine, so I'll get in touch with him. In the meantime, take a look at the basement and let me know what you think."

"Yes, Sir, right away."

"I can line up some contractors to give you estimates on the renovations. It's always a good idea to get three or more bids, so you can show why you made the decisions you did for tax purposes."

"I can't thank you enough."

"No need to thank me. Benita and I had a long talk before she passed away, and I promised I would help you whenever I could. Being new in the area, it would take you a week to accomplish what I can do in a couple of hours. Oh, as you know, tomorrow is Thanksgiving. If you don't have plans, you're welcome to come to my house and celebrate with my family. All the kids and grandkids will be there. It's one of the few times a year we all get together. We have a big dinner, so adding another plate isn't a problem."

"Thanks for the invitation. I'll think about it and let you know."

After they'd hung up, David started carrying some of his things into the house. The more he looked at his measly possessions, the more ridiculous he felt; his things didn't belong in Aunt Benita's mansion. He opened and inspected box after box, and then started two piles in the garage; one for trash, one for charity. He didn't need these things anymore. They were part of a life he'd traveled half way across the country to escape. Things were going to be different from now on. No longer was he David Miller, the only biological child of the serial kidnapper. Now he was David Miller, entrepreneur. It was time his wardrobe and belongings mirrored his new image. He did, however, fold Mikey's Winnie the Pooh blanket and place it in his top dresser drawer. Some things had a way of fitting in, no matter where you were.

Where there's a will, there's a way.

~ Old English Proverb

Chapter Three

David, excited about his brand-new living arrangements, was sad when he couldn't think of a single person he could share his feelings with. Then, two days later, he decided to call Officer Butler.

When he recognized David's voice, the first thing he asked was, "Did you get to see your mother?"

The subject of his mother put a bit of a damper on David's excitement. "Yes. I stopped by on my way out of town."

"How was she?" Officer Butler seemed like he really cared, which David couldn't figure out. He had arrested Bea, and was responsible for her being in prison. He was the one who calmed David during the trial, telling him to place his trust in the justice system, and he was so happy when the final verdict was guilty. It didn't make sense.

"She seemed okay, physically, but the whole visit was very odd."

"Odd? How so?"

"She seems to have no recollection of anything that's happened. She kept talking about Grandpa as if he were still alive, and asking about my brothers and Maggie. When I told her Aunt Benita died, she asked if Grandpa killed her. More than once she referred to the prison as a hotel. Then she said something that was pretty chilling."

"Chilling? What did she say?" Rich was curious.

"She told me to remember that things aren't always what they seem. I asked her what that meant; she didn't elaborate. Do you think she's trying to tell me I was kidnapped too? That I'm really not my mother's son?"

David was standing in the kitchen, looking out the French doors at the pool, which was still empty. Next to it was a bird feeder, an exact replica of Aunt Benita's house, where two squirrels were raking the bird seed onto the ground. *Wonder who filled the bird feeder?* he thought.

"No, that's not it."

"How do you know?" David was curious how Officer Butler could be so sure—and part of him hoped it was true. It would explain a lot.

"I know for a fact you are. Just after the arrest, when Chief Felder and I secured that search warrant and went through the trailer, I saw your birth certificate. It showed Bea as your mother and Henry as your father." David heard Officer Butler release the foot rest on his recliner as Max barked in the background. "Then there was the DNA test that further confirmed it."

"Then I have no idea what she meant. But I did speak to someone in charge. They said she was on antidepressants, which could affect her short-term memory and cause her to act the way she did."

"I've heard of that. Being sent to prison is a big adjustment, and your mother still feels she didn't do anything wrong. She's in denial and that, coupled with the medication, is probably wreaking havoc on her brain."

"I wonder if she'll be like that forever." David tapped the granite countertop, scratching at the flecks of gold with a fingertip.

"No, I'm sure she won't. Once she's been there a while, they'll ease up on the medication and she'll be back to her old self. But there are stages she has to go through with something of this magnitude. She's probably still in denial, thinking it didn't really happen."

"Yeah, that sounds like her. Then what? What comes next?" David placed his foot on the rung of a bar stool and leaned on the countertop.

"Then she'll get angry. She'll blame everyone and everything, except herself. This may be the hardest stage, at least in my experience. It's the hardest stage to watch someone go through, especially someone you care about. Then, after the anger subsides, she'll start bargaining.

She'll talk to anyone who'll listen, promising never to do another bad or illegal thing as long as she lives if they'll let her go home."

"Does that ever work?"

"No, not for someone in her situation. After she realizes she can't bargain her way out of this mess, she'll become very depressed. That's typically when they start the antidepressants. I was surprised when you said they've already started them. Maybe she's further along than I thought."

"I don't know. All I know is that she was acting and talking crazy. Is depression the final stage?"

"No. The final stage is acceptance, understanding the ramifications of what she did and realizing she screwed up. Showing some type of remorse usually comes along with it."

"Well, she's not there yet. She still thinks she did nothing wrong."

"Everyone is different, and every situation is different. Maybe she's going through the stages in a different order. I'm sure there are medical professionals monitoring her, and they know what they're doing. Oh, before I forget, I got a call from Hildebrand."

"What did he want?" David sat up straight, thinking Officer Butler had some bad news.

"To tell me Bea was sentenced yesterday. She got fifteen years for each of the kidnappings. If she stays out of trouble, she could be released early for good behavior. While she's in there, like I said, she'll be monitored. I'm sure they'll send her to therapy to be sure she's rehabilitated so this doesn't happen again."

"Why didn't she get the maximum?" David had to admit to himself that he was a little disappointed.

"Hildebrand said that because she didn't physically harm any of the children, they went a little lighter on her."

"Maybe she didn't harm them physically, but they'll all suffer for a long time because of her. Heck, I'm her kid and I'm suffering."

"True, but it could have been much worse. All in all, I think she's in the best possible place right now. She'll also have to participate in a work program of some sort."

"She already does. She mentioned something about sewing scrubs and stuff like that. You should have seen how excited she was about watching television. She was like a kid with a new toy."

"Well, enough about your mom. How are things in Phoenix?"

"The weather is awesome, warm and sunny all the time. And you would not believe the house Aunt Benita lived in. It has seven bedrooms, seven-and-a-half bathrooms, and three fireplaces. There's a pool and a hot tub. There's a pantry larger than our living room in the trailer, and it's stocked from ceiling to floor with all kinds of food. The four-car garage has a funny stone-type floor, and there's a really nice silver car parked in it. The whole set-up is amazing!"

Officer Butler couldn't help but chuckle at David's description.

"I even found out Aunt Benita used to have a cook, maid, chauffeur, and a gardener. Can you believe that?"

"It sounds really nice."

"The basement is enormous! It's as big as a bowling alley. I spoke to Aunt Benita's attorney, and he suggested I turn it into offices for my foundation. There's already a bathroom and a fireplace down there. With Mr. Cooper's help, I've lined up a couple of contractors to come by and give estimates for constructing a few walls and a little kitchen area."

"What about school?"

"I'm going to register today. I know they make you take a lot of required courses, like math and English, but I'm hoping to be able to start off with some small-business classes, so I can understand what's involved. I know I'm young, and probably very naïve, and I'd hate for someone to take advantage of me because I don't understand the mechanics. Aunt Benita's attorney has been a wealth of knowledge. He even recommended some classes I should start with."

"Great! I thought once you distanced yourself from Bunting Valley and had some time to think about things, you might change your mind about school."

"Nope. I'm more excited about it now than I was then."

"Are you still planning to major in criminal law?"

"I don't know. When I said that, I was still angry with Mom's attorney. But now that the dust has settled, I might pick something else. I'm going to meet with an academic counselor and see what she has to say. I understand Aunt Benita established a scholarship for me, so all I have to do is choose my classes and they're paid for. I can't believe she thought of everything." David picked up a pen and clicked the point in and out.

"Sounds like you have a pretty good handle on things so far. What did you do for Thanksgiving?"

"Aunt Benita's attorney invited me to his house. I didn't know anyone, but they made me feel very welcome. There were a lot of people, seventeen in all. It looked like something from a movie. We all sat around a huge dining-room table, and Mrs. Cooper carried a perfectly browned turkey out from the kitchen. I think that was the first time I had a turkey dinner on Thanksgiving since Dad passed away. Mom wasn't much of a cook so after that, we didn't celebrate any more. She always said we didn't have anything to be thankful for anyway. What about you?"

"I went to my parents' house. They don't live very far from me. The older Mom gets, the more she reminisces about the past. She had all of our old home movies transferred to DVD, so we watched home movies after we ate."

"I have nothing like that from my childhood. Not even a photograph. Of course, most of the stuff wouldn't have been fit to film anyway."

"Have you had a chance to read the journal?"

"No. I picked it up a few times and read the inscription, but I just can't bring myself to read more. I know I should, but I'm just not ready."

"It talks a lot about your father and when he died. Do you remember any of that?"

"Not really. I remember Mom telling us the baby was coming, and then Josh and I went to stay with our neighbor, some old lady who lived near us. A few days later, Mom came and got us, and said Daddy had died in an accident. That's when I first met John. He was just a couple days old. Do you know where she got him?"

"Yes. She took him from a hospital called Mercy West. I think she worked there."

"Yeah, I think you're right. I remember her working at a hospital; I'm just not sure which one."

"It's all in the journal."

"When I think about all the lives she ruined, I get so angry at her." David gritted his teeth.

"Maybe you should look into counseling. It's a lot to deal with, and being alone may not be the best thing for you right now. Talking to a therapist will help you heal, and you need to heal before you'll be well enough to help others. The stages will work in this situation, too."

"Yeah, you're probably right. Not to change the subject, but I need to ask you something."

"What's that?"

"I don't know the first thing about running a business or searching for missing kids."

"You'll learn. It takes time."

"Some of these kids may not have time." David's words rang true.

"What are you saying? You've changed your mind about the foundation?"

"No, nothing like that. I was wondering…hoping, really…that you'd consider leaving your job in Bunting Valley and come to work with me. I would pay you whatever you're making there, plus a little more. You can live with me; this house is plenty big enough. Not only would it be a big help, I'd love the company."

"I don't know, David. I'm very flattered you think so much of me, but I'm not sure I'm the right one for the job."

"I think you're perfect. Just promise me you'll think about it. I want this foundation to start off on the right foot and I think that with your knowledge and experience, and Aunt Benita's money, we can't go wrong."

As they hung up, Officer Butler promised to give it some thought. David hoped he'd decide to do it. Having an ex-police officer, the one who was key in finding and returning Maggie Taylor safely to her family, would give the foundation the credentials it needed. It was imperative that the community take him seriously for the foundation to be successful.

~

David wandered into the living room to look around. There was a curio cabinet filled with antique-looking figurines. He opened the door and gently picked one up. It was made of some type of ceramic or glass, and he flipped it over. The bottom had an imprint that read, "M. I. Hummel." Not having the slightest idea what that meant, he placed it back in the cabinet and shut the door. He stood back looking, guessing there were at least twenty-five to thirty of the figurines on each shelf, and the cabinet had six shelves. That meant whatever they were, there were over one hundred and fifty in the cabinet.

The furniture, made of inviting leather, seemed to call his name, and he sat in a corner chair with a high back. He ran his hands over the brown leather, so soft and warm. The drapes, made of satin, were also chocolate brown, graced with multi-colored embroidery. The tops were very ornate, with roping and tassels showcasing each pleat and curve. David stood and ran his hand over the fabric. He couldn't remember ever feeling something quite so fine. Knowing Aunt Benita as he did, he guessed the curtains probably cost a small fortune.

The only curtains David remembered were the ones hanging in the trailer when they moved in: Teenage Mutant Ninja Turtle curtains in one bedroom, and Pink Panther curtains in the other. Then there were the curtains Bea made for the kitchen. Never having been one to pay attention to that sort of thing, as far as he knew, they were all still hanging there when he moved out.

David noticed a wall plate with six switches. He'd never seen such a thing. Curious, he went over and flipped the first switch. The marble fireplace came to life with huge gold, red, and orange flames licking at the fake logs. The second and third switches operated the enormous ceiling fan and light fixture. When he flipped the fourth switch, it wasn't immediately apparent what it was, but then he felt his feet getting warm. *What the…? It's as if that switch warms up the floor.* He bent over to feel it, and sure enough, the floor was warming under his touch. *Only in Phoenix would someone put a heated floor in a house.* David shook his head. The fifth switch operated the blinds encased between the window panes. It was the coolest thing ever. He turned it on and off several times as the blinds went up and down. When David flipped the sixth switch, he couldn't believe what happened. Out of nowhere, a big-screen television came out of the floor, stand and all.

Never having had a TV, and no idea how to operate one, David grabbed the manual and searched for directions. Before long it was turned on and speaking to him. Flipping through the channels, he paused when something looked interesting. There was a Golf Channel. *Nothing but golf, all day, every day? Seriously?* He flipped again and stopped to watch some comedian. He was pretty funny, but used vulgar language. He started flipping again and stopped when he saw a picture of his mother in the corner of the screen. They were talking about her trial and sentence. Hildebrand had given a brief statement—nothing about his mom, mostly about other kidnap victims and the similarities and differences.

Next on the screen was a video of Joshua getting off a plane in New Orleans, being met by his biological family. It had been filmed several months prior, but they were running it again because they were talking about the trial. Joshua had twin sisters. When David saw them all on the screen, all the damage his mother had done hit him again. *Damn you, Mom. How could you?* Not wanting to see any more, David turned the TV off and sent it back under the floor where, as far as he was concerned, it could stay.

He picked up the journal, one of the key pieces of evidence at the trial. His mother had been writing in it on and off for most of her life, intending to give it to David someday. He opened it up, hoping to get past the inscription inside the front cover this time. David knew from reading the words that some of the earlier entries in the journal were written from memory, based on what his mother had been told by Aunt Benita. David hoped once he read about what his mom went through, it might help him to heal.

Returning to the leather chair in the corner, he turned to the first page, which bore a child's scribble. This first entry, dated August 17, 1965, was the day Bea was born. David chuckled when she described herself as looking like a troll, or at least that's what his grandpa had said when he saw her. David learned his grandma passed away three days after giving birth. *I knew Grandma died, which is why Aunt Benita moved in with them, but I didn't know it was when Mom was three days old.* He continued reading for a while longer, and saw that his grandpa was a smoker. *That's why Mom hated it so much.* Looking up at the grandfather clock, David realized he was about to be late for his appointment with the academic counselor. He gently closed the journal and placed it in a drawer in one of the end tables. Now that he'd started it, he was curious about the threads that wove the fabric of the person who was his mother.

~

A few days after David asked Officer Butler to move in and help him with the foundation, Officer Butler left a message on David's answering machine. When David arrived home, he saw he had a message, but he couldn't figure out how to retrieve it. After looking through the manual, he read that entering star-twenty-nine would automatically redial the last number. He tried to give that a whirl, but couldn't find a star on the telephone. *What in the world?* After giving up and slamming the manual shut, the telephone rang. It was Officer Butler. "David, did you get my message?" he asked.

"No. You wouldn't believe this telephone. There are so many buttons, and I can't figure out what any of them do. I must have spent a half an hour trying to figure out how to retrieve a message. I'd just given up when you called." David could hear Officer Butler laughing. "It's not funny. If you saw this telephone, you would sympathize with me. It looks like something out of a science fiction movie. Where in the hell is the star?"

"I'm not laughing at your situation, I just love the way you explain things. The star is the asterisk."

David exhaled sharply. "So why didn't it just say asterisk?"

Still laughing, Officer Butler confessed, "I have no idea."

David, finally seeing the humor, relaxed a bit. "So, why are you calling? Did something happen to Mom?"

"No, it has nothing to do with Bea. I've been giving your offer some thought and decided I'd like to work with you. You're a bright young man with a bright future ahead of you, and your cause is something near and dear to my heart. If the offer still stands, it would mean the world to me to become part of your team. The task is bigger than both of us, but together I think we can make a difference."

"Really? Are you serious?" David had a hard time controlling himself; he felt like jumping up and down with excitement.

"Absolutely! I'm looking forward to it. I discussed it with my parents, and they pretty much said I'd be crazy not to. Of course, they've always been very supportive of anything I wanted to do."

Hmm. I wonder how that feels.

"So, when do you want me there?"

"The sooner the better. I selected a contractor and construction will be starting by the end of the week. There'll be two offices…one for you and one for me. The rest of the staff will sit in an area with cubicles. He's going to make eight of them and then build a kitchen area for breaks and stuff. He said it should take him and his crew about a month, give or take. The blueprints just blew me away and I'm pretty pleased with everything they plan to do. I can't wait to see it when it's finished."

"Okay, then. I'll turn in my two-week notice at the station tomorrow. It's going to be hard, but the chief knows how much I enjoyed working on the Maggie Taylor case, so I'm sure he'll understand. He'll have to find someone else to head the K9 unit, but hopefully that won't be difficult. I'll need to put my house up for sale and put some things in storage. How long was the drive?"

"I can't remember exactly, but it was long. Why don't you just catch a plane and I'll pick you up at the airport?"

"What about my car? I'll need transportation."

"We'll worry about that when you get here. When do you think that will be?" David was doodling on a note pad next to the phone. Even though the phone was cordless, David was so used to the old-fashioned kind that he always stuck close by when using it.

"You're making this too easy for me. If all goes well, I'll be there about mid-December."

"Awesome! I can't wait to see you. Officer Butler, you're not going to believe this house. I know I told you all about it, but really, words can't describe it!"

"David, if we're going to share the same house and work together every day, call me Rich. Once I leave the Bunting Valley Police Department, I'll no longer be an officer."

David grinned from ear to ear. "I like the sound of that, Rich. But I'm telling you right now, for the foundation, we're going to advertise the heck out of the fact you were a police officer."

"I understand completely. What about Christmas? Do you celebrate?"

"Not since Dad died. Wait, I take that back. Mom always got each of us a stocking, but we didn't put up a tree or do other traditional things. There was no room in the trailer, and Mom didn't have the money. In our stocking she always gave us stuff we needed...a new toothbrush, a pair of socks, deodorant. And she'd get us each one special item, like our favorite candy bar or a pack of gum."

"Hopefully this Christmas will be different. The holidays are my favorite time of year."

It was David's turn to laugh. "That sounds like something a girl would say."

"Well, they are. They typically bring out the good in people. Even in my line of work, people are friendlier around the holidays."

"I'll see what I can do about decorations. I'm not sure what Aunt Benita has and what she may have done in the past."

After they hung up, David was in a good mood. Everything was falling into place and he had another phone call he needed to make. He found Aunt Benita's business cards in the decorated box, and called Lou Cooper's office. While he sat listening to the music, waiting for Mr. Cooper to get on the line, he flipped through the remaining contents of the box. There was a death certificate for Patrick Adams. *That must have been Aunt Benita's husband.* There was also the title for the car in the garage, which was called a Mercedes E350 sedan, and a deed to the house. There were several business cards in the Rolodex: an accountant, tailor, dry cleaner, custom window treatments, carpet cleaner, caterer, car repair, et cetera. A few photos, no one David recognized, and a couple of keys, one to a safety deposit box. *Hmm, I wonder what she kept in there.* David heard a click on the line and closed the lid of the box.

"Hello, Lou. This is David Miller."

"David! I was just thinking about you. Are you getting settled in?"

"I guess you could say that. This house is so huge, I think it'll take me a year or longer to figure out where everything is."

"I'm sure that's true," he chuckled. "What can I do for you?"

"I was wondering if you could contact some of my aunt's former staff, to see if they're interested in coming back to work."

"I thought you'd need some help."

"I don't have the slightest idea how to maintain the lawn, and keeping the house clean is overwhelming. Even though it's just me, things have a way of getting dirty, especially the floors. I don't think I'll need the chauffeur, but I'm willing to give him some money to hold him over until he finds something else, if you can help me determine what would be fair."

"David, what a generous offer! I'm sure he'll be thrilled. Benita had the gardener stay in the guest house behind the pool."

"The guest house? I was wondering what that little building was."

"Anyway, he's not married and his sister lives nearby, so hopefully he's still in the area. I'll contact her to see. The housekeeper is a young, single Latino gal, in her mid-to-late twenties. She lives with her family, so she only works forty hours a week and goes home every night. You didn't mention a cook. Are you all right with that?"

David could hear Lou shuffling papers.

"I'm not sure. A good friend of mine is moving from Bunting Valley to help me with the foundation. He's a police officer, or he was, and a super nice guy. I asked him to move in here since I have so much room. Why don't we wait until he gets here and I'll let you know then? He may enjoy cooking, and I wouldn't want to take that away from him."

"That sounds like a good plan. While you're making up your mind, I'm sure Miss Lopez can help you with the cooking, as long as it's not anything too difficult. Her English isn't the greatest, but she and Benita were able to communicate quite well, so I'm sure you'll get along."

"I have another question."

"Shoot."

"Do you know if Aunt Benita put up a Christmas tree?"

"Oh, my gosh, yes. We were there every year for a Christmas party. Benita always had a fifteen-foot tree in the foyer, and a smaller one in the living room. They looked like Martha Stewart decorated them herself. Every light, ornament, and trinket was hand-selected and perfectly placed."

"Were they artificial?"

"I don't believe so. Benita always pre-ordered her trees from the nursery. It was the only way she could get what she wanted."

"Damn. I promised my friend I would decorate for Christmas, and I don't know the first thing about it. I thought an artificial tree might make things easier. Do you know where I can reach Martha Stewart to ask her to come and help me?"

Lou laughed out loud. "Martha Stewart is an entertainer, an entrepreneur. She has a cooking and interior design show on television. I don't really think she is available to come and help you decorate. But Benita had a lot of decorations she kept in storage. Let me make some phone calls. I think there are companies that will decorate your house for you."

"Really?" David had never heard of such a thing. "Rich people are so lazy!"

Lou laughed, and they hung up.

Having nothing but time on his hands, David decided to go back and read a bit more of the journal. So far, he'd read about the day his mom was born, and how her father refused to let her celebrate her birthday because he blamed her for the death of his wife, Marcy. These were all things Aunt Benita had told him, so there hadn't been any surprises so far. His opinion of the journal had changed. He thought it would be filled with one horror story after another, but it wasn't like that at all—at least, not yet.

Things, however, quickly changed. In February, there was an entry about Bea being beaten black and blue when she was two years old. Having never been hit by someone bigger and stronger, David could only imagine how scary this must have been for his mom. He wondered if that was why she never hit him or the other kids, and why she was so angry the single time David raised his hand to her. Thinking back to that day, David remembered the warning his mother had given him: "Don't you ever raise your hand to me again! I took that from one man, and I'm not going to take it from another." He felt sorry and ashamed that he'd never believed her when she spoke of her childhood. She only did so rarely, but when she did, her stories were of how horrible it had been and how badly she was treated. David always assumed she was exaggerating just to make him and his brothers feel bad.

He finally got to the part where Aunt Benita and his grandpa argued, and he kicked her out. When Aunt Benita told the story, he thought there must have been more to it than that. How could he force Aunt Benita to leave over something so small and trivial? But reading about it, David was heartbroken—for his mom, who at the vulnerable age of six, lost the only mother figure she'd ever known, and for Aunt Benita, who loved Bea and doted on her as if she were her own child. And why? Simply because they chose to celebrate a birthday.

Disgusted, he decided he'd read enough. He gently closed it and studied the cover for a while, wondering how many people had touched and read it over the years. Some of the pages appeared rippled, as if they'd gotten wet. David wrapped his arms around it and held it close to his heart. He pictured his mom, crying, hiding to write in her journal, hoping someday to give it to her own children so they would understand.

Anyone can give up; it's the easiest thing in the world to do. But to hold it together when everyone else would understand if you fell apart, that's the true strength.

~ Unknown

Chapter Four

Rich Butler's plane was scheduled to land in about four hours. David was so excited he couldn't sit still. He paced, trying to keep himself busy while waiting to leave for the airport. David had already given Officer Butler's name to the security guard at the main entrance, and informed them he would now be living at Pembrooke Gardens.

Lou had rehired the staff members David requested. Miles, the chauffeur, paid David a visit and cried about the severance package Lou had helped David assemble. Not knowing how much Aunt Benita had paid him, and not knowing how much a chauffeur makes, David was once again grateful for Lou. Miles spoke with a thick British accent, which was more pronounced when he was crying, but somehow David understood that he thanked God for Miss Benita's family.

The gardener, Mr. Kniffee, who also took care of the pool, admitted to stopping by a time or two to fill the bird feeder. He was a middle-aged, silver-haired, balding man with a rotund midsection. When Lou contacted him to see if he was interested in coming back to work, he was overjoyed.

"Miss Benita loved to watch the birds. God rest her soul," he said while making the sign of the cross over his chest. He continued, "I don't think she would be happy knowing their feeder was empty—especially with all the birdseed we have in the shed." Soft-spoken, with beautiful steel-blue eyes, David liked him immediately and trusted him explicitly when it came to the landscaping and what needed done. Funny as all get-out, he was always in a good mood, whistling and humming as he worked.

Since Mr. Kniffee returned, he'd used three days to decorate the outside of the house. He hung strands of clear icicle lights on the angles and pitches of the roof, and more clear lights outlined the branches of the palm trees and the window frames. At night it looked like a small Christmas village, minus the snow. As David looked around the front yard, he couldn't believe what a difference a year could make; twelve months ago, they'd been knee-deep in snow and he was arguing with his mother over some stupid thing as she plotted to get a little girl. David still missed his brothers, and hoped they were doing well and adjusting better than he'd last heard. *I should try to reach them. I'd like to wish them a Merry Christmas and let them know how to get in touch with me, in case they ever need anything.*

Back indoors, David glanced at the clock and saw it was finally time to leave for the airport. He waited patiently for Rich to deplane, and was elated when he finally saw him. *He's here! He's really here!* David ran to meet him.

"Officer Butler!" David said. "I'm so glad to see you!" David stood awkwardly, not knowing what to do. Then, giving in to his instincts, he rushed over and gave Rich a big hug. Remembering the shy teenage boy who climbed out of the back of the van, dressed all in black, just a few months ago, the gesture touched Rich immensely.

When David pulled back, Rich said, "Good to see you, too, David. And remember, no more Officer Butler. I'm Rich from this point forward. Deal?"

Not able to wipe the grin off his face, David shook his head and said, "Deal!" It was the first time David had seen him out of his policeman's uniform. He somehow didn't seem as tall and intimidating. Seeing him in worn blue jeans and an ivory crewneck sweater with the sleeves pushed up, David thought he looked younger.

Rich was carrying a small, soft-sided black leather bag. "Is that all you brought?" David asked.

"No. I checked two bags and had some things shipped. I didn't know what to bring."

After collecting his suitcases, they headed home, talking non-stop about Bunting Valley and the things going on in that sleepy little town.

When they waited for the gate arm to retract at the entrance to Pembrooke Gardens, Rich raised his eyebrows. "My gosh, where are we, Fort Knox?"

David chuckled and couldn't wait to see his reaction to the house. When they pulled into the driveway, David stopped, making a point not to open the garage door. Rich climbed out and shook his head.

"David, this place is unbelievable. I mean, you told me about it on the phone, but never in my wildest dreams did I ever picture anything like this. When I saw the guard at the front of the development, I had no idea what to expect."

"I know. Wait till you see the inside."

"It's hard to wrap my mind around it being December fifteenth and it's seventy degrees! When I left Bunting Valley, I felt like I was in a snow globe. White, fluffy flakes coming down and the temperatures in the twenties. I didn't bring a heavy coat with me. I can see that I won't need one."

"Don't let this nice weather fool you. Sometimes it does get down in the sixties at night," David smiled.

Anxious to see the rest of the house, Rich said, "Well, what are we waiting for? Let's go inside."

"I have a surprise for you." David hit the button on the garage door opener, and there it was—the silver Mercedes, his gift to Rich for coming to help him accomplish his dream. Rich's mouth fell open.

"Is this for me?" He was almost speechless.

"Yep. It's the silver car I told you about. It's a Mercedes. I don't really know much about it, but Lou said it's a nice car."

"Yes, it's a nice car. A very nice car! Are you sure you don't want to sell it? I can get something smaller and more economical."

"Nonsense. You need a car and I have this one. It's yours as a thank-you for coming to work with me."

"I don't know what to say." Rich walked towards the car.

"You don't have to say anything."

Rich climbed inside. It was immaculate inside and out, with soft leather seats and a panorama sun roof. David handed the keys through the open door, and Rich turned the ignition to hear it purr to life. He wrapped his hands around the leather steering wheel and couldn't believe it was his. Pushing buttons and opening compartments, he was like a kid in a candy store.

"The title says it's a 2010. I hope that's okay," David said.

"Yes! Fantastic!" Rich glanced at the dash. "It only has seven thousand miles on it."

Finally, Rich was willing to leave his car to go into the house, which they entered through the garage. After a quick tour and introductions to the staff, David took him to the basement, the area he was most proud of.

"Welcome to the offices of 'Never Give Up,'" David said, proudly spreading his arms wide.

The contractors had worked nothing short of a miracle, and the place still smelled of fresh paint and new carpet. There were two offices on the perimeter, the interior walls and doors made of glass. Each already had a gunmetal gray desk and matching cabinet. It was nothing fancy, but it would work well.

"This is your office," David pointed to the door on the left, "and this is mine."

Already hanging on the doors were name plates. Under each was another plate that read "President."

Rich was taken aback. "What's this?" he asked. "We can't both be president. Besides, this is your foundation and your idea. You can have the title. I came to work for you, to pitch in wherever my experience and expertise would be most valuable."

"We're in this together. I couldn't do it without you, and you couldn't do it without me…or at least without me and Aunt Benita's inheritance."

After a quick tour of the rest of the house, David explained they'd be open for business after the first of the year.

"There's still a few last minute things the contractors have to finish up; and then next week, the telephones, a copy machine, and computers will be installed. Lou told me what we needed, and he also helped hire the staff. He found four people with previous telephone and customer service experience. One used to be a nine-one-one operator, so that's pretty exciting. The local news has run a few interviews with me, and in that frame," David pointed to a framed black and white newspaper article hanging on the wall, "is a story that ran in a local paper. Word is getting out. I contacted the FBI to introduce myself and tell them about the foundation. I told them we're always available to help if there is a missing child in the area. Even with my lack of experience, it never hurts to have another set of eyes and ears. Besides, with your years in law enforcement, and my unconventional upbringing in a house with a serial kidnapper, it's not exactly like we're completely clueless. Any exposure we can get will be a learning experience for all of us. I thought the more we can get our name out there, the better."

"Absolutely. I'm amazed at how much you accomplished in such a short time." Rich glanced around in awe.

"I couldn't have done it without Lou, Aunt Benita's attorney. He's been a rock. Any time I had a question, or couldn't find something, or didn't know something, I just picked up the phone. If he couldn't help me, he found someone who could."

"David, I don't think he's Aunt Benita's attorney anymore. She's no longer with us. He's your attorney now."

"I know, but I have a hard time thinking that people work for me."

"Well, they do, and pretty soon you'll have several more, so it's time you got used to it," Rich said, pointing to the empty cubicles.

"No. There will be several more people added to our staff. They'll work for both of us."

"Whatever you say." Rich made a fist and knocked on the glass wall in front of his office.

"It's bulletproof glass. The FBI suggested it."

Rich frowned. "Sad, isn't it? We're trying to do a good thing, yet there are always people against that."

David shook his head. "I hate to say it, but the publicity surrounding my mother helped. Everyone seems to know who I am."

"I guess that's a good thing…just as long as they know that while you may be her biological son, you're nothing like her." They stood in silence for a moment. "Well, if you don't mind, I'm going to go upstairs and get settled. All I packed were clothes. My house is up for sale, so I left the furniture behind for staging. After I get cleaned up, let me take you out to dinner as a thank-you for your generous offer."

"What generous offer? You're the one helping me."

Rich put his arm around David's neck and, as they climbed the stairs side-by-side, teasingly rubbed his knuckles across his scalp. With Rich there, David finally felt he was home, and Rich felt he finally had the younger brother he'd always wanted.

~

The holidays were soon over, and Mr. Kniffee and Miss Lopez were busy taking down the decorations. Miss Lopez was the most beautiful woman David had ever seen. She was absolutely stunning. Her flawless skin was the color of iced coffee; her dark brown, almost black, eyes gave her an exotic appearance. David had to remind himself to keep his distance; she was an employee, but she wore a lily-of-the-valley perfume that drove him crazy. One of David's favorite flowers, he fondly remembered looking forward to May, when he knew they would be in full bloom and the wonderful scent would waft through the air. Miss Lopez spoke little English, and David worried about how easily she seemed to trust others. When he mentioned his concern to Mr. Kniffee, he was assured Eva Lopez grew up with seven brothers and could take care of herself, but it still didn't stop David from fretting.

David and Rich were trying to be helpful, offering to lend a hand in taking down the Christmas decorations, but they seemed to be more in the way and underfoot than anything else. However, neither Mr. Kniffee nor Miss Lopez complained, saying they both thought having David and Rich there was a nice change of pace. As the four of them worked side-by-side, Mr. Kniffee and Miss Lopez told countless stories about how Christmas was Miss Benita's favorite time of the year. They said the holiday music, piped in through the intercom, began in early December, and continued throughout until New Year's Eve, and even then, Miss Benita was reluctant to stop it.

Once the Christmas decorations were down, they were wrapped with care and Mr. Kniffee took them to a nearby storage facility for safekeeping. This is the reason why David couldn't find them when he first moved in.

David's opinion of TV changed a little when Rich talked him into watching some classic Christmas shows. His favorite was *A Charlie Brown Christmas*. There was something about Charlie Brown and that pitiful little Christmas tree that reminded David of his childhood. He also liked *It's a Wonderful Life,* but he sure didn't understand what that pretty woman saw in cantankerous old George Bailey. The only time he was nice was at the very end of the movie, and by that time David didn't much care for him.

David, Rich, and the household staff had exchanged Christmas gifts. David gave Miss Lopez and Mr. Kniffee a few days off, in addition to a nice holiday bonus. Never having had much money, David was surprised how easy it was to get used to it. At times he felt like he was playing a board game and using pretend money.

Lou told David that Benita always celebrated with parties every weekend the entire month of December. There was one for her political friends, one for the board members of the various charities she held positions on, and another for the staff and other people who worked for her. He had known Benita for many, many years and knew she had hoped for children of her own someday, but she found out early on that her husband's sperm count was extremely low. They were told by more than one fertility specialist that if she were to become pregnant, it would be a miracle. Unfortunately, it was a miracle that never happened. Lou said she always hoped for a little girl, just like Beatrice.

David was childlike and innocent in his reactions to things other people took for granted. The Christmas trees were some of the most beautiful he had ever seen. The one in the foyer was tall and statuesque, every branch perfectly shaped and decorated. Then there were the bubble lights. Never having seen anything like them, David could and did watch them for hours. And when Christmas carolers came to the door he felt like someone was playing a practical joke on him, as he had no idea people actually did that.

More than once, Rich had said his favorite decoration was the nativity scene in the front yard. David often found him staring at it; the baby Jesus, cradled by his loving mother, was so lifelike. The reason Rich liked it so well was because Mary reminded him so much of his own mother. David disliked it for the same reason—because of the loving mother, the loving mother he never had.

David thought of his brothers often, and wondered how they were doing. After talking to Rich, he decided not to contact them. This was their first holiday with their biological families, and Rich felt it best if David didn't dredge up old memories. He assumed it was hard enough for them to adjust, and hearing from David, Rich felt, would be a step in the wrong direction. Rich assured him that he should contact them someday, but now was too soon.

After thinking about it and looking at it from their point of view, David decided Rich was probably right, but that didn't stop him from trying to locate them. Mikey was easy to find. In his mother's testimony, she indicated they'd moved to New Mexico. It looked like they'd moved a total of five times since 2003 and once since the trial. Their last known address was Joplin, Missouri.

Locating John was not quite as easy. He knew he was originally from the Seattle area, but he couldn't find any information about a John Miller. Of course, David knew that wasn't his real name, and assumed his parents probably changed it back. *Oh, well. I'll try again some other time.*

David was equally curious about how his mother was doing. She'd been writing him letters, and when time allowed he wrote back, trying to keep the conversation light. Usually she told him about TV shows she'd watched or how she was doing in school. She'd managed to get her GED and was now in a book club. There were also exercise classes, and Bea went to pass the time. David couldn't tell whether or not she realized she was in prison, but she still referred to it as a hotel from time to time. One thing that never changed, though, was the way she closed every letter. "Remember David, things aren't always what they seem." David still had no idea what she meant, but once the foundation was up and running, he planned to take a few days off to visit her. It would be the first time he'd flown in an airplane, and the very thought unnerved him a bit.

The phones and computers had been installed and they were working out the kinks, preparing for their first day at the foundation. David hired a firm to come in to teach both him and Rich the software. David never used a computer much, except at school, and even Rich commented that the programs were different than any he'd used before. It was an intense two-day training, which was enough for them to teach the rest of the staff.

The kitchenette had a full-size refrigerator and microwave. David decided against having vending machines and instead bought the kind of things a vending machine would offer, things Bea would never allow him and his brothers to have. He had a small, flat-screen television mounted in the corner so the staff could watch it when time allowed.

David was anxious to meet the staff, and tried to think of little things that might make them feel more at home. For the foundation to be successful, he needed a cohesive, content staff. Rich warned him that talking about missing children every day might be hard for some of them, so David arranged for a therapist to stop by once a week to talk and see how everyone was doing. They could meet with the therapist privately or as a group. It didn't matter to David, as long as they could deal with the ups and downs of their job, keep their emotions intact and do what was expected of them.

David's first semester of college started in mid-January, giving him about ten days to get the foundation started and make sure things were running smoothly before he had to leave for a few hours every day to attend class. He was confident Rich would be able to run everything in his absence, and Rich stressed that David's education should be his first priority.

The thought of going back to school gave David a queasy feeling. Never having had many friends in high school, he felt he was opening up his world for more disappointment. When he left high school, his self-esteem was very low. But now he tried convincing himself college was different; it wasn't about who was popular, the better athlete, the prettiest, or whose family had the most money and influence. It was about acquiring the skills he needed to follow the path before him. This was where learning became serious.

David and Rich were becoming good friends, and he told Rich he'd started reading the journal, which made Rich happy. David learned that Rich had decided to become a police officer after he saw his best friend, Buster, shot and killed in Detroit when they were in high school. They'd gone to the movies, and were laughing and talking about Axel Foley, the main character in the film. Waiting for their ride to pick them up, they started walking down the street, and when they crossed at an intersection Buster was gunned down, simply because he'd put his foot down on the wrong side of town.

Rich pulled Buster back across the street, cradling his head in his lap, holding and rocking him until the ambulance arrived, but it was too late. Still, after all these years, Rich could picture what happened so vividly. It was as if he were watching it unfold before him on the big screen: Buster walking slightly in front of him, carrying a white paper cup; the old red-and-brown graffiti-laden brick buildings; the flashing "walk/don't walk" sign; the steam rising from the manhole covers; the background noise of sirens and people yelling; the way he tossed his head back every time he laughed. Then the bang and the sound of Buster's head hitting the concrete so hard that blood splattered up, hitting Rich in the face. It happened so fast that Rich wasn't sure what had taken place for a split second. But when he realized what had happened, it didn't take him long to figure out that if he had been the one in front, he would have been killed instead of Buster. Because of that brush with death, and the lack of closure because the person responsible for Buster's death was never caught, Rich knew he was meant to do something meaningful with his life.

David shared more stories of what it was like growing up with Bea Miller. "I remember when she screwed up and kidnapped Mikey, thinking he was a girl. When I refused to get rid of him, she was so angry with me, as if it were my fault. She demanded I apologize. 'David,' she said, with her hands on her hips, 'we're in this together, and I demand you apologize for defying me. I told you to get rid of that baby and I expect you to do as you're told.' "

"What did you do?" Rich said, mesmerized, both hands around the insulated coffee mug in front of him.

"I refused. I told her I wouldn't do it and I wouldn't apologize. I said that if I owed anyone an apology, it was God."

"God?"

"Yeah. I felt awful about what Bea did and thought I should apologize…if not for myself, for her."

"Did you?"

"I thought about it for a long time, and I finally wrote a note and gave it to her."

"What did it say?"

"I'm sorry, God. Love, David."

"What did Bea do?"

"She looked at it and said, 'Well, I guess that'll do, even though I don't understand what God has to do with it.' "

Rich could only shake his head in disbelief. His family was very religious, and knowing God was just a prayer away gave him solace like nothing else. He called upon Him when things got tough, asked for His help countless times, and always remembered to thank Him when things were going well.

David also told Rich about the year he turned sixteen and was dying to get his own car. Bea, not having any extra money, explained they couldn't afford it, and told him to do what she had when she was his age—shoplift.

"No!" Rich said, shocked.

"Yes, she did. At first I was appalled she would suggest such a thing, but then the more I thought about it, the more I decided to give it a try. I asked her what would happen if I got caught." David stopped a moment, remembering. "She said, 'Just don't get caught,' like that was the answer."

"So you stole something?"

"Yes. It was a few months after she told me that, so on this particular day Bea had no idea what I planned to do. She took me to Music Mart, which was when I stole that CD I told you about before the trial. When I climbed back in the van and didn't have a shopping bag, she was so angry. 'Money doesn't grow on trees, David,' she said. 'Gas is expensive. I can't believe you had me bring you all the way over here and you didn't buy anything.' That's when I pulled the CD out from under my coat and showed it to her."

"What did she do?" Rich, having had such a normal childhood, with parents who taught him right from wrong, was very curious.

David hung his head, ashamed at her reaction. "She told me she was so proud of me. Can you believe that?" He looked up. "I took something without paying for it, and my mother was proud of me. I remember sitting in the van, feeling so small. It was half-raining and half-snowing, and you could see it coming down in the beams from the parking lot lights. All the way home, I stared out the window, and the snow looked like it was coming right at us. Mom was happy and smiling, and I felt like shit. She even said she wanted to tell my brothers when we got home so they could see how stealing helped you get what you wanted in life. I told her I didn't want my brothers to know, I didn't want anyone to know. That was the first time, and the last time, I ever did anything like that. I was so disgusted with myself that I opened the window and flung the CD out like a Frisbee. I still have nightmares of the police knocking on my door, asking if I took a CD from Music Mart."

"I'm proud of you, too. Of course, for a different reason than Bea, but I'm very proud."

"Why?"

"I'm proud of you for realizing, early on, that living that kind of life was not for you. Just think how differently things could have turned out. Everything happens for a reason, and at that moment, you were at a fork in the road. You could have gone in either direction, but you made the best decision. Especially with a mom like Bea, who was encouraging you to go down the same path she did. It's always easier to do what's wrong in life; it takes guts to do what's right."

"I don't think my mom knew how to be a mother. I don't remember her ever telling me she loved me, or hugging me for no reason."

"I agree. She never had that type of role model in her life, besides Benita, and even that, from what I read and remember from the journal, was not what I call a normal situation. I don't think she really had any idea what she was supposed to do, how she was supposed to act. I remember an entry in her journal seemed odd when I read it, and I've thought about it several times since. I'm not sure if you've gotten to this part yet, and I'm paraphrasing, but there was something Bea said about dressing you and your brother in matching outfits for the first day of school. Then she said she packed your lunch, walked you to the corner to wait for the bus, and took pictures—something she assumed a loving mother would do."

David was dumbfounded, not knowing how to respond.

"You know, people can take a test and get a driver's license; they can pass a bar exam and become an attorney; but not everyone becomes a loving parent because they have a baby. Your mom provided for you and put a roof over your head. Even though she wasn't the best at showing her feelings, she didn't physically abuse you, and that, in itself, speaks volumes. I think your mom loved you in the only way she knew how."

"You're pretty good at reading people. What do you see in me?"

"I see a young man, lost for many years, who has finally found his way, finally knows what he was meant to be."

David smiled and nodded. "Why haven't you gotten married?"

"I haven't found the right girl. The older I get, the more I'm set in my ways. I don't know if marriage is right for me. And being a police officer, I would hate to have someone worry about me every time I left the house, wondering if I would come home safe. I sacrificed a lot for my career, but I'm not sorry I did. When I was sworn in as a police officer, I promised to serve and protect and I meant it." Rich paused a moment to reflect. "Gosh, it's been a long time since I thought about the day Buster died, but I can still remember it like it was yesterday. I sometimes try to picture what he would look like now. What would his life be like? Where would he live? Would we still be friends? He was like the brother I never had and I continue to miss him, even after all these years."

David, feeling a bit uncomfortable at the heaviness of the topic attempted to add a little levity to the conversation, "Buster? Are you seriously telling me the kid's name was Buster?" David laughed.

Rich grinned as he shook his head. "That was his nickname, smart ass." The trust and camaraderie between them was growing stronger every day. Soon, it would be put to the test.

"When the world says, "Give up," hope whispers, "Try it one more time."

~ Author Unknown

Chapter Five

Time has a way of slipping away, and soon it was March. The foundation had been up and running for over three months, and they were getting their fair share of publicity. Most of it was positive, but on occasion, when some reporter had nothing else to do, they would dredge up the details of Beatrice Miller and the horrific things she did, always tying them to David. Then it was broadcast as if it were news no one had heard before. But donations were coming in, some large and some small. Each was appreciated and was a clear testament that people supported what they were trying to accomplish.

At the suggestion of the FBI, they'd purchased some high-tech equipment—bugging devices, cell phones with internet access, a police scanner, computer programs that allowed them to do intensive and elaborate background and other types of checks, wireless earphone walkie-talkies, and bulletproof vests. Even though they'd not been involved in any violence, Rich insisted they purchase the vests, saying that you never know when you might need one. As word spread about their foundation, Rich was certain they'd be called to assist at a hostage situation involving children, and it was better to plan ahead.

The first time they were contacted about a serious situation was in mid-January, about thirteen days after the foundation opened. David and Rich were sitting in the break room enjoying a fresh cup of coffee and looking at the newspaper when the call came in. Kayla, one of the operators, came to get them as they all excitedly crowded around to listen to the details via speaker phone. Rich took notes, so as not to miss anything.

It was a kidnapping resulting from a bitter custody battle. The young father, who was distraught after being denied visitation because of several recent DUI convictions, kidnapped his two children, a boy and a girl, both toddlers. Because he was still listed as a contact at their daycare facility, he was able to pick them up, no questions asked. He'd done so two days earlier, and no one had seen or heard from them since. The FBI thought the foundation might be able to offer some insight where others had failed. Once they hung up, Rich and David ran around grabbing what little equipment they had, to try to aid in the safe recovery of the children.

About an hour after the call, the FBI phoned again to say they'd found them. The father had been holed up in a rundown motel and planned to take the children out of the country. After seeing his picture on television at the airport and realizing everyone was looking for him, he had second thoughts. Several hours later, still not sure what to do, he turned himself in to the police. The children were returned safely to their mother, and the father was taken to jail. Last they heard, he was under suicide watch. Even though "Never Give Up" didn't get to assist, it was a valuable learning experience and taught Rich and David how quickly things could happen.

Not long after, a young autistic girl wandered away from daycare, got on a city bus, and rode all over town before someone realized she was missing. The bus driver, an older man, thought it seemed a bit strange, but she was happily rocking back and forth and humming while looking out the window. She didn't cause any trouble, so he let her stay on the bus for six hours, until his shift ended. As luck would have it, David was leaving the dry cleaners on the strip where the bus depot was located and overheard the driver talking about the girl. Having heard something earlier on the police scanner, he quickly got involved. The owner of the daycare was charged with child endangerment, and when it was discovered that the child-to-adult ratio was over the legal limit, the facility was shut down with no plans to reopen.

On the first day of spring, a mother contacted them from a local park claiming that she'd turned away from her daughter to read a text message, and when she looked back, the child had vanished. She phoned "Never Give Up" before she called the police. By the time David and Rich arrived at the park, however, the police were there questioning her. They were searching for the little girl when Rich spotted a tiny white-and-pink athletic shoe, lace undone, stuck in the mud on the other side of the playground where the park butted up against a wooded area. As he bent to pick it up, he thought he heard whimpering. Following the direction of the muffled sound, he found the child hiding in a hollow log, still wearing one shoe and a muddy Hello Kitty sock on the other foot. When she saw Rich, her eyes brightened as she said, "I lost my shoe. I'm in big trouble. Mommy will be mad." Rich smiled, picked her up, and returned her to the appreciative open arms of her mother.

In late April, a call came into the police station from the manager at a local big box department store. He explained a three-year-old boy was missing. The police immediately called "Never Give Up" since the foundation offices were less than two minutes from the store. David and Rich arrived and the mother explained that since he was old enough to walk, he liked playing hide-and-seek under the clothing racks. Not realizing his shoes were in plain sight, she always played along pretending she couldn't find him and when she did, he always laughed hysterically. For a time it was a fun game, but now that he was getting older she was tired of it. So on this particular day she thought if she didn't *find* him, he would learn a lesson, get scared, and hopefully not do it again. She watched him as he crawled under the rack with all the slacks and stood back and waited. She waited and waited and when he didn't come out, she pushed the slacks back and he was gone. Frantic, she told the manager and they immediately put the store on lockdown. The manager called the police who then called "Never Give Up." David and Rich found the boy moments before the police arrived. Always fascinated by loud machines and roaring engines, he had followed the sound of the trash compactor and became mesmerized by all the boxes and trash it appeared to be eating. The sound coming from the compactor was so earsplitting he had not heard them calling his name over the loudspeaker. Thankfully, there was a wire fencelike partition that sat in front of the compactor for safety reasons, so he could not get really close to it.

One case made David and Rich chuckle, and their main contact at the police station even seemed a little embarrassed. Two-and-a-half-year-old Kendra Kindle had just graduated from her crib to a big-girl twin-size bed. Never one to like taking a nap, she whined and cried, but once she quieted down she was out like a light and typically slept for three to four hours.

About ten minutes into the nap, her mother, a twenty-five-year-old stay-at-home mom, went to check on her and Kendra was gone. She searched everywhere: closets, cupboards, under beds; anywhere Kendra could fit she looked at least twice. Frantic, she called the police who also came out and searched. It was going on three hours when they called "Never Give Up." Explaining the situation, David asked if someone may have snuck in and kidnapped her. At about the four hour mark, two-and-a-half-year-old Kendra wandered out of her room, sleepily rubbing her eyes to find her mommy sitting on the sofa in the living room sobbing. "Why are you sad, Mommy?" she asked.

Turns out Kendra slid out of her bed, which was up against the wall. The side of the bedspread had also fallen down and was touching the floor. Kendra was lodged between the wall and the bedspread so when you looked under the bed, you saw nothing but the bedspread. David and Rich were on their way when they got the call. They all had a good laugh over it.

The stories, however, didn't always have a happy ending. A twenty-one-month-old boy was missing, and they found him face down in the family swimming pool. His mom was on the phone, and took her eyes off of him for a minute. She explained that when he was tired, he would sometimes climb into his bed and take a nap, and that's what she thought he did. She thought nothing of it when she hung up and didn't see him. After a while, she went to check on him and he wasn't in his bed. She looked everywhere and couldn't find him, but found the front door slightly ajar. She called the police, thinking someone had kidnapped him, or he'd opened the door and was wandering around the neighborhood. David and Rich were contacted and went to the house. David noticed the side gate was unlatched. Shortly thereafter, David discovered the toddler in the pool. His mother, sobbing so violently she could hardly catch her breath, fell to the ground, pounding it with her fists. As they drove away, David could still hear her shouting, "No! No! No!" over and over again.

In a similar incident, a baby boy was found in the family vehicle. He climbed in and shut the door, and no one knew he was missing. With temperatures inside the car reaching over one hundred ten degrees, it didn't take long for him to become hyperthermic and die. The police were called and a search was conducted, but nothing turned up. "Never Give Up" was contacted as an afterthought, hoping David and Rich might think of something the police had not. Unfortunately, the little boy's body was found the following day when his mom numbly walked out to get the newspaper. Passing the family car, a flash of bright yellow fabric caught her eye. It was then that she saw her son lying in a heap on the floor, swollen and bloated. When Rich and David heard the outcome, they were both grateful they weren't there.

In cases like these, David wondered if he had more experience, or if the foundation had been contacted sooner, the outcome would have been different. Rich, having been a police officer, knew things didn't always turn out favorably, but David had to learn to deal with it in his own way. David was reminded again and again how a poor decision made in a split second could reap such negative results. David just couldn't fathom what caused people to do the sick and twisted things they did, especially when it involved an innocent child.

Lou had done a fantastic job in helping to hire the perfect mix of people, and their ability to work together during a crisis proved helpful again and again. The FBI called on several occasions, asking them to help locate missing children in and around the Phoenix area. They also suggested both Rich and David apply for a passport, just in case they were asked to leave the country quickly.

David and Rich hung a bulletin board in the office, where they proudly displayed photos of children they were contacted about and sometimes helped recover. There was always a big celebration when they added another picture; the staff cheered, and David usually had a special lunch catered in.

As David was learning the order and process of how things worked, he was frustrated to see the amount of red tape necessary to get anything done, especially when working with the FBI or other government agencies. He felt that because they had to wait for search warrants or approvals, precious time was wasted, which may have changed the outcome.

A lot of calls came into the foundation, and they were busy doing one thing or another most of the time. David and Rich had been on local morning talk shows, and as word got out regarding their experience and success rate, they started to get calls from other parts of the country.

David grudgingly went to school every day, despite feeling he was missing so much at the foundation. After meeting with the academic counselor, he changed his major. His passion now was forensic science. He loved looking over the reports provided by the medical examiners, and was amazed at how much could be determined by blood splatters, skin abrasions, debris found in the tread of a pair of shoes, or even the contents of a victim's stomach. Those were the people he admired, not a dime-a-dozen blowhard attorney like Monroe. He just wished he could skip all the intro classes and concentrate more on the criminal justice side of things. Classes such as criminal investigation, scientific crime scene investigation, laws of evidence, laws of arrest, search and seizure and ethical issues in criminal justice were on his schedule, but not until his junior and senior years.

David was making plans to go visit his mom in mid-May, when the spring semester ended. He'd read more of the journal, and for the first time was looking forward to seeing her. The more he read, the more he began to despise his grandfather. He was a cruel, heartless bastard who deserved the hand fate had dealt him. When he saw his mother, David made up his mind to apologize; for what, he didn't know, but he felt a need to tell her how sorry he was. It might be the first difficult step in mending their dysfunctional relationship, but it was a step he was ready to take.

~

It was Friday, May thirteenth, when David went to the airport for his first flight, filled with trepidation. He arrived two hours prior to his departure time, and when he told the agent it would be his first time on an airplane, she insisted he take a window seat so he could thoroughly enjoy every aspect of the experience. Taking his shoes off and going through the metal detectors at the security checkpoint, David was amazed by how friendly everyone was. He took every opportunity to tell them this was his first flight. Looking out the floor-to-ceiling windows at the planes landing and taking off, David didn't understand how a thing so enormous could fly. The more he thought about it, the more nervous he became; and so he decided to sit with his back to the windows as he waited for his flight to begin boarding.

The majority of the seats at the gate were now full, and people excitedly chatted about where they were going or where they'd been. He kept pulling out his boarding pass and checking his seat number, trying to take his mind off things. Finally they called his row. Once on board, he was shocked at how narrow the seats were, but more shocked by how much stuff people tried to cram into the overhead bins.

When the plane finally lifted off, David had himself so worked up he felt like he was going to puke. Listening intently as the flight attendants explained where the emergency exits were, he couldn't believe that no one else seemed to care. As he looked out the window and watched the ground withdraw and the houses, pools, and parcels of land turn into little squares, his nerves settled a bit. Surprised when the flight crew pushed a cart down the aisle and offered him something to drink, he ordered a ginger ale. When he offered to pay for it, they wouldn't accept his money. But after watching the top of the clouds for the majority of the trip, he decided flying wasn't anything special. Once you were airborne, it was almost like riding on a bus, potholes and all, although in the air they were called "turbulence."

His flight landed late that afternoon, and he was waiting for his mother when visiting hours began at six-thirty. Bea looked unhappy. "It's about damn time you got here. I've been sending you telepathic messages. Didn't you get them?" she blurted before she even took her seat.

David stood and hugged her. "It's good to see you, Mom. How have you been?"

"I'll tell you how I've been. My precious little girl came for a visit, and I asked if she could spend the night. I didn't know what harm there would be, but they flat out refused. What kind of a hotel is this? I can't have anyone stay over? The same customers are here day after day, night after night. You would think they'd want to increase business by bringing in some new people." Bea shook her head in disbelief.

"What little girl are you talking about? Who came to visit you?" David was thoroughly confused. Her statements were becoming more and more bizarre.

"Why, Maggie, of course. She's the only little girl I have, unless you know something I don't," Bea chuckled.

David hesitated, trying to decide if he should acknowledge what she'd said or ignore it. He opted to ignore it. "Mom, I have something to tell you."

"What? You aren't dying, are you?" Bea's eyes were wide with fear.

"No, I'm not dying. I just wanted to tell you I'm sorry."

"Sorry? Sorry for what? What did you do? Are the kids all right? You didn't hurt one of them, did you? If you did, please tell me it was Mikey. I never liked him anyway."

"No, Mom, I didn't hurt one of the kids. As far as I know, they're all fine. I've been reading your journal." When David said the word journal, it was as if Bea's mind got back on track.

"Oh, David, I'm so glad. I wrote that journal for you, you know? I hoped one day you would read it so you could see I'm not really a horrible person. Everything I did, and will continue to do, is because I loved your father so much. Whatever he asked for, I tried to give him. Don't you see that?" Tears were welling up in her eyes.

"I know, I know. Don't cry. Everything will be okay. I'm just sorry you had to go through so much, and I'm sorry I never believed you. I can't believe all the horrible things Grandpa did. What an awful man he was."

Then, just like that, she was gone again. "This place has gone downhill. I don't know if it's under new management or what, but I think there are people here who are out to get me. I saw someone putting poison on my breakfast the other morning."

"Poison? What are you talking about?" David furrowed his brow, unable to understand how she could change so quickly.

"They were sprinkling my donuts with white powder. I know it was poison."

"Mom, I think they call those powdered donuts. Did it taste sweet and sugary?"

"Yes, it did, but the people who use poison know how to make it taste good so they can get you to eat it, and then you die." Bea was so matter-of-fact.

"I'm sure it wasn't poison." David shook his head.

"Would you at least ask them about it?"

"Ask who?"

"The management. They should know, don't you think?" She was serious.

"Okay. Before I leave, I promise to ask the management if they are trying to poison you."

Bea let out a huge sigh of relief. "Thank you, David. You have always been my rock."

David stuck with small talk for the rest of the visit. When she talked, he listened, pretending to take everything she said seriously. She told him what her days were like, and how she looked forward to the day when she could check out. "Boy, I hate to see what that bill will look like," she said, laughing.

"Don't worry about it, Mom. I have it covered."

She wanted to know what the other kids were up to. She asked him to bring her a picture the next time he came so she could hang it in her room. "See if you can find one without Mikey in it." He promised he would. Before long, visiting hours were over. She stood to leave, turned, and said, "David, remember, things aren't always what they seem."

He was baffled again by that statement, but as he promised, David asked to speak to someone in charge. "My mom claims she saw someone sprinkling white poison on her donuts. I tried to convince her it was sugar, but when that didn't work I told her I'd ask about it. I know it's not true."

"What donuts? We don't serve donuts here. This is a prison, Mr. Miller, not a Holiday Inn."

David, caught completely off guard, didn't know how to respond.

~

Shortly after David returned to Arizona, red-and-blue flashing lights were everywhere as police cruisers barreled into the main entrance of Pembrooke Gardens. Curious as to what was going on, David and Rich took a walk to get a better view of the activity. There were a total of six police cars, over a dozen uniformed officers, vans bearing the call letters of several local news and radio stations, reporters, and a few bystanders. Everything was positioned facing a two-story, red-brick mansion a few streets over from their house. David wasn't sure who lived there, but he was sure something horrifying was going on. Once they made their way through the crowd to where the police officers stood, they introduced themselves and were given the details known so far.

The owner of the house was Suzanne Snyder, a forty-something woman who was a vice president at a national bank. Earlier in the week, it was discovered one of the employees, a bank manager, had been embezzling small amounts of money over a long period of time at one of the area branches. Because he never took much at one time, it was hard to pinpoint where the money was going and who was responsible. It seemed to disappear just after someone new had been hired and their training began. After weeks and weeks of record keeping and video surveillance, the culprit was confronted and immediately fired.

After bearing the shame and disappointment of his family, the angered and disgruntled employee, armed with a revolver, parked on the main street and took off on foot to bypass the main gate and guards. He was determined to confront the vice president and make her pay for ruining his life. He felt that after all the years of service he'd given to the bank, taking a few hundred dollars now and again wasn't enough to warrant the treatment he received. Humiliated and embarrassed, he'd never be able to find another job in finance, and he felt banking was what he'd been born to do. Without it, he had nothing.

When he arrived at the house, Suzanne wasn't at home, but her four children were. They ranged in age from four to fifteen years. The fifteen-year-old was babysitting while Suzanne ran some errands. The disgruntled bank employee elbowed his way through the French doors of the patio and demanded to see his ex-employer. When he discovered she was not at home, he took the children hostage and wouldn't allow anyone to enter or leave the house. In return for not harming them, he wanted his job back and a public apology so his name would be cleared.

The negotiations were going very slowly. When a gunshot rang out, two police officers positioned on the perimeter of the back yard saw a small, lifeless body heaved through the broken glass of the French doors. Blood was everywhere.

Suzanne had since returned home and was outside the house with the police, David and Rich, and the news media. She was very polished and even though she was wearing a jogging suit, she had matching sneakers and big gold hoop earrings. Her perfume smelled like plumeria and her makeup was impeccable—in a different situation, she could easily be confused for an anchor on the nightly news or an entertainer of some sort. When the gunshot rang out, she screamed and her fancy mascara ran and caused black smudges around both her eyes. Not knowing what was going on inside the house, she was a basket case. As David watched her pace back and forth, wringing her hands, he realized no amount of money or wealth could compensate for what she was going through.

David and Rich were discussing their game plan, and decided to go back to the foundation to retrieve their vests, hoping one of them could enter the house to talk to the angry man.

"Where are you going?" Officer Pruitt, the policeman in charge, asked when they turned to leave.

"We're going to get our bulletproof vests. Rich has been trained in handling situations like this, and we hope you'll let him enter the house and try to reason with the man." Sometimes when David spoke, he seemed much older than he was.

"Absolutely not. If anyone is going in, it will be a uniformed officer," Officer Pruitt said.

"But he's been trained!" David almost yelled.

Officer Pruitt placed his hand on David shoulder and motioned for him and Rich to walk away from the commotion so they could talk privately.

"It doesn't matter if he's been trained. Both of you are civilians. We can't send you into a home where you'll be in harm's way. Imagine the repercussions if something went wrong. Absolutely not!"

"But this is what we do! We run a foundation to help find missing children." David wouldn't give up.

"I'm fully aware of your foundation and what you do, but these children are not missing. We know where they are. It takes a special person to be able to negotiate with a cold-blooded killer."

"A cold-blooded killer? Did he kill someone?" David blinked hard, not sure he wanted to hear the answer.

Officer Pruitt shook his head, berating himself for saying too much. "Yes. The gunshot we heard killed the youngest child, a four-year-old female."

David placed his hand over his mouth. "Oh, my God. Does she know?" he pointed at Suzanne Snyder.

"No. She's already at her wits' end…no sense making it worse. It could be hours before this is over and we need her to remain composed, or as composed as she can be."

Another gunshot rang out, and Suzanne fell to the ground. David, Rich, and Officer Pruitt rushed back over to where they'd been standing earlier just in time to see the front door open. Out walked the three children in single file. Suzanne ducked under the yellow police tape and ran to them.

"Where's Emily?" she asked.

"She's gone," the oldest daughter replied, wiping her eyes.

"Gone? Gone where?" Suzanne's eyes were wide with fear.

Finally, one of the boys said, "He killed her. Emily was scared and confused; and when she wouldn't stop crying, he shot her. We tried to quiet her down, honestly we did."

Suzanne let out a howl that reminded David of a wounded animal. The four of them stood hugging, trying to console each other.

The policemen rushed into the house to find the deranged man dead, a single gunshot wound through the roof of his mouth. His brains were splattered on the wall, his body was hunched over on its side, and a pool of blood surrounded his head.

David decided against entering the house. He watched Suzanne with her remaining children, sobbing for the one she lost. He knew she'd give up everything to have that child back. Her heart had been shattered, and no amount of money or power could put it back together. David was reminded again of how he'd always been told that money doesn't buy happiness. Now he believed it.

Hope is a waking dream.

~ Aristotle

Chapter Six

On a bright, sunny day in late May, David was on his way out when the phone lines in the call center started lighting up. It was a detective from Mesa, a suburb of Phoenix, calling to ask "Never Give Up" to assist in the search for a fifteen-year-old girl, Julie Hartley, who had been missing for over forty-eight hours.

David asked for the details, and after getting Rich in the room, put the detective on speaker phone.

"The missing girl's name is Julie Hartley. She's fifteen, soon to be sixteen. She's Caucasian, about five-foot-two, 107 pounds, shoulder-length light brown hair and green eyes. She's a ninth-grade student at Conrad High School in Mesa."

"You said she's been missing for over two days? Why did it take you so long to contact us?"

"We had a couple of leads and thought we could handle it ourselves, but when we hit one dead end after another, we decided to contact you. We've heard good things about the foundation and thought you might be able to help."

"Yeah. We could have helped just as well two days ago." David was pissed; precious time had been wasted.

"Anyway, if you'll get down off your high horse, here are the details. Julie recently started 'dating,' if you can call it that, a seventeen-year-old boy named Johnny Logan. He's a troublemaker, or has been for at least the last ten months or so. He's been in and out of juvenile detention, getting involved in one criminal activity after another, mostly shoplifting and other misdemeanors." David could tell the detective was reading from a list.

David interrupted "How did they meet?"

"Julie and Johnny met one night after a high school dance. Julie was standing outside, waiting for her mom to pick her up, when Johnny drove up on a motorcycle. They exchanged numbers and began texting non-stop, talking at least once a day. Never having had a boyfriend before, Julie loved the attention. He was a player...always knew the right thing to say and when to say it. He was always buying her things...a stuffed animal, a necklace, perfume...stuff like that. I use the word 'buying' loosely, because I imagine most of the items were hot. I think Julie is what you'd call a goody-two-shoes, and she found Johnny and his bad-boy persona exciting."

"How did her parents feel about the relationship?" Rich was taking notes.

"Probably exactly the way you'd feel if she was your child...not thrilled. Her parents think she's too young to have a serious relationship, especially with a boy like Johnny."

"Tell me more about him," David said.

"What would you like to know?" David heard the detective sigh.

"Is he the main suspect or just a person of interest?"

"There's no suspect yet. We're still trying to sort things out."

"She's been missing for two days and you still don't have a suspect? Have you questioned anyone?" David was angry.

"Of course we've questioned people, Mr. Miller. We aren't completely incompetent, and I resent your tone. I've been doing this longer than you've been alive."

"I'm sorry. I get frustrated when I have to ask all the questions."

The detective cleared his throat and began again. "We talked to her mom, dad, and best friend from school. We tried to talk to Johnny, but he's a slippery bastard. We can't pin him down."

"Does he go to the same school?"

"Nope. As far as we know, he's a dropout."

"Does he have a job?" David looked at Rich, shaking his head, not wanting to say what he was thinking for fear of offending the detective again.

"Nope. Deadbeat. He's also Goth. You know the type...lots of black clothing and makeup. He wears one of those dog-collar-type things with spikes around his neck, big earrings, and piercings in his nose, eyebrows, and chin. He also has a black spider-web tattoo across his lower left arm and hand. Probably has more tattoos, but they aren't visible, at least not in the photo. If it weren't for the getup, it appears he would be a relatively good-looking kid. He's very intelligent or lucky, I don't know which. He breaks the law on a regular basis, but always just short of a felony," the detective chuckled.

They continued to talk, and found out the last time Julie was seen was when she climbed on the back of Johnny's motorcycle after school, two days ago. They drove off and she never made it home. The police promised to e-mail a photograph of both. Rich and David explained that once they received the photographs, they would do some digging and get back in touch with them, if and when they found anything.

While David waited for the e-mail, he and Rich used their database to do a little research. They found Johnny Logan didn't have a permanent address, and assumed his parents were dead since he was put up for adoption as a pre-teen. He'd been in and out of foster homes ever since. His rap sheet was a yard long and included just about every imaginable minor offense, including shoplifting, breaking and entering, petty theft, disorderly conduct, public intoxication, vandalism, and so on. They occurred in several states, but most were committed within the last ten months. David wondered out loud how a kid could get in so much trouble in such a short amount of time, but before that, nothing.

Rich speculated, "Maybe there's a glitch with the database, or he managed to stay under the radar and not get caught."

He shrugged and then turned to leave taking the rap sheet so he could study it and start profiling Johnny Logan. This was the part of the investigation Rich enjoyed: piecing together clues from someone's past to determine the story it told. Like a jigsaw puzzle, it doesn't come together until the final piece is clicked into place.

David, growing impatient, checked his e-mail again, wondering what could be taking so long. Time was of the essence, and the longer the girl was missing, the less likely they were to find her alive. It irritated him that it took the police so long to contact them. Finally, a few minutes later the e-mail popped up. He opened it up and looked at the photos. Looking back at him was his younger brother, John. John Miller was Johnny Logan, the newborn baby Bea had kidnapped from the hospital shortly before they left Seattle and moved to Bunting Valley. John looked horrible in the photo. His eyes were bloodshot and sunken, and his skin was ghostly white. He looked like the walking dead.

"Did you get the e-mail?" Rich burst into his office.

"Yes."

"What's wrong?"

"Johnny Logan is my brother. He's the baby Mom took from that hospital in Seattle. He's not seventeen. He's only thirteen."

Rich came around the desk to see John's photo. "Oh, my gosh. I remember now. His hospital ID bracelet was in the safe we confiscated at the trailer. It said Baby Boy Logan. He must be using a fake ID."

David turned very pale, then stood and vomited into the trash can.

"David, are you all right? Maybe I should call them back and decline due to the circumstances?"

David grabbed a tissue and wiped his mouth. Once he caught his breath he said, "No. He was the last one to see Julie alive. If he did anything to that girl, or knows anything about her disappearance, it doesn't matter who he is, he needs to be located and questioned."

"I can work on it alone, if it's too difficult for you," Rich volunteered.

David shook his head and took a deep breath. "I'll be okay. It was a bit of a shock, that's all."

As Rich stayed behind gathering facts and information to help in formulating some type of game plan, David decided to go out and look for either John or Julie. He didn't know where to begin looking as he headed his car in the direction of downtown Phoenix. If nothing turned up there, he would head over to Mesa. He tried to recall what his interests were but couldn't really remember. He was quite a bit younger than David, which made it more difficult. Since they didn't have a television and they didn't play video games, David had difficulty remembering the activities John liked. David recalled that they'd gone bowling once, and John wasn't very good at it. He did watch Joshua play softball, but that was only because Bea made him. She made all of them go. Wandering around downtown Phoenix, he hoped he could find him. He prayed John was not involved in Julie's disappearance, but his gut was telling him otherwise. The vacant, distant look in John's eyes was so sad. *So help me, if I'm responsible in any way for how he turned out, I'll never forgive myself.*

David walked in and out of nightclubs, pool halls, movie theatres, tattoo parlors—anywhere he thought a thirteen-year-old-kid who was pretending to be seventeen might hang out. He showed John's photo around, and no one could recall seeing him. David left his business card with all the establishment owners, just in case John showed up or they remembered something after he left.

It was growing late, and David was no closer to finding the missing girl—or John for that matter—than he had been. He couldn't remember the last time he'd eaten, so he went into a fast-food restaurant and ordered a cheeseburger and fries. After taking the wrapper off the cheeseburger, he dropped it, cupped his face in his hands, and started crying. *He was from Seattle. Why would he be in Phoenix? Was he here looking for me? This wasn't how it was supposed to happen. After the kids were returned to their real families, their lives were supposed to be better, not worse.* He took a bite of his sandwich, shoved one fry in his mouth, and gave up. Food was no longer a priority.

Lying in bed that night, he thought back to his childhood and what a good kid John was. It didn't seem possible that things could go downhill so quickly. David remembered it was John who lay on the floor next to the rabbit cage for a week straight, holding his brother's hand so Mikey didn't feel alone during one of Bea's extreme punishments. After tossing and turning, David decided to catch the first flight out of Phoenix to see his mother. Maybe she could shed some light on where John might be, or at least tell David some of the things he enjoyed as a child. It was sad that he'd lived with John for twelve years and couldn't remember anything important about him.

David thought it would be a good idea if either he or Rich talked to the girl's parents, too. The police had done such a bang-up job so far; it wouldn't hurt to backtrack and see if they could find more information. Maybe her parents could tell David where John and Julie went on dates. Something—they needed something.

Finally drifting off to sleep, David dreamt of John curled up outside the rabbit cage, holding on to the tiny hand that came through the bars. But instead of Mikey, it was Julie in the cage.

In what seemed like ten minutes later, there was a light knock on his bedroom door, jolting him awake.

"David?" It was Rich.

"Come in." David sat up, turned on the bedside lamp and rubbed his eyes.

Rich barged in. "We got a call about Johnny Logan."

"What did they say? Do they know where he is?"

"He's in the hospital." Rich paused, trying to read David's reaction.

David stood up and started pulling on a pair of jeans. "Hospital? Is he all right?"

"He's stable." Rich stood back, still wearing his pajamas, allowing David room to move around and gather his things.

"What happened?" David asked, pulling a navy blue sweatshirt over his tousled hair.

"Apparent drug overdose."

Arriving at the hospital twenty-five minutes later, it appeared the police had been searching for David for several hours. They found an "in case of emergency" card in Johnny's wallet that just listed David Miller; Brother; Phoenix, Arizona. With a common name like David Miller, the police dispatcher practically went through their entire database calling each and every one trying to find *the* David Miller John was referring to; not realizing it was *the* David Miller from "Never Give Up." Upon arrival David immediately confirmed his relationship as Johnny's brother, who was unconscious in the ICU. Since it did not appear Johnny had any medical insurance, David told them he would be responsible for all his medical bills.

As the details were provided it seemed an anonymous call was phoned into 911 around seven o'clock the prior evening. Without knowing for sure, it appeared John had taken an entire bottle of Rozerem, a prescription medication most commonly prescribed for insomnia. Where he got them no one knew, but the name on the bottle was that of a Stephanie Herminy. The empty bottle, lying near his unconscious body, which was found under a highway overpass, was brought to the staff in the emergency room by the paramedics. Not knowing if this was all he took, or how many he took, at least they could try and reverse the effects of the overdose. His stomach had been pumped, but most of the pills had already dissolved. Only time would tell; they hoped he would wake up.

Rich stood outside the ICU and continued to talk to the medical professionals as David went in to see his brother. Hooked up to tubes and wires, John looked awful. Pale and skinny, his skin was ghostly white, his eyes sunken with little veins visible across his eyelids. An IV hooked up to his scrawny arm was dripping a clear liquid. David checked his arms for track marks but didn't find any. *Thank God for that.* There was a spider web tattoo on his left hand, but on closer inspection, it seemed to be temporary. David sat beside his bed, took his small hand, and squeezed it.

"Oh, John, what have you done to yourself?" David noticed his fingernails were gnawed down to the quick. He reached up to smooth down his jet-black hair, but it was so dirty it wouldn't do anything but stick straight up. He also noticed dirt and grime on his neck and between his fingers. "Why didn't you contact me? Or is that why you were in Phoenix? Wake up, John; wake up and talk to me. Tell me what happened to that girl." There was no response. David just continued sitting, holding John's hand and stroking his hair.

Some hours later Rich was back, and he knocked on the window to John's room to get David's attention. David walked out to see what Rich wanted. "I contacted the detective to tell him Johnny Logan was in the hospital, unconscious. I also ran the name Stephanie Herminy through the database to see who she was. She lives in the area and it turns out her house was one he'd ransacked."

"Did you tell the detective who he is?"

"No. I thought if he knew, he may not want our help. How is John? Has there been any change?" Rich, his arms crossed in front of him, shifted his weight from one foot to the other.

"No. Still unconscious, but they did find he has brain activity so he's still with us."

"Well, that's good news. Why don't you go home and get some rest? I can wait here and call you if there's any change." Rich glanced at his watch. "You've been here for almost five hours."

"I'd like to stay just a little longer. When he wakes up I want him to see me, to know that he's not alone. I'm sure he's scared."

"Okay. Just call me when you need relief. Before I leave, would you like me to get you something to eat or drink? I'm sure the cafeteria doesn't have a full menu at this hour, but I could get you a cup of coffee and maybe a Danish."

"No, I'm fine. I don't have much of an appetite anyway."

"You know, it could be a while before he wakes up. Even then, there's no telling what condition he'll be in."

"I know. I just want to wait until his doctor gets here so I can talk to him. So far I've just spoken to the staff from the emergency room."

After Rich left, David stood just inside the door of John's room, watching his chest go up and down with his breathing. He'd had a nasal cannula placed on his face to deliver extra oxygen, a blood pressure cuff on his upper left arm, and a pulse oximeter on his right index finger. A catheter disappeared under the blanket and the bag was about half full of urine that was dark yellow, almost orange, which was a sure sign of dehydration. About every fifteen minutes, the blood pressure cuff would automatically inflate, and his blood pressure and pulse would appear on a digital monitor beside his bed as well as at the nurse's station right outside the door. The hospital staff came in often to listen to his heart, shine a light in his eyes, and check the fluid in his IV. They also gave John a sponge bath, which was long overdue. David figured he hadn't had a hot shower or a good meal in quite some time.

David kept thinking back to the day when he and Bea were arrested for kidnapping Maggie Taylor. He was so worried about himself and his own well-being that he didn't even bother to say goodbye to his brothers, the brothers he'd spent the majority of his life with. As John lay there, David prayed he would pull through so he could talk to him again.

~

Rich and David had decided it would be best if the foundation did some investigating on its own to try and determine if Julie Hartley was still alive. They didn't have the luxury of waiting for John to wake up and tell them what they needed to know. Wherever she was, she might be hurt or need medical attention. They had to find her—and the sooner the better.

Early the next morning, Rich entered the room. David glanced up, happy to see him. Even though David had chosen to stay with John, it was still stressful and lonely.

"Want to go grab a cup of coffee?" Rich asked when David looked up.

"Sure. A cup of coffee sounds really good about now."

As they walked to the cafeteria, Rich asked if there was any change in John's condition. "No, still the same. Still waiting for him to wake up. It's hard sitting there, seeing him unconscious. I was thinking that up to this point in my life, I don't recall ever being in a hospital. My mom was when she fell down the steps and split her head open at some factory where she worked, but I don't think we went to visit her. If we did, I don't remember it."

"I guess you're making up for lost time." Rich smiled.

Arriving at the cafeteria, both Rich and David got a cup of coffee and took a seat at an empty table by the window, which overlooked a small creek. The sun was starting to peek through the clouds, and it looked like it was going to be another beautiful Phoenix day. The hospital had hung bird feeders just outside the wall of windows, and birds of every size, shape, and color were busy fighting over the seed mix. Watching them was quite peaceful.

David removed the lid from his cup and dumped in three creamers. As he stirred it in, the liquid going round and round almost hypnotized him in his fatigue.

"Well," Rich said suddenly, causing David to jump. "I talked to Julie's best friend, Katie Lambert, before school this morning."

"Yeah? What did she have to say?"

"Katie said she was there when Johnny pulled up and Julie took off with him. Julie told Katie she had to break it off with Johnny because he was asking her to do things she wasn't comfortable with."

"What sort of things? Don't tell me sexual things. He's only thirteen years old!"

"No, I don't think so. Not that she told me. She did say that Julie and John were at the mall once, and John asked her to create a diversion while he stole a black leather jacket. Julie always did what he asked, but his requests were getting more dangerous, and she was starting to get scared. Lately he'd been talking about robbing a bank, and he wanted Julie to help him. Julie knew she had to end it, and she knew it wouldn't go well."

"Why did she think it wouldn't go well?"

"I guess John had become quite attached to her. He told her time and time again how much he loved her, and asked her to run away with him."

"The kid's only thirteen. How far did he think they could get?"

Rich shrugged. "He managed to get this far, so I don't think that would have deterred him."

"What about Julie's parents? Have you spoken to them?" David glanced over Rich's shoulder to see the staff serving breakfast. The bacon smelled so good.

"No, not yet. I plan to call them after I leave. You look so tired, David. When was the last time you had something to eat?"

"Early this morning. When they handed out the breakfast trays, they gave me one. I didn't eat much, but the hospital food is pretty good."

"You must be exhausted. I can sit with John for a few hours. If there's any change, I promise to call you."

"I've been sleeping on and off in his room. If I go home and lie down, I won't be able to stop thinking about him, and I'll feel like I should be here. I'd rather stay."

"If you change your mind, you know how to reach me."

~

Later that afternoon, Rich finally got David to leave for a few hours. While he was back at the foundation, Mrs. Hartley phoned, and David arranged to meet with her and her husband. Driving his SUV down their tree-lined street, he saw kids playing, riding their bikes, or walking their dogs. The cookie-cutter houses looked very similar, as about every third one had the same look except for a different color; there were split-levels, bi-levels and colonials. David smiled, thinking it looked like the perfect place to raise a family.

The Hartleys lived in a tan, split-level house with maroon shutters and a big bay window. As soon as David entered, he was greeted by an old Basset Hound who sniffed him and went back to his bed. He caught the aroma of brownies or chocolate chip cookies, and they smelled delicious.

Photos of Julie were everywhere: on the walls, end tables, and mantel. David walked over to have a closer look. She was a gorgeous girl, and so photogenic; she had beautiful blue eyes, a perfect smile, and tiny freckles across the bridge of her nose. Mrs. Hartley offered David something to drink, but he declined. She explained she had a hard time sitting and doing nothing and was an anxious baker; when something was bothering her she tended to make cookies, cupcakes, and the like. She told him she'd just taken a batch of brownies out of the oven; they were what David smelled as soon as he entered the house. His mouth began to water and when Mrs. Hartley asked if he would like one he was not able to resist. He said yes, and before the visit was over he'd eaten three.

Mr. and Mrs. Hartley, both in their forties, told David they'd created a neighborhood task force and had spent the majority of their waking hours, since Julie's disappearance, looking for their daughter. Mrs. Hartley had short brown hair, with highlighted, wispy bangs. She wore fashionable teal-blue framed glasses. Her earrings were enormous and looked so heavy David wondered why they didn't tear her earlobes.

She had Julie's eyes, but hers were red and swollen. Several times Mrs. Hartley looked like she was going to break down, but she just moved her glasses and dabbed at her eyes, managing to hold it together.

Mr. Hartley was a big man with broad shoulders and thick, dark brown, almost black, hair that had glints of silver at the temples, and equally thick eyebrows and mustache. He, too, looked like he'd been crying.

"Julie has a good head on her shoulders, and instinctively knows right from wrong," Mrs. Hartley said.

"She sounds like a wonderful girl," David responded.

"She is. She really is. Her empathy for others is unbelievable. She has even gone so far as to attend funerals and send sympathy cards when she didn't even know the people involved. She's always giving of her time. She's received several humanitarian awards from the mayor, but being recognized isn't important to her. She just wants to leave the world a little better than she found it."

"There should be more people like her," David said, wetting the tip of his finger and picking up the last of the brownie crumbs from his plate.

Mrs. Hartley smiled. "Since Julie met Johnny, her priorities changed, or at least it seemed they did. She didn't care about anyone or anything, except when she could see Johnny again. Julie was always a chatterbox and we could talk about anything, but once Johnny entered the picture she became very quiet and secretive. We asked her if she was doing drugs, but she told us she wasn't that stupid. We wanted to trust her and we wanted to believe her, but it was getting more and more difficult. She would disappear for hours, and we didn't know she'd left. When she came home and we asked where she had been, it was always the same answer. 'With Johnny.' When we pressed her, she went into her room and locked the door."

"I'm so sorry. This must be very hard for you." David leaned forward and placed his empty plate on the coffee table, next to the newspaper.

"You have no idea, Mr. Miller. We live and breathe for her. She's our only child, and we planned it that way so we could give her all our attention. We never intended for her to want for anything. If something has happened to her, our world will crumble."

"Well, we're doing everything we possibly can. John is still unconscious, which is a good thing; it's giving his body a chance to rest and heal. While we wait for him to wake up, my business partner and I are following some leads and talking to people on our own. Do you have any idea where John and Julie went on dates?"

"Not really. As I told you, she didn't share much about Johnny with us because she knew how we felt about him. I did find half a movie ticket in her coat pocket, so I'm assuming they went to the theater at least once."

"Hopefully we'll find her, and hopefully she will be okay."

"We hope and trust in the Lord. That's all we can do." Mrs. Harley broke down, and her husband put his arm around her as she wept. It broke David's heart knowing his brother might be responsible for their misery, and there was nothing he could do about it.

Be faithful in small things because it is in them that your strength lies.

~ Zen

Chapter Seven

Minutes turned into hours, and David remained vigilant, staying by his brother's side as much as possible and napping when he could. He took a leave of absence from school, and Rich ran the foundation to give David as much time as he needed. He was determined to be there when John opened his eyes. He just had to be.

Thinking back to when they were younger, David remembered a time when Bea left Joshua and John at the Miracle Mart and he made her go back to get them.

"I told them they had twenty minutes, and if they weren't in the van in twenty minutes I was going to leave without them," Bea explained, as if that made everything okay. David could still feel how angry he was and how he threatened to drive the van back to get them, even though he didn't have a license. The way home from the Miracle Mart was about two-and-a-half miles on busy three- and four-lane roads with no sidewalks, and it was already beginning to get dark. That was one of the few times he stood up to her and looking back, he wished he'd have done it more often. Maybe if he had, he wouldn't be sitting here waiting for John to wake up after a drug overdose.

David brought the journal with him, and had managed to read the entire thing. He read some of the passages again—especially the one where his grandpa sold his mother's virginity to a stranger for a mere one hundred dollars, and then took her to get an abortion when she got pregnant. His mother, being young and naive, didn't even know she was pregnant. There was also an entry about his grandpa raping his mother when he was angry at her. It also described the day she shot and killed him when he barged into the trailer, drunk as a skunk, when she was cleaning. He and his brothers, Joshua and John, were in school at the time, and Bea had dropped his youngest brother, Mikey, off at day care.

What a screwed up family he came from. He discovered, by reading the journal, that his own father was killed by his grandpa. Even though he believed in an eye for an eye, David wished there could have been a more civilized way to deal with it. If there were, he would still have an intact family, and things would not have gotten so far out of hand. If only his grandpa hadn't treated his mother so horribly. If only Henry had been happy with one son. If only Bea hadn't wanted a girl. If only…

~

Thirty-six hours after the ambulance brought John to the emergency room, he woke up. He was disoriented and surprised when David called his name. David stood when he saw John's eyelids fluttering, calling, "John? It's David. Can you hear me?"

John attempted to talk, but his throat was so dry, it came out as a gurgle.

David pressed the call button and a nurse appeared almost immediately.

"He's awake. He's trying to say something," David said, excited.

John was back. He was alive and he was back. David walked out into the hallway, not wanting to be in the way of the medical team, to call Rich. Within seconds, several medical professionals had surrounded John, taking his vital signs and checking his pupils with a small light.

After a long drink of water, John spoke in a scratchy voice. "Where am I?" he croaked, as David watched from the doorway.

One of the doctors spoke up. "You're at the hospital, Johnny. You took quite a few sleeping pills but were found in time. You've been out of it for a while, but all your vital signs look good. How are you feeling?" He placed the stethoscope in his ears to take a listen to Johnny's chest.

"My throat hurts, and the light seems so bright." John squinted.

"Yes. We had to pump your stomach, and passing the tube through can irritate your throat. The light probably does seem bright since you've been in darkness for several hours, but your eyes will adjust. Anything else?" The doctor draped the stethoscope back around his neck.

"I'm hungry!" John tried to sit up.

"Whoa, easy there. Being hungry is a good sign, but you lay there for a while until you get your bearings. Once the cobwebs clear, we'll get you some liquids." The doctor nodded at the nurse, who left the room, presumably to order some food.

A short time later a tray was delivered and the medical staff left while John tried to eat his soup, which appeared to be more broth than anything else. David hesitantly entered his room, and as soon as John saw David in his peripheral vision, he smiled.

"I thought I heard your voice when I first woke up, but then you were gone and I thought I'd dreamed it."

"No, you didn't dream it. I've been here for a while, waiting for you to wake up. Once you did, the medical staff came in. I didn't want to get in the way, so I left to make a phone call. How are you feeling?"

"Okay, but much better after seeing you. I've missed you. That's why I came to Phoenix…to find you."

"Where are your parents?" David was curious because he was told John had been returned to his parents in Seattle

"Hell if I know," John shrugged, slurping up his soup.

"What? You don't know where they are?" David was still standing at the foot of the bed.

"When I got back to Seattle, the welcoming committee wasn't waiting with open arms for the return of the prodigal son. They only located my mother, who wanted nothing to do with me. So I was placed in a foster home, which was awful."

"What was so awful about it?"

"The family had a small, two-bedroom house, and six or seven foster kids. I think I was number eight. We all slept in one room; the girls got the bed and the boys had to sleep on the floor. There were cockroaches and rats everywhere. I never had a decent meal while I lived there. My foster parents collected the money and used it to buy drugs. I don't think I saw them clean the whole time I was there. One of them would sober up and put on a happy face when they knew they had a meeting with the child welfare people, but I couldn't stand it. I wanted to report them, but I didn't. I just realized I'd be better off if I got out of there."

"So how did you get here? It's practically fifteen hundred miles from here to Seattle." David made a mental note to contact child services in Seattle and let them know where John was. He also planned to tell them what John said about his foster family.

"You won't believe it, but I lucked out and won a used motorcycle in a game of cards." John stopped eating long enough to smile.

"Really?" David didn't believe it.

"Yeah. Beginners luck is what they called it."

"So you rode a motorcycle all the way from Seattle?"

"Yep."

"But you don't have a driver's license."

"Sure I do."

"John, this is David. I was there the day Bea brought you home from the hospital. Unless my math is really off, you're thirteen. You aren't old enough to get a driver's license."

John hesitated. "I got a fake ID. It says I'm seventeen."

David shook his head. "How long have you been in Phoenix?"

"Not long. Wait a minute, what day is it?" John started playing with the remaining soup, filling his spoon and turning it over to spill it back into the bowl.

"It's Wednesday morning. You've been in the hospital since late Monday. Where have you been staying?"

"Just around. Under overpasses, in cardboard boxes, dumpsters, railroad cars. Wherever I could find a dry place to stretch out. I've been on the road for quite a while, because I started out in Seattle."

"Why didn't you come to me?" David's heart was breaking, thinking of his brother being homeless, resting his head wherever he could.

"I tried, but that guard took one look at me and wouldn't let me in. I told him I was your brother, but he didn't believe me."

"Oh, John, I'm so sorry. You should have called. I would have told him to let you in."

John shrugged. "Oh well. At least you're here now."

"Yes, but do you know why I'm here?"

John was silent.

"John, look at me. Do you know why I'm here?"

"Because you're my brother?" John looked up from his soup bowl and locked eyes with David for the first time.

"No, I'm afraid not. Do you remember Rich Butler?"

John furrowed his brow. "No, I don't. Should I?"

"Rich and I have a foundation to help find missing children. We're working on a case right now; a girl named Julie Hartley." The expression on John's face told David everything he needed to know. "I've been told you and Julie are close and you might know where she is."

"We were close," John corrected.

"Tell me what you know about her. Do you know where she might be or what may have happened to her? Her parents are worried sick."

"Tell me this: are you asking as my brother, or as an owner of some do-good foundation?"

"Maybe a little of both. The police will be here soon, so please talk to me." David took a few steps forward.

"The police? You dickhead. Did you rat me out?" John shoved the soup bowl onto the floor. The plastic bowl bounced, the spoon clanked, and soup splattered everywhere.

"No, I didn't rat you out, but my hands were tied. I didn't have a choice. They had to know where you were," David said, sitting down in the chair where he'd spent the last couple of days.

"You always have a choice. Didn't Bea teach you anything?" Still attached to tubes and wires, John swung his legs over the side of the bed, trying to get up. David jumped to steady him. "Whoa! Make the room stop spinning!" John said, turning to lie back down.

"Forget about Bea, and forget about the police. Just talk to me. As far as we know, you were the last one seen with Julie. Tell me what you know, John, before the police get here. I'll help you if I can, but if you aren't honest with me, there's nothing I can do."

John let out a huge sigh, and then laced his fingers behind his head. David could tell he was carefully choosing his words.

"I picked her up at school and we went for a ride. The wind was in my face and she was sitting behind me on my motorcycle, holding on to my waist, and it felt so right. Did you ever have a moment like that, David?" Avoiding eye contact, John used his hands to scoot to a sitting position. "A moment of clarity when everything seems right? That's what it was like with Julie and me. We were riding through the park, and stopped for an ice cream cone. That's when she told me she couldn't see me anymore."

"Why would she say that?" David knew what Julie's best friend had said, but he wanted to know what John thought.

"I don't know. I thought she loved me. She said something about her dad's company transferring him to another state so they were moving, but she wouldn't tell me where. She said she didn't know where. I think it was a load of shit. How could you not know where you were moving?" David noticed John clenching his fists. "I know her mom and dad didn't like me and told her to break it off with me."

"How do you know that?" David was hoping Julie had not shared with him how much her parents disliked him.

"I could tell by the way Julie acted. And the fact that she never let me pick her up at home. She always walked to the corner or insisted we meet somewhere else."

"Okay, so she said she wanted to break up with you. What did you do?"

"I couldn't bear the thought of living without her. I snapped." John smiled, looking down.

"Snapped? What does that mean?" David thought it was a new slang word the kids were using.

John glanced up and looked David in the eye. His eyes were still the same color, but now they lacked the human aspect of a soul. "Her pretty little neck, that's what."

David could not believe John was capable of such an act. "What? You broke her neck? You killed her?"

"Yeah. We finished our ice cream and got back on the bike. I drove and drove, and when we were deep into the park, I stopped the bike and told her I wanted one last kiss. The setting was perfect: big trees growing over the road, creating a shaded arch." John paused with a peaceful look on his face, as though he were in a trance.

David furrowed his brow and waited for him to snap out of it. "So what happened next?"

"I went around behind her and..." John grabbed his own hand and pulled it toward him, pretending to have someone's head in the crook of his elbow. He made a noise to simulate bones breaking.

Speechless for a moment, David swallowed hard and finally asked, "Then what?"

"Then I threw her body over the embankment. The more I thought about it, the worse I felt, so I decided suicide was my only option. I mean, it wasn't like anyone would miss me, so I took some sleeping pills I lifted from some old lady's house."

"How many pills did you take?"

"I don't know. There weren't that many in the bottle...maybe six or eight. I wasn't sure if it was enough to kill me or not, but I was willing to try. Imagine my disappointment when I woke up here."

"So you threw Julie over the embankment. Was she dead?"

"I assumed so. She wasn't moving and her eyes were wide open. She was limp, like a rag doll. When I tossed her over the side of the road, she rolled about fifty feet until her shirt got hung up on some brush. I figured if I couldn't have her in life, I would have her in death."

"You left her there?"

"Yeah. I got back on my motorcycle and rode around a little while, trying to decide how I was going to kill myself. I thought about driving off a bridge but that seemed a little too dramatic. That's when I remembered I had the sleeping pills."

"Oh, John. What have you done? What happened? You weren't like this growing up. You were such a good kid. For God's sake, you protected Mikey from Bea!"

John was angry. "You have no idea what I was like growing up, David. You never gave me the time of day."

David knew he was right. He'd been so consumed with his own life and how horribly Bea treated him that he never thought about his brothers. He wished again that he could go back and change things. "I'm sorry, John. Truly I am."

"As I sat there under the bridge waiting for the drugs to kick in, I thought back to my childhood. When I was finally rescued, everyone thought being kidnapped and forced to live with a different mom should have been a horrible ordeal, but it wasn't. I wish Bea would never have been caught. We were doing okay. Why did the police have to screw everything up?"

"Taking you from that hospital was wrong, no matter how it turned out. And what you went through doesn't give you the right to harm others."

Before John had a chance to say anything more, a policeman entered the room and handcuffed him to the side rail of the bed. The policeman, Rich, and the detective were standing out in the hallway and had heard every word of John's confession.

David turned to leave, hearing the last words John yelled at him. "Bea left me, my real mom and dad left me, Julie wanted to leave me, so now it's your turn, David. Go, just go! I don't need any of you!"

As he left the hospital, David had to admit that maybe Bea was right about John; she'd rescued him from an unpleasant situation, and when he was forced to return to it, things didn't go well. One thing for sure—as awful as David felt, he couldn't wait to get away from the hospital.

Not long after John's confession, the body of Julie Hartley was pulled from a ravine in the state park, just as John had described. The medical examiner estimated she'd been dead for at least five days. The preliminary cause of death was hypoxic brain injury, so it seemed she'd died instantly or shortly after John snapped her neck. David was grateful he was not the one who had to tell Mr. and Mrs. Hartley; Julie was their only child, and David hated thinking his brother was responsible for destroying their world.

~

A few days after the Hartley case concluded, David left to visit his mother. It was his third visit. Each time he went to see her, it seemed like she remembered more about what had happened, but she still vacillated between being her old self, and seeming crazy.

"Next time you come visit, David, can you bring me some aluminum foil?" Bea almost whispered.

"Aluminum foil? For what?" David leaned in, thinking it was something serious.

"To wear on my head at night so the radio waves will bounce off instead of penetrating my brain and melting it. That's what they're doing now. The poison on the donuts wasn't working, so now they're trying to kill me by melting my brain."

David didn't know if he should laugh or cry. "Sure, Mom. If I remember, I'll bring some."

Running out of things to talk about, David decided against telling her about John. It was still too fresh in his mind, and he didn't want to upset his mother. He decided instead to share some good news with her, so he told her about his foundation. She threw her head back and laughed.

"What? A foundation to help recover missing kids? You're pulling my leg! David, you are part of the problem, not part of the solution. You're such a silly boy."

"No, Mom. I'm dead serious. This is something I need to do. Aunt Benita left me a lot of money when she died, and I feel like I need to do something good with it."

"I'll tell you what you can do with it. Stop being so damn stingy and let me stay at a nicer hotel. This place is horrible. I only get to shower once a week and my toilet is right next to my bed. It's so close I can reach out and touch it when I'm lying down. The rooms are filthy and the beds are so uncomfortable. When I place an order with room service, it never comes."

David let her vent. When she was done, he told her about school and how he was hoping to graduate with a degree in forensic science. Then, just like that, she turned into her old self again.

"Where in the world do you get it?" she asked, leaning back and crossing her arms, as he continued to talk.

"Get what?"

"If I didn't know better, I'd think I kidnapped you too. Maybe you were switched at birth. You're nothing like me…or your father, either. I almost don't recognize you anymore. You don't behave like my son."

"I'll take that as a compliment," David smiled, which made Bea angry.

"I mean it, David. You've turned into the type of person I hate…smug, rich, and arrogant. You act like you're better than everyone else. But don't forget where you came from and remember your shit still stinks, just like the rest of us."

"I'm sorry I'm a disappointment, but I've never been happier. Maybe I inherited some of Aunt Benita's traits. Things are going well for me and the foundation. We're getting a lot of donations. People know about us and take us seriously. We've helped in the recovery of almost two dozen children. Rich and I work really well together…"

"Rich? Who's Rich?"

"Officer Butler. You remember him, don't you? He's the one who..."

Bea's face turned red and a vein throbbed on her forehead. "Yes," she said, through gritted teeth. "I remember him. He's the one to blame for my life falling apart. He took my children. He took my home. He took my life. He took everything. I can't believe you can look at that man, let alone work with him. Have you forgotten, David? He arrested you too."

"He was only doing his job. And he should have arrested us. Hell, I should have called the police myself but I never did. You know why?"

"Because you love me?" Bea showed her gummy smile.

"No. Because I was afraid. But I'm not afraid anymore. I've learned that you can't control me." *Two people can play this game, Mom.* David crossed his arms in front of him.

"Don't be so cocky, David. It doesn't suit you. Remember what I told you, things aren't always what they seem." Bea stuck her hand out in front of her and started looking at her fingernails as if the conversation was boring her.

"What does that mean? You keep saying it, but you never tell me what it means."

"You'll find out when the time is right. Besides, I made a promise and it's not up to me to tell you."

"A promise to whom? Who else is left? Dad is dead. Aunt Benita is dead. Grandpa is dead. Does John know? Does Joshua know? What about Mikey? Who else is there, Mom? Who else knows?" David was growing tired of her antics.

Bea pretended to zip her mouth shut and throw away the key.

"Well, I guess if your mouth is zipped, this visit is over." David stood.

"Suit yourself, David. I never invited you to come in the first place." Bea stood as well, pushing her chair back in under the table.

"I never thought I had to wait for an invitation."

"Next time, think again." Bea turned, not looking back.

David left knowing his mother didn't really mean what she said. He wished he knew what was wrong with her and why she acted so crazy. He never knew his mother to keep secrets, especially from him. *Why is she being so secretive now?*

The difficulties of life are intended to make us better, not bitter.

~ Anonymous

Chapter Eight

David's twenty-first birthday was just a couple of months away, and Rich was busy planning what they should do. He tossed around the idea of having a surprise party, but he wasn't sure how David would react. Not knowing how the Miller family celebrated in the past, Rich thought it would be a good idea to plan a special evening and take him out for his first legal glass of alcohol. But when he mentioned it to David, he was not prepared for his reaction.

Rich had fond memories of the day he was legally allowed to drink alcohol. Back then, the legal drinking age was eighteen, and his parents took him out to one of his favorite Mexican restaurants. The atmosphere was bright, cheery, and loud and the chips and salsa were great. Rich still smiled thinking about the wait staff crowding around him, placing a sombrero on his head, clapping, and singing "Happy Birthday" in Spanish.

When the waitress asked what he wanted to drink, he started to order a soda like he always did, but his dad interrupted and ordered him a beer. It seemed so odd, drinking a beer with his parents, but it was something he would never forget.

David, however, didn't understand what the big deal was. "Absolutely not! I have no desire to go out drinking if it's legal or not!" David said, shaking his head.

"What? I thought it was a rite of passage everyone looked forward to, like turning sixteen and getting a driver's license." Rich was confused.

"Maybe everyone else, but not me!" David was still shaking his head to drive his point home.

"Why? What could have happened to make you feel this way?

There's nothing wrong with drinking alcohol in moderation."

"I'll tell you. It was July, the same day Mom kidnapped Maggie Taylor from Lake Gerber. On our ride home, Mom announced that we weren't allowed to go anywhere for a week or so because she wanted all of us to get to know our new sister and vice versa. I was tired of Mom telling me what to do and when to do it. I was nineteen years old, and most of the time she treated me like an adult, but there were occasions when she played the mom card to let me know she was still in control. I'd already made plans to see a movie with my friend Gus, and I meant to keep my plans, with or without her blessing. Even though Mom didn't like him, Gus was my only friend…until that night."

"What happened?" Rich frowned.

David continued, "As soon as Mom and Maggie went to bed, I took the van keys from Mom's purse and set out to show her she couldn't control me."

"You took the van without her permission?"

"Yes, I did. If I'd asked, she would have said no, so I just did it. Anyway, I pulled into Gus's driveway and he came running out, sheltering his head from the downpour. It was raining like crazy, great big drops hitting the windshield, the wipers trying to keep up.

"Gus and I had the type of relationship where no words were necessary. We were the same age, in the same grade, and he came from a good family. His parents were both doctors; his mom a pediatrician, and his dad a general surgeon. Being an only child, Gus always had a nanny, but mostly he was left to raise himself, which had its pros and cons."

"Go on." Rich was now extremely interested.

"Well, as soon as Gus slammed his door, he smiled and pulled a completely full bottle of Jack Daniels out from under his jacket, and told me maybe going to see a movie wasn't the best idea."

"Where did he get it?"

"I think from the liquor cabinet at his house. It was usually locked, but either they left it unlocked, or Gus found the key. I didn't care; I was up for anything that got me out of the trailer and away from Mom. Gus told me he thought we should go somewhere and enjoy a little Jack D."

"I don't like where this is heading," Rich said, shaking his head.

"I turned into the state park. I was driving slowly because the rain was coming down so hard that it was almost impossible to see the road. The park closed at dusk, but I didn't care. I picked a parking spot near a picnic area, and we sat there listening to the radio and talking about things. Even though his family was wealthy, I always felt sorry for him. He never saw his mom and dad, and if he wanted to speak to them he had to make an appointment. Even though Bea wasn't the best mom in the world, at least she was always around if I needed her.

"An hour and a half later, both Gus and I were completely drunk. I remember having to pee, and when I opened the van door, I fell to the ground, laughing like a hyena. I stood up with mud all over my pants. Gus thought this was hysterical, and came out to join me out by the picnic tables. As we stood there urinating, getting soaking wet from the rain, Gus asked me what Bea would say if she could see me."

"Good question. What did you tell him?"

"I told him I didn't care and then I fell down again, this time with my pants around my ankles. Gus helped me up and back into the van. We both continued giggling, and I told Gus I'd better get him home and get the van back in the driveway before Bea noticed it was gone. I often called her Bea when I was with friends; I thought it made me sound more grown-up. So that was the first, and the last, time I drank that much alcohol. Not only did it give me a nasty hangover, but it made me feel stupid and silly. I also felt invincible, like I could do anything."

"Yeah, drugs and alcohol have that affect. So what happened next?"

"Gus didn't say anything; he just leaned up against the inside of the door moaning and holding his stomach. I told him not to get sick in the van, because Bea would kill me. I threw the van in reverse, backing out of the parking spot as I hurried to get Gus home before he vomited everywhere. Being defiant and stealing the van was one thing, but being forced to clean up Gus's puke was quite another. As I sat at a red light, Gus was turning greener by the minute, so I made a split-second decision to run the red light and get him home."

"That was the night you were arrested for drunk driving, wasn't it?" Rich finally remembered the evening David was talking about.

"Yes. Before I was a half-mile down the road, red and blue lights were flashing behind me, and the realization of what was going on hit me. I cupped my hand and blew into it, testing it to see if I smelled like liquor. I sat straighter in the seat and pulled off to the side of the road. Gus, who's passed out, was of no use. As I sat there waiting for the police officer to come to the window, I wondered what Bea would do when she found out. After several minutes, my heart racing the entire time, an officer knocked on the window with the butt end of a flashlight.

"I rolled down the window, and he asked me why I was out so late. I told him Gus and I had gone to Bakersfield to see a movie and we were on our way home. He asked me if we'd been drinking, and I lied and said no. Then he shined his flashlight into the van and saw the empty bottle on the floor. When I gave him my license, he saw that I was only nineteen and reminded me that the legal drinking age in North Dakota was twenty-one. I told him Gus wasn't feeling well, hoping he'd let me go to get my sick friend home, but that didn't happen."

"Yeah. That wouldn't have worked on me, either."

"He asked me if I knew why he pulled me over and I said no. Then he reminded me of the red light and made me climb out of the van for a sobriety test, which I failed miserably. Twenty minutes later I was sitting in the back of a police cruiser, shivering and drenched, with Gus sound asleep in the van. As I sat there, I watched Gus's dad drive up to get him. I could hear yelling, but couldn't make out the words. All I knew was that whatever happened to Gus was nothing compared to what Bea was going to do to me. That was the last time Gus and I hung out together. I can only imagine what he told his dad. I bet he blamed the whole thing on me."

"Well, that doesn't seem so bad. No one got hurt, and the only downside was that you lost a friend," Rich said, trying to put a positive spin on it.

"I haven't gotten to the bad part yet. The van was impounded, and I had to call Bea to come get me. She was livid; she never liked being disturbed in the middle of the night. After she took a taxi to the police station, she paid my bond and got the van out of the impound lot. When we climbed inside, the stench was awful."

"What was it?"

"At the time, I assumed Gus had puked. I moved my feet around, trying not to step in it, but it was so dark I couldn't tell where it was. For all I knew, I could have been sitting in it. Bea lectured me the whole ride home about how stupid I was and how I could have killed someone or myself. At that point, I did feel bad about the way it turned out, but when I tried to apologize, she didn't care and didn't want to hear what I had to say.

"The next morning I woke up with a mammoth hangover. My head felt like it was going to explode, and any noise made it worse. Bea knew this and took every opportunity to yell or speak loudly; she even got right up next to my ear to talk to me. She woke me up at some ungodly hour to clean out the van. Like I said, I was hung over and tired and I didn't understand why it was so urgent that I clean the van at that moment but, as she was with everything else, she wouldn't let up. Finally I got up and she handed me a toothbrush. My toothbrush. She told me to clean out the van with my toothbrush and, when I was done, I had to brush my teeth with it." David almost gagged thinking about it.

Rich covered his mouth. "She did not!"

"Yes, she did."

"What did you do?"

"What else could I do? With Bea, you never had a choice. I scrubbed the van the best I could and then I brushed my teeth with the same toothbrush as she stood by, watching and smiling that stupid gummy smile. I gagged the whole time, but she was so proud of herself. Another Kodak moment."

"Okay, now I understand. But turning twenty-one is a big event. What would you like to do instead?"

"How about a nice quiet dinner at home? We could invite the foundation staff, Lou, Miss Lopez and Mr. Kniffee. Just promise me there'll be no alcohol! To this day, I can't even stand the smell of it!"

Rich smiled. "Forget I brought it up."

Enjoy life. This is not a dress rehearsal.

~ Anonymous

Chapter Nine

Much to David's surprise, Joshua, now eighteen, phoned him one evening. He'd Googled Beatrice Miller on the Internet, and found out about the foundation. After a bit of small talk, he asked David if he could come for a visit. David was excited about the chance to see his "brother" again and felt overjoyed when he offered to pay his airfare.

"No, thank you. Mom and Dad said they'd buy me a ticket. They know how important this is to me."

It was odd to hear Josh talk about his mom and dad. They'd shared the same parents for so many years, but now Josh had a real mom and dad. David, still stuck with Bea, couldn't help feeling a bit jealous. They made plans for the following week, and Joshua was due in Phoenix on June fifteenth. David offered to meet him at the airport, and could hardly wait to see him.

When David spotted Josh, he recognized him immediately. He was a little bit taller, a little bit thinner, and had a bit of a suntan, but still the same thick, dark, naturally curly hair, now cut short. He looked contented and healthy. Smiling broadly, David helped Josh get his bags, and before long they were pulling into the driveway at David's house.

"Oh, my gosh. This is where you live?" Josh's eyes were huge.

David never grew tired of the reactions. "Yep. It's my Great Aunt Benita's house. When she died, she left it to me, and I've been here since last November. It's a big house, but considering where I came from…where we both came from…I've learned to appreciate it."

"You live by yourself?"

"No. Rich lives with me. We also have two full-time staff members; Miss Lopez, the housekeeper, and Mr. Kniffee, the gardener. Mr. Kniffee lives in the guest house behind the pool. Miss Lopez lives nearby, so she works here Monday through Friday. I've been told it's a full-time job keeping a house this huge running, and I believe it. I tried to do it myself when I first moved in, but I fell more behind every day. You need a degree in horticulture just to keep the grass green," David chuckled. "Let's go inside. I'll introduce you to everyone, and then we can sit and chat."

Josh, still amazed at the house, nodded. He was surprised to see Officer Butler, unaware that Officer Butler and Rich were the same person. He'd met Rich twice: the morning he came to the house to talk to Bea, and when they all climbed out of the back of the van in the abandoned parking lot a few hours later. Rich, on his way out the door, didn't stay to talk, but told Joshua it was good to see him and they'd catch up later.

Soon after Rich left, Joshua and David went out to dinner. Although happy to see Joshua, he wasn't sure what to talk about; their lives had made such a drastic turn and progressed so differently. Finally, Joshua broke the ice. "Did you know Bea was sentenced to thirty years? Fifteen for Mikey and fifteen for Maggie."

"Yes, I know." David turned on his blinker to switch lanes.

"I read it on the Internet. Have you seen her?" Joshua nervously tugged at his seatbelt.

"Yes, I saw her at the trial. I was a witness. Then I visited her before I left Bunting Valley to let her know I was moving to Phoenix, and again in April and just last week. I try to see her when my school schedule allows. I'll be going again soon. You're welcome to come along if you want. I'm sure she'd love to see you."

"I don't know. I don't think I'm ready yet. Besides, I don't know how Mom and Dad would feel about it, so I think its best I keep my distance for now. That doesn't mean I won't go with you at some point…just not yet."

David understood completely.

"How is she doing?" Joshua asked.

"She seems okay. The first visit was odd. She had no recollection of anything that had happened and kept referring to the prison as a hotel. Then she asked how the kids were doing...meaning you, John, Mikey, and Maggie, as if you were all at home waiting for her. The prison staff said she's on some pretty strong antidepressants, and that could be causing her short-term memory loss."

"Wow. That seems pretty far out there, even for Bea. How was she the last time you saw her? Better I hope." Josh reached over to lower the volume on the radio. He didn't want to miss a word of what David had to say about Bea.

"Better, but still not herself. Sometimes she's okay, and other times she's completely crazy. It's so weird that I don't know how to describe it. We talk, and she'll carry on a conversation, but then she gets a funny look in her eyes and her personality changes, and she starts saying things that I don't understand."

"Really?" Joshua furrowed his brow.

"Yeah. She thinks the other 'guests,' " David made imaginary quotation marks in the air, "are out to kill her. Sometimes it's funny and it's hard not to crack up. But there's one thing she keeps saying to me."

"What's that?"

"Remember, David, things aren't always what they seem."

"What does that mean?" Joshua seemed puzzled.

"I have no idea, and she won't elaborate, which is so unlike her. She used to tell me everything. My first guess was that she was trying to tell me I'd been kidnapped too, and I'm not really her son, but when I ordered a certified copy of my birth certificate so I could apply for a passport, it listed Beatrice Miller as my mother. Rich also told me he saw my birth certificate right after Bea and I were arrested; and remember when they did that cotton swab on the inside of our mouths?"

"Yes. What was that for?"

"It was for a DNA test to find out which of us was actually related to Bea. As you know, I was the 'lucky' one so I know that's not it." When David said the word lucky, he made air quotes.

"Have you asked her what she means?"

"Yes, several times. She says I'll find out when the time is right, and she's not the one who should tell me."

"That's creepy, isn't it?"

"Yeah, but we're talking about Bea."

Both boys chuckled. Each could write a book about growing up with Bea Miller, but they didn't know if it would it be considered a comedy or horror story.

David took Joshua to one of his favorite Italian cafes. As they entered, the smell of garlic and Italian spices greeted them at the door. They were shown to a table midway across the restaurant, and as soon as they sat, a waiter appeared to take their drink orders. As they looked over the menu, David recommended the fettuccini Alfredo, which was his favorite.

When they'd placed their orders, Joshua talked about his twin sisters, Monica and Erica. They were older than he, and were already in college by the time he arrived at his home in New Orleans. Joshua found it odd that he was related to them.

"I see them, and I think they're really hot, and then I remember they're my sisters and I shouldn't be thinking that way."

David laughed, picturing Joshua flirting with his own sisters. His mom and dad were both attorneys, and had looked for him a long time after he disappeared. Even when the police stopped, they wouldn't give up. Their nanny, Yvonne, felt horrible that she'd trusted a stranger to watch him while she took the twins to the swing set. When the police questioned her, she realized she knew nothing about the woman who'd identified herself as Robin. And when the facts came together, they realized Robin probably wasn't her real name.

"Speaking of names, are you telling me your birth name was Joshua and Bea didn't change it?" David was surprised. That didn't sound like something Bea would do.

"Oh, she did. My real name was Bryan, but after being Joshua for so long, I asked Mom and Dad to change it legally. Since they didn't want to make the transition any harder for me, they agreed. My legal name is now Joshua Johnson. Has a nice ring to it, doesn't it?" Joshua smiled.

"Yes, it does. What are they like, your parents?" David asked.

Joshua shrugged his shoulders. "I guess they're nice. I don't really have much to compare them to. They're nothing like Bea, but then again, I never really thought Bea was that bad."

"What was it like being back home?" David was curious.

Their food arrived and they dug in. "Well, it was awkward at first. Mom and Dad treated me like a visitor, taking me to see the sights: the French Quarter, Bourbon Street, museums, zoos, cemeteries, gardens...you name it, we saw it. After that, they started spending money on me, buying me stuff I didn't even want. They even bought me a car, and I don't even have a driver's license. I guess they were trying to make up for the sixteen years I was gone, the sixteen birthdays they missed, the sixteen Christmases without presents. Then they didn't really know what to do with me. I wasn't a visitor, I had everything I needed, and I wasn't going away."

"It must have been difficult for all of you."

"Yep. Imagine giving birth to a baby, and the doctor says, 'It's a healthy baby boy. Oh, and, by the way, he's sixteen years old.' "

David shook his head. "I can't even begin to imagine..."

"My sisters were gone, and Mom and Dad were planning the next phase of their life. Then I came back and messed it up."

"Don't you think they were glad to get you back?" David asked.

"No, no. They were glad I was back, and they were glad I was healthy, but by then, I was already the person I am now. They didn't get to shape me and teach me. They want me to be a lawyer, but I have no interest. I played softball through school and Dad hates softball. He wishes I would have played football, like he did. It's things like that I see on their faces; the disappointment, the letdown, the realization that they can't change who I am."

"Did you get any counseling or therapy? The environment we work in at the foundation can get very depressing, so I have a therapist come by once a week in case anyone needs to talk. It's done a world of good for the staff."

"Yes, we tried therapy. I went by myself for a while, and then Mom and Dad joined me."

"Did it help?"

"In some ways, yes; in other ways, no. It just made us realize they don't know me, yet they're my parents."

"I'm so sorry, Joshua." David pushed his plate back, having lost his appetite.

"Sorry for what?"

"I was there when she took you, and I had no idea."

"David, you were two years old. Of course you had no idea. And people told us we looked alike so often over the years that we never questioned it. It wasn't a bad life; I got to grow up with three brothers. I wish I could remember what Henry was like. I just can't remember him at all. But I do remember that trailer we lived in." Josh chuckled at the thought. "Boy, did that place stink! What was that odor, anyway?"

"You wouldn't believe me if I told you. Besides, it's not important. The important thing is we're here now and we're okay."

The waiter took their plates, and asked if either wanted dessert. Both declined and had French vanilla cappuccino instead.

"Have you heard from John or Mikey? I'm curious how they're getting along."

David shook his head.

"What? What's wrong? Did something happen?"

David looked at Joshua. "I was hoping not to get into this so soon, but since you asked, John's in jail."

"Jail! What for?"

"It's a long story." David's shoulders drooped, and he looked sad.

"I've got all night."

Joshua removed the napkin from his lap and tossed it on the table. He scooted his chair closer and rested his elbows on the table, waiting patiently for David to start.

David started from the beginning, with the phone call about the missing girl, and ended with the events at the hospital. The longer David spoke, the more transfixed Joshua became, unable to believe David was talking about John, his younger brother. When David finished, Joshua was speechless.

"I'm sorry you had to hear that, but I thought it best if you heard it from me. I planned to tell you, but wanted to wait a few days."

"Are you sure? Maybe John just made the whole thing up. Maybe he didn't do it."

"He admitted it. He even showed me how he broke her neck. I was stunned, but after working at the foundation, I guess nothing much surprises me anymore. The only part that shocked me was that it was John."

"So what's going to happen to him?"

"I'm not sure, and I don't want to know. He's no longer the John we grew up with. Early on, John pled not guilty, and I was contacted to appear as a witness. But a few weeks after that, I was contacted and told he'd changed his plea to guilty so there was never a trial. I've thought of going to visit him, but I'm not sure I want to. If he asked to see me, I'd go, but otherwise, I've washed my hands of it. The last thing he said to me was, 'Bea left me, my real mom and dad left me, Julie wanted to leave me, so now it's your turn, David. Go, just go! I don't need any of you!' It broke my heart to leave him, but he made a decision and now he has to live with it."

Joshua shook his head. "I can't believe it. As sad as it is, maybe Bea was right."

"Right about what?" David sipped his cappuccino, leaving a little foam on his upper lip.

"It seems like she did rescue him from an unpleasant situation."

"I can't believe you said that. I thought the same thing."

"So, maybe Bea wasn't as bad as we thought?"

"Oh, little brother, I wouldn't say that." The mood shifted, and they were laughing and again. "How long are you going to stay in Phoenix?" David asked.

"Well, I wanted to talk to you about that. I just graduated from high school, a year sooner than I should have."

"How did that happen?"

"I was tested when I got home and scored higher than expected, so they put me in twelfth grade. As I said, I don't aspire to be a lawyer. I was hoping that I could work for you at the foundation. Being a victim, I may be able to sympathize and help more."

"Oh, my gosh, Joshua! That's a fabulous idea. I can't believe I didn't think of it! You'd be able to relate to victims better than any of us, since you've been there. This is so exciting! My brother is home! I can't wait to tell Rich. An ex-police officer, an ex-911 operator, and a former kidnap victim; the staff is getting better all the time. Once I get my degree, there'll be no stopping us."

Fortune knocks once, but misfortune has much more patience.

~ Dr. Laurence J. Peter

Chapter Ten

In late June, the foundation received a frantic, teary call from a woman who identified herself as Beverly Smith. Although a lifelong resident of Phoenix, she was calling from Portugal, where she was vacationing with her family. She explained that as they exited the plane, she was holding the hand of their six-year-old daughter Trudy, and her husband, Matthew, was carrying their toddler, thirteen-month-old Eliza. When they reached the baggage claim area, Matthew put Eliza on the ground so he could grab one of their bags, telling her to stay put. She hung on to his pant leg. He retrieved the bag, and when he turned back another kid was hanging on to him and Eliza was gone. It had happened so quickly. Matthew looked around, but she was nowhere in sight. They notified the police, but with the language barrier, they were getting nowhere and growing more and more frustrated with each passing minute.

Kayla, one of the operators at the foundation, transferred Mrs. Smith to Rich. Within minutes, he called David, who was in the break room, into his office and they had Mrs. Smith on speaker. Through tears, she retold her story, and added that she'd heard wonderful things about "Never Give Up," that she'd stored the number in her cell phone, hoping never to need it. But now she did, thousands of miles away from home. When the call ended, Rich and David decided to fly to Portugal to see if they could help. Joshua, who didn't have a passport, would stay behind to remain in charge.

Never having flown outside the United States, both David and Rich were apprehensive about going through customs and immigration. The flight crew handed paperwork to the passengers to complete en route and present upon landing. Knowing neither had anything to hide, and they'd each brought only one small carry-on bag, they hoped they'd be processed quickly; the longer it took them to reach the Smiths, the less likely they'd find the missing child.

After clearing customs and immigration, David and Rich were met by the Smiths. Rich suggested they discuss the case with the Portuguese police present, but Mrs. Smith insisted they proceed without them. Her patience was wearing thin, and she didn't want to waste any more time with them. Mrs. Smith, who stood about five foot tall, was a blubbering mess, unable to put two words together without breaking down in tears. Mr. Smith, however, was unusually calm. A tall, handsome, stoic man, he apologized profusely and said more than once that he was sorry to bother them. He told them the details of the incident without emotion.

"...and after I grabbed the bag, I turned around. Eliza was gone and a little Portuguese boy about her size was holding on to my pant leg."

"Do you remember feeling Eliza let go?" Rich asked as he started to jot down notes. Always the designated note-keeper, he spent countless hours working with David training him in interrogation so David knew in exactly what order to ask the important questions. Rich usually got the ball rolling and then backed down and let David take over.

"No. Someone was holding it the entire time. If I had felt her letting go, I would have turned to see where she was."

"How long would you estimate you weren't looking at her?" Rich glanced up, still surprised by how calm Mr. Smith was.

"Not very long. I sat her down as soon as I saw our bag and told her to stay put. The bag took about ten to fifteen seconds to round the corner of the carousel, and I grabbed it. I put it down in front of me, turned back, and saw another child."

"What did you do then?"

"I asked, 'Who are you?' but realized he didn't speak English when he smiled and started babbling in Portuguese. Then I looked back to find her, but it was so crowded."

"Mrs. Smith, where were you when this happened?" David jumped in, turning his attention to Mrs. Smith. He could tell she was on the verge of hysterics.

Holding a tissue, she dabbed at the tears that would not stop flowing. She took a deep breath and blinked a few times, then began.

"I was standing on the other side, looking for our other bags. We always work in tandem." She stopped to catch her breath and blow her nose. "If Matthew misses them, I grab them. I'm the second string."

"How far away were you?" David asked.

"Maybe fifteen feet, but there were probably five-to-ten other passengers between us, so I couldn't see Matthew."

"And you didn't see Eliza, either?" Rich continued to take notes while David did the majority of the talking.

"No, not since we arrived at the baggage claim. I didn't know she was missing. I stood there, waiting for our bags, talking to Trudy, when Matthew told me." Retelling the details, Mrs. Smith began sobbing again.

"When was that?" David asked, but she couldn't answer through her tears.

"About five minutes after the incident," Mr. Smith said. It was obvious his wife had been pushed to the limit and could no longer speak coherently.

"Why did it take you so long to tell her?"

"I didn't want to scare her, and I thought I'd look around first to see if I could find her." He shrugged, and then placed his arm protectively around his wife.

"So you waited a full five minutes to alert your wife that your daughter was missing? In a foreign country?" David said in an accusatory manner.

"Yes. That sounds about right, but it may have been a little longer. We were on vacation. I didn't want Beverly to panic. Especially if Eliza was nearby."

"What happened to the little boy holding onto your pants?" David was starting to sound skeptical.

"He walked away when I started searching for Eliza."

"Mrs. Smith, did you see the little boy?" Rich asked.

She could only shake her head.

"Take us to the baggage claim area so we can get a better feel of where this happened," David said.

When they arrived, it was like nothing Rich and David had ever seen. Small Portuguese children, probably five to ten years old, were everywhere, offering to help tourists with their bags for a price. There were mobs of people talking and yelling, swarming around two to four deep, huddled around the turnstile, waiting for their luggage. Other children at tables offered handmade flower necklaces to all the pretty women. A small boy took Rich by the hand and offered, in very broken English, to give him a ride to his hotel. With all the activity, Rich could see why Mrs. Smith had no idea what was going on, even though it happened such a short distance from her.

Rich asked the Smiths if they had a photo of Eliza. When he looked at the picture, the child reminded him of Maggie Taylor—blonde hair, blue eyes, and a smile that could light up the world. Mr. Smith said he was hungry and was going to take his wife and daughter to get something to eat. Rich and David told them they'd be in touch when they had some news.

~

As soon as they left the Smiths and began to talk, they agreed something was unusual about the story—especially Matthew Smith's version. It didn't make sense. As they walked through the airport, they continued reviewing the details.

"If it were my daughter, I'd have started screaming bloody murder," Rich said. "But he waited a full five minutes, maybe longer, before he said anything. His wife could have helped him search for her."

"Yeah," David agreed. "And when he turned and saw the wrong kid, all he could say was 'who are you?' He didn't even follow the kid;

he just let him walk away. The odds of us finding the child he's talking about are remote at best."

After settling into their hotel, they phoned Joshua. After relaying the series of events, Joshua agreed things did not seem on the up-and-up. They asked him to do a little leg work—checking bank statements and phone records to see if he could find out anything else about Matthew Smith. Something didn't seem right; he was too calm and uncaring. He talked about Eliza's disappearance like it was a routine trip to the grocery store.

Not thirty minutes after they hung up, Joshua was back on the phone. "You're not going to believe this. Two days before the Smiths landed in Portugal, one million American dollars were wired into Matthew Smith's bank account from Caixa de Crédito Agrícola Mútuo de Pernesa, a Portuguese bank. Then, on the day they arrived in Portugal, another one million American dollars were wired from the same bank. I attempted to contact said bank to see if I could find out more information, but due to the time difference, the bank was closed. I'll try again as soon as I can. There were also phone calls placed from Mr. Smith's cell phone to a number using the country code for Portugal. I called it to see if I could determine who it was, but the man who answered didn't appear to speak English.

"Great job, Josh." David was very proud and Joshua was proving to be such an asset to the foundation.

"Wait, that's not all. Matthew Smith filed for divorce a couple of weeks before this vacation. The papers haven't been served, so it appears Beverly Smith has no idea."

"This is getting more and more interesting. Did he think we wouldn't be able to find this stuff out?" Rich asked, reading back over his notes.

David said, "Remember, he kept saying he hadn't wanted his wife to call us? I bet he knew we'd find out. He probably wanted to leave things to the Portuguese police, who were, as Beverly Smith described, just wasting time."

As soon as they hung up Rich contacted the Portuguese police, and through broken English and repeating several of the facts more than once, they were able to relay the information they'd unearthed.

Early the next morning, Matthew and Beverly Smith were at the police station in separate interrogation rooms. The station, a small, one-story, cinderblock structure, lacked central air conditioning; box fans, placed randomly, circulated the hot, humid air from one area to the next. Most of the staff was wearing shorts, and Rich couldn't blame them. Beverly Smith was in a small room with a huge open window, which allowed the steamy air to billow in, making the room even more stifling. However, she never backed down; through her tears, she repeated the same story she'd told from the beginning.

Matthew Smith, sitting just down the hall in a smaller room with no windows, was having a different experience. He was sweating profusely—from guilt, the heat, or both. There were huge sweat stains under his arms, and his forehead was beaded with perspiration, which streamed down his face. At first he claimed he was carrying Eliza, but then said he was holding her hand as she walked beside him. He said it was a few seconds before he grabbed his bag; then it turned into two to three minutes. He'd told Rich and David a small Portuguese boy held his pant leg, and then it became a small Portuguese child, and he didn't know if it was a boy or girl. He now said he'd alerted Beverly as soon as he found Eliza missing, as opposed to the five minutes or longer he'd described in his original account. There were so many inconsistencies in his story they were beginning to wonder if his name was really Matthew Smith.

In the meantime, Joshua e-mailed the copy of the bank statement showing the pair of one-million-dollar deposits. When Rich placed it in front of Matthew Smith, his face turned ghostly white.

"Mr. Smith, can you tell me where this money came from?" Rich was ready to take him down.

Matthew picked up the statement, looked at it, and then placed it back on the scarred table. Regaining his composure, he said, "I have no idea. Smith is a very common name. It's either someone else's bank account, or someone transferred it to my account in error. Now, can one of you get me something to drink?"

"That's your answer? One million dollars, two days before your vacation, and you have no idea where it came from or how it ended up in your bank account? Unbelievable!" Rich turned a chair backwards and straddled it.

Matthew did not respond.

"Well then, can you tell me when you planned to tell your wife that you filed for divorce?" Rich asked.

Matthews's mouth was agape. "I told her not to call you. I told her to let the Portuguese police handle it, but she never listens to me!" He stood up and banged his hand on the table, leaving a damp palm print.

"Mr. Smith, sit down and tell us what's going on. The sooner you tell us the truth, the sooner we can find your daughter, and the sooner we can all get out of here." Rich just wanted this whole ordeal to be over so they could go home.

Matthew took a deep breath. "You'll never find her, so just go back to Phoenix." Rich and David looked at him incredulously, and when they didn't speak, Mr. Smith began. "It started two years ago. We came to Portugal on vacation, and while we were here I met a man involved in human trafficking. He commented on my daughter Trudy, but said she was too old. He told me they like kids to be young…two years or less. I asked how much a person could get for a child like that. He told me one million dollars, but if they had blonde hair with blue eyes, the price doubled to two million dollars. I couldn't believe it. Two million dollars!

"So we went home and luckily, Beverly got pregnant right away. When Eliza was born, I insisted we return to Portugal for another vacation. When we started making plans, I got in touch with my contact, told him about Eliza, and sent a photograph. When he saw it, he agreed to transfer one million dollars into my bank account two days before our trip. As soon as we got off the plane, the switch would be made, and the remaining one million dollars would be wired. It's good to see he is a man of his word."

Rich shook his head in disbelief. This man bought Eliza and Matthew was glad to see he was a man of his word?

"What were they going to do with her?"

"I don't know, and I don't care."

Rich took a deep breath. It took all the self-control he could muster not to punch Matthew Smith.

"What do you mean, you don't care? This is your daughter we're talking about!" Rich screamed, leaning over the table.

"No. It's two million dollars we're talking about. Eliza was just a pawn." Matthew smugly leaned back and interlocked his fingers behind his head.

"You make me sick." Rich turned his back before he did something he knew he would regret. Thank goodness David was there to pick up where Rich left off.

"What about the divorce? What does that have to do with this?" David asked.

"Do you think I wanted to share two million dollars with her?" Matthew pointed towards the door. "She's so boring and practical. For Christ's sake, just look at her. I knew that if I divorced her, I'd get the two million bucks and, since we only had one kid left, the child support payments wouldn't kill me. Especially on my income—which will be nothing when I quit my job." Matthew smiled. "What can I say? It's a win-win."

Rich didn't care about maintaining composure any more. He rushed at Matthew Smith and punched him, full on, in the face. Mr. Smith bent forward, cupping his hands to catch the blood pouring from his nose. Rich stood back, shaking his stinging hand. David was speechless.

The police handcuffed Matthew and led him away. When they walked out of the room, Beverly was standing there, eyes red and swollen, her hair tousled, as if she didn't even think to run a brush through it. She panicked at the sight of all the blood running down Matthew's face.

"Matthew, what happened? What's going on?" she asked, following them. "Where are they taking you? Where's Eliza?"

Since the police spoke very little English, Rich and David led her back into the room she just came from to explain what happened. While they thought she'd been upset earlier, it was nothing compared to now. "No! No! No!" she kept saying, her head down on the table, pounding it with her hands as her shoulders jerked with sobs.

The police explained that when human traffickers buy a child, that child is sold to another group who typically sells it to another group, and so on. The toddlers are blindfolded, gagged, and placed in a crate, sometimes with three to six other kids. The crate is then sent by rail, water, or air, whichever is most convenient. The conductor, captain, or pilot is paid off to keep quiet. The children who make the most noise are severely beaten, so they quickly learn there are unpleasant consequences for their actions. The police estimated that, by now, Eliza had probably changed hands close to a dozen times; finding her now would be virtually impossible.

Rich and David returned to Phoenix, and David had never been so happy to be in America. The first night back, he dreamed of Portugal, and kept seeing Eliza Smith's blindfolded face in a window. Just when he was able to reach her, she was gone, across the street in another window, always just one step ahead of him. He was never able to reach her.

With this case still fresh in his mind, David stopped to look at the bulletin board each time he passed it. He wished he was able to hang Eliza's picture there. Although he was glad they were able to find out what had happened to her, he was sad because Beverly Smith's heart had been broken, and there was nothing they could do to mend it. He vowed to contact her regularly to see how she was holding up and ask if there was anything he could do for her. Short of finding and bringing Eliza back home, he doubted there was.

God does not ask about our ability, but our availability.

~ Anonymous

~ Chapter Eleven ~

David had not seen his mother since mid-May. He continued to get letters from her, and every now and then she'd send something she'd made in arts and crafts: a keychain, a watercolor, or a potholder. They were simple gifts, but it was sweet just the same. She seemed to be doing better and spoke more positively about her future. She occasionally managed to apologize for something she'd done when David was younger; he didn't remember some of the things, but if she was willing to apologize, it was a positive step. Rich told him her therapist was probably encouraging her to do it. Although she was still taking antidepressants, her dosage had been cut in half, and it seemed that the less she took, the more she seemed her old self. However, David didn't know if that was who he wanted; she hadn't been a model citizen or a good mother.

David flew first class this time, and arrived in Bunting Valley earlier than he'd anticipated. With a couple hours to occupy before he could see his mother, David decided to pay Mrs. Brown, his old neighbor, a visit. He could probably spend fifteen minutes with her, and she would get him caught up on all the news in Bunting Valley and the surrounding cities since he'd left, which had been about eight months.

When he pulled into her driveway, he sat for a moment looking at his old trailer. It had been painted and some of the windows were replaced. There was a "For Rent" sign in the front yard. David hoped it hadn't been vacant since he left, but knew Mrs. Brown would tell him all about it.

As soon as he climbed out of his rental car, a horrible smell assaulted him. It was a stench like that of a dead, decaying skunk. He had to hold his nose to keep from gagging. He pounded on Mrs. Brown's door, hoping she'd open the door as soon as possible.

"I'm coming, I'm coming. I'm an old lady. Hold your horses," he heard her say as she walked towards the door. She was annoyed at first, but when she saw David, she seemed happier and invited him in.

It was the first time David had ever seen her appropriately dressed, wearing a light-blue, fleece long-sleeved top—with an appliqué of a curled-up cat playing with a ball of yarn—and pants. Of course, the big, furry, cotton-candy house slippers had not changed.

"David, it's so good to see you!" She seemed as though she meant it as she slammed the door behind him. "When I heard the pounding, I thought you were another one of those people running for public office, out soliciting votes. They annoy me to no end. I'm not going to decide who to vote for based on a conversation that lasts a minute or less through the crack of an open door."

"Oh, my gosh, Mrs. Brown. What in the world is that odor outside?" David asked as he wiped his feet on the rug by the front door.

"I believe it started out as a dead deer, or at least that's what they told me. Then it turned into a dead body. It's a long story."

"A dead body?" David was shocked.

"I'll tell you all about it. I'm still livid about the whole situation, which is another reason I'm not in the best mood. The way these elected officials turned a blind eye to what's been going on here! I can tell you right now, I won't be voting for any of them!"

"I'm so sorry."

"It's not your fault, so you have nothing to apologize for. Besides, it seems like it's getting a little better."

"The smell is sometimes worse?" David could hardly believe it.

"Absolutely! I could barely go outdoors a few months ago. I'm hoping the worst is behind us; I can't take much more of this. Oh my goodness, where are my manners?" David was still standing at the door. "Why don't you have a seat in the living room while I pour us a nice glass of lemonade? Would you like that?"

"Yes, that would be nice." David left his shoes by the front door and walked to the sofa. "I'm sorry to have stopped by without phoning first. I came to visit my mom, and I got here a little sooner than I thought

I would. I still forget about the one-hour difference and calculate the time wrong. Visiting hours at the prison don't start until six-thirty," David said, feeling small as he sat on a big, floral-upholstered, oversized couch.

"Hold that thought. I'll be right back," Mrs. Brown said, holding her index finger up.

David had never been inside Mrs. Brown's trailer before, but based on how meticulously she'd always kept her flower beds, he imagined it would be spotless—and it was. As soon as she was out of sight, David walked around, looking at her photos and trinkets. The walls were neatly papered, and there were cat figurines everywhere: on shelves, in shadow boxes, and in a curio cabinet. After living in a house with high ceilings, the low ceiling of the trailer was making him feel a little claustrophobic.

There was a black-and-white photo in an oval, vintage-looking frame, sitting on a high rectangular table pushed up to the back of the couch, next to a brass table lamp. It was a younger version of Mrs. Brown, apparently at her a wedding, and she looked so happy. David smiled, looking at the people in their old-fashioned clothing, smiling ear-to-ear without showing their teeth.

Mrs. Brown returned with a tray and said, "That's a picture of me and my Howard. June 11, 1954."

David smiled and placed the photo back on the table. He joined Mrs. Brown on the couch as she placed a tray with a glass pitcher full of lemonade, two glasses full of ice, and a small plate of store-bought chocolate chip cookies on the coffee table.

"Do you have a cat?" David asked.

"No. Why do you ask?"

"I noticed all the figurines."

"No. I love cats, but I'm highly allergic. Since I can't have a real one, I decided the ceramic version was the next best thing. I thought about getting an outdoor cat, but our winters are so brutal. I couldn't do that to an animal. So, you mentioned you're here to visit your mom. How is she?" Mrs. Brown grabbed a cookie and took a small bite. She seemed a little embarrassed when crumbs sprinkled all over her lap.

"Wait. Before we get into that, tell me about the dead body." David was anxious to hear her story.

"Do you remember the people who lived two doors down from your trailer? Three down from mine?"

David shook his head. "No. I don't know anyone here except you."

"Well, it was an older lady and her mentally-challenged adult son. He's in his early seventies, so she must have been close to ninety years old."

"I had no idea."

"Yes. They lived there for years and years. His name was Jimmy and her name was Silvia. She was taking care of him which, from what I heard, was no easy task. I heard he was strong as an ox and Silvia was afraid of him. Anyway, she passed away last fall."

"I'm sorry." David took a gulp of his lemonade and wiped his mouth with a napkin.

"Jimmy, having about the intelligence of a six-year-old, didn't know what to do with the body, so he kept it in the bathtub for a while…five or six weeks, from what I remember reading in the newspaper. When the body started to decompose, he put it in a black trash bag, cinched the top, and sat it out behind their trailer."

"Good God, he didn't!" David almost choked on his cookie, which was extremely dry. It reminded David of some of the cookies Bea had baked over the years, using only half the amount of oil called for in the recipe, in order to save on ingredients.

Mrs. Brown nodded. "Yes, he did. There was just a smidgen of an odor, so I called city hall and, a few days later, animal control came out and found a dead deer. The carcass was just starting to decompose, so they hauled it away."

"Did that help?"

"I don't know. I was trying to convince myself the deer was the source of the odor so I could move on."

David finished the last of his lemonade. "What happened next?"

"Winter came and the temperatures dropped. I stayed indoors for several months, just like everyone else, so I didn't notice it for a while."

David chuckled. "Yeah. I remember how we all had to hibernate."

"So, this past spring, the smell came back. I called city hall again, but as soon as they found out where I live, they just tuned me out. Apparently," Mrs. Brown raised her eyebrows, "our concerns are not taken as seriously as the hoity-toity residents in their million-dollar homes. Would you like more lemonade?" Without even waiting for David to answer, she stood and poured both of them another glass.

"So, what happened next?" David said, as he helped himself to another cookie.

"This went on for several weeks. I must have called them a dozen times." Mrs. Brown paused to shake her head. "Finally, last week animal control came out again; then the health department was here, with several police cars, the coroner, and a number of other people. I was told they came out when someone else complained. Anyway, they found Silvia in the trash bag. She died of natural causes, and due to the circumstances, Jimmy is now in a state home. So much of this could have been avoided if they'd taken me seriously when I called the first time. As you can imagine, I'm irritated, but enough about that. I'm dying to know. How is your mother?"

David shook his head, wondering how much of the story was fact and how much Mrs. Brown fabricated. "She seems to be doing all right. At first she was having a hard time, but I think she's finally coming around."

"A hard time, you say? How so?"

"Just lost and confused. Not sure where she was or why she was there. She kept asking about my other siblings, the ones she kidnapped, as if they were at home, waiting for her to return. I was a little concerned at first, but was told she was on some strong medicine, and her short term memory loss was expected."

"Oh, dear. That's horrible. Please tell her I said hello when you see her. Despite her being a cold-blooded killer, I always liked your mother. She was a good neighbor, and a good friend," Mrs. Brown smiled.

David didn't know how to respond. Finally he said, "That's kind of you to say. Hey, I noticed a 'for rent' sign next door." David pointed with his thumb. "Has the trailer been empty since I left?"

"Heavens, no. There have been two different tenants since you moved out. The first was a man, a woman, and a little kid. I'm not sure if it was a boy or girl. They didn't stay very long, so I never got to know them. The next ones moved out last month. I guess they couldn't stand the odor. I watched them pack the moving truck from my living room window. It seemed to be just a man and woman, both relatively young...probably in their early- to mid-thirties. I was amazed at all the stuff they had. Musical instruments like you wouldn't believe: a piano, guitars, drum sets. They must have been in a band or something, even though I never heard music coming from their trailer. I have no idea where they put it all."

David rolled his eyes. *Some things never change.* "How are things in the neighborhood? Anything else going on...besides the dead body?"

"As a matter of fact, there is. Someone finally bought that old warehouse at the end of the street. I can't begin to tell you how happy I am. It's been an eyesore for years. They're going to tear it down, and a large supermarket chain is building a brand new store. I'm so excited." Mrs. Brown slapped both her thighs with enthusiasm. "Now I don't have to go all the way across town when I run out of milk or bread. Heck, once the smell goes away, I can even walk there. Tell, me, how are things in Phoenix? It is Phoenix, isn't it?"

David was certain she knew it was. "Good. Things are going really well. I opened a foundation to help find missing kids."

"Yes, I know. I saw some mention of it on the local news...you know, one of those 'local boy makes good' segments. I also heard that police officer from here joined you. Butler was his name, wasn't it?"

"Yes, it was Officer Butler, but we just call him Rich now."

"How is that going?"

"Great. Besides Rich, my brother Joshua recently came out to lend a hand. We have a wonderful staff, and get calls day and night asking for our help. It's such a joy to have a part in helping to find a missing child and return him or her safely to their parents."

"Yes, I imagine it would be. Can I ask a question?" Mrs. Brown seemed to have her own agenda, as always.

David knew she'd ask, so he said, "Absolutely."

"Where did you get the money to open the foundation? Your family was never...how shall I put this...wealthy by any stretch of the imagination. I assume something like that would cost a pretty penny."

David said, "Yes, that's true; it wasn't cheap, that's for sure. I had a great aunt who passed away and left me her estate. I used some of her money to open the foundation, but we run it solely on donations."

"A great aunt, you say? The one who came in for the trial?"

"Yes. I'm surprised you remember that. It was my Great Aunt Benita. She took care of my mom for the first six years of her life. She was Grandpa Edward's younger sister." As soon as he said it, he regretted mentioning Edward.

"Oh, I see."

"I'm sorry, Mrs. Brown. I didn't think about your relationship with Grandpa before I spoke."

"Don't be silly. That was years ago. I'm over it. Even though your mother shot and killed the only man I ever loved, besides my Howard, I'm over it."

The rest of the visit took a turn for the worse. It was obvious that Mrs. Brown was not "over it." Her tone of voice changed from friendly and inviting to annoyed and intrusive.

"How long are you planning to be in town?" Mrs. Brown asked as she stood and started clearing away the lemonade glasses, setting them back on the empty tray. David wasn't even finished drinking his.

"Not long. I usually just come in and visit Mom and then go home, either the same night or early the next morning."

"I'm surprised your beloved foundation can survive without you," Mrs. Brown said sarcastically.

"Rich knows what he's doing. Heck, he knows more than I do."

Suddenly the tension in the room increased and David started feeling uncomfortable, making a comment that he had taken up enough of her time. When he stood to leave, Mrs. Brown invited him to stop by anytime, and she reminded him not to forget to tell his mother she said hello.

"Will do," David said as he waved and walked to his car. *Oh my God, that smell is horrible!* He jumped in his car, threw it in reverse, and sped away, gravel and dirt flying everywhere. It was funny how David had lived on Crimson Lane for years and never thought anything of it, but now, looking in his rearview mirror, he could understand why Aunt Benita turned up her nose at his living conditions when she visited. David was told his entire life never to forget where he came from. He hadn't forgotten, but he knew one thing for sure—he never wanted to go back.

~

Bea was happy to see him. She surprised him by giving him a hug and kissing him on the cheek. "Oh, David, I'm so happy to see you. Thank you so much for sending the aluminum foil. It worked wonders, as you can see. My brain hasn't melted." Bea seemed almost giddy as she smiled, showing off those big pink gums.

Knowing he hadn't sent any foil, he decided to play along. "You're very welcome. Oh, before I forget, I paid Mrs. Brown a visit this afternoon. Do you remember her?"

"Of course I do. How is the old biddy?" Bea asked, taking a seat.

David laughed, sitting down beside her. "She's fine. As nosy as always. She asked me to tell you hello. Oh, and you would not believe the smell in the old neighborhood. Absolutely horrible. Makes your eyes water. We got out of there just in the nick of time."

"Really? Do they have any idea what it is?" Bea gasped, her hand covering her mouth.

"Mrs. Brown said it was a dead body."

"A dead body!"

"Yeah. She said it started smelling really bad in the spring. Turns out some man a few doors down from where we lived put his dead mother in a trash bag and set her out behind their trailer."

Bea released a sigh. "Really?"

"Yep. Mrs. Brown said that was just a week or so ago, and the smell is getting better. It almost reminded me of the odor we had in the trailer, but about a hundred times worse."

The rest of the visit went surprisingly well. Near the end, Bea asked David if he would bring her a pillow the next time he came.

"A pillow? What for? Don't they have pillows here?"

"Don't be silly. Of course they have pillows, but since the poison on the donuts didn't work, and they failed to melt my brain, they're now putting crushed lime in my pillow. When I lay down, they hope I'll inhale the fumes and powder, and they'll make me sick and I'll die."

David said, "You've got to be kidding me."

"No, I'm serious. They won't give up. When they find something doesn't work, they waste no time moving on to something else."

"Do any of the other inmates have these problems?" It was the first time David actually called them inmates instead of guests, and he wasn't sure how Bea was going to react.

"No. I seem to be the only one they want to get rid of. It's quite distressing. I've never done anything to these people."

David nodded in agreement. "Okay. Next time I come I'll bring a pillow."

"Good. And bring Maggie. I haven't seen her in such a long time. What is she now, four or five years old? Before we know it she'll be starting kindergarten. I can't get over how quickly the time passes."

"Yes, it does. A pillow from home and Maggie. Will do." Just when David thought his mother was better, she wigged out again.

When it was time to leave, Bea gave David a great big hug and whispered, "Remember, David, things aren't always what they seem."

Concerned that Bea wasn't getting any better, David asked if he could speak to her therapist. Of course, bound by the doctor-patient relationship, there wasn't much he could share. David asked if he should agree with his mother when she said strange things.

"What types of things?" her therapist was curious.

"Oh, I'm sure you know. Like people are trying to kill her and asking how my siblings are doing."

"What do you say when she says these things?"

"I play along because I don't want to upset her."

The therapist had a strange look on his face. "Hmm, she never says anything like that during her sessions. I find that very interesting."

"Interesting? That's all you have to say? My mom is acting completely crazy and all you can say is interesting? What kind of doctor are you?" Every time David spoke to a professional at the prison about his mother's mental state, he was the one who ended up looking and sounding crazy.

The whole world steps aside for the man who knows where he is going.

~ Anonymous

Chapter Twelve

In early August, a detective from a small suburb outside Dallas, Texas called "Never Give Up." A twenty-eight-year-old mother of three with an estranged husband claimed someone had stolen her car. She'd left it running at a gas station when she went in to pay the cashier. When she came out, her car was gone, along with her one-year-old-daughter Mikayla, two-year-old-son Carlos, and his twin brother Miguel. They were all asleep when she left them, and she thought the person who stole the car didn't know they were in the back seat. An Amber Alert was issued immediately, but nothing turned up.

On the second day, she held a press conference on national television and pleaded for the safe return of her children. She promised whoever took the car that they could have it; she just wanted her babies back, safe and unharmed. She sobbed and clutched a photo to her chest.

David, Rich, and Joshua reviewed the footage, and then David and Rich caught a plane the same day. They met first with a detective, who reviewed what little evidence they had. He showed them pictures of the children and gave a little background on Tina Torres and her estranged husband, Phillip. The kids were adorable. Mikayla had the perfect features of a china doll; the twins didn't resemble Mrs. Torres in the least, so David and Rich assumed they looked like their father. Tina had been working at Burgers and More, a local fast food restaurant, but her last day was the same day the children disappeared.

The detective asked David and Rich to speak privately with Tina, hoping she might have some additional information. He admitted the department was shorthanded. He was bombarded with several cases and wasn't able to devote the amount of time and energy to this case as he would have liked. Not only that, his brother was terminally ill. With so much on his mind, several possible suspects had not been contacted and things had a way of falling through the cracks.

A heavy-set, short woman with walnut-colored wavy hair and dark, coffee-colored eyes, Tina Torres was Latino, but spoke perfect English. She was wearing cut-off shorts made from grey sweatpants; her yellow t-shirt was too small for her frame, and her belly fell over the top of her waistband. Black flip-flops and a brown suede handbag completed her outfit. Mrs. Torres took a seat in the interrogation room and retold the same story she'd conveyed at the press conference. She said she hadn't been able to eat or sleep since their disappearance. Her twins were so afraid of the dark that she couldn't sleep imagining how scared they must be. She hoped wherever they were, they were allowed plenty of light.

David and Rich contacted the gas station where the alleged abduction took place, to see if there was security footage from the day in question so they could try to identify the person who drove off with Mrs. Torres' automobile. They were told the police already had it. While they waited for it to be located, they tried to reach Phillip Torres. He and his wife were separated, and according to Mrs. Torres, there were no plans for a divorce. She couldn't afford it, and now that her babies were missing, it wasn't a priority.

After a few phone calls, they were able to track down Mr. Torres and ask him to come to the police station. After complaining and giving every excuse he could think of, he finally arrived about two hours later. Both Rich and David were with him in a windowless interrogation room for quite some time.

"I haven't seen those kids since she kicked me out," Mr. Torres said angrily.

A mid-sized, stocky man, he looked like he was stuck in the 1950s; slicked-back, jet-black hair with long, thick sideburns. Despite his appearance, his hands were immaculate; not a callus or scar, and his fingernails were manicured. His arms, however, bore several tattoos. He wore a tight, short-sleeved, black t-shirt, a pack of cigarettes outlined in the pocket, with black pants and a wallet attached to his belt loop with a long chain. Completing his outfit were a gold pinky ring engraved with the head of a lion, a chunky, finely brushed gold watch on his left wrist, and a pair of dark brown Bruno Magli shoes. He sat, relaxed, his legs crossed with his ankle resting on his knee.

"And when was that?" David asked.

"Shortly after the doctor gave us the okay to have sex." Mr. Torres spoke with a slight New Jersey accent—very rough around the edges. He kept cracking his knuckles, which David assumed was a nervous habit.

"What? When was that?"

"After a kid is born, you have to wait six weeks before you can jump her bones again. Well, the doctor gave us the all-clear, and that's when she kicked me out."

David shook his head. "Why would she kick you out then? That makes no sense."

"The doctor said she couldn't have sex for six weeks; he didn't say anything about me. Bada bing." Mr. Torres leaned in and hit the table as if it was a drum, waiting for some type of reaction from David and Rich. When none came, he leaned back and recommenced cracking his knuckles.

David blinked a couple of times. "Okay, so we've established you're a pig." David looked over and saw Rich smiling. "When was the last time you saw your kids?"

"I told you, not since she kicked me out."

"Mr. Torres, we need a date, a time, a place. Something else besides when you got the okay to have intercourse."

"I don't know the exact date. What do I look like? A freakin' calendar?"

"You look like a man who has three small children missing, and until he can give me some facts, he's looking like he's hiding something and is guilty of more than being a pig."

"Okay, all right. Let's see. Mikayla was born on August seventeenth, last year. Six weeks after that was...does someone have a calendar?"

"Mr. Torres, you aren't helping matters." David shook his head.

"Wait a minute. I know. I know the date because it was the same day I moved into the fun house."

"What?" David asked. "Are you part of a carnival or something?"

"No. That's the nickname I gave my bachelor pad."

David rolled his eyes.

"I moved in on October second." Mr. Torres paused to admire his pinky ring.

"October second? Where is your apartment? We'll have to check with the landlord to verify your story."

"You go right ahead. I told you I had nothing to do with their disappearance. I've got nothing to hide." For the first time Mr. Torres smiled as he leaned back in his chair, looking smug.

It seemed to David that Mr. Torres was more concerned with proving them wrong than distraught by his three children being missing. "Just so I know we're on the same page here, you know we called you down here because your three children are missing, correct? And until you can prove otherwise, you are considered a suspect."

"Of course I know that. I'm not a moron. I watch those crime shows on TV. I know how things work."

After getting the name of his apartment complex, Rich phoned the landlord and Mr. Torres's story was confirmed. However, that didn't mean he was innocent of any wrongdoing.

After Mr. Torres left, David and Rich reviewed the notes to see if they could come up with anything.

"It was so out of character for you to call him a pig. I didn't see it coming, and it was pretty funny," Rich commented.

"Thanks. I feel like I should remain a little more professional, though. But some of the things these idiots tell us make me want to knock them upside the head. I mean, the man admitted he was having an affair. He seemed relieved when his story about moving into the apartment was verified. Yet, where is the concern over his children? Some psycho could have them this very minute, doing horrible things to them, and all he cares about is jumping someone's bones? Bada bing!"

Rich laughed out loud. "Well, at least you didn't punch him in the face."

"No, but that doesn't mean I didn't want to." Someone knocked lightly on the door and David rose to open it.

It was a department employee. "Here's the security tape from the gas station. You can play it in the next room." The detective who had contacted "Never Give Up" was now out on bereavement leave, so David and Rich were working independently on unanswered questions.

Both went into the next room, and couldn't believe what they saw on the tape. It was Tina Torres who climbed back into the car and drove off. No one stole her car; the story was a lie. They called Tina back to the police station for further questioning. Since she didn't have a car, they sent a police cruiser to pick her up.

"Mrs. Torres, we know you lied to us earlier. Your children weren't kidnapped by someone at the gas station, were they?"

"Yes. Yes! Why would I lie about such a thing?" Her dark eyes were wide, darting from Rich to David and back again. Her accent became more apparent when she became nervous.

"I don't know. You tell us," David said, leaning back and folding his arms in front of him.

"Why are you calling me a liar? Did you talk to my worthless, dumb-ass husband? What did he tell you? He doesn't know where they are. He left them. He left me. He left us. He hasn't tried to see them for months. He doesn't care. He has no idea."

"No, Mr. Torres didn't tell us anything. We requested the video surveillance tape from the gas station on the night you claim someone took your car. We thought if we could see the person on camera, we might be able to use a facial recognition system to get an ID. When we watched it, we saw you climb back into your car and drive off. It wasn't the best angle, but it looked like all three of your children were in the back seat, sound asleep, just like you said in your original statement."

"You must be mistaken. I was at the same gas station the day before. Maybe they gave you the wrong tape from the wrong day. Check back with them. I didn't do anything to my children. I love my children. I would give my life for them. I miss them and I want them back."

Mrs. Torres sounded so sincere that David wanted to believe her, but he was having a hard time. "Okay, Mrs. Torres. We'll contact the gas station to see if they sent the wrong tape. Give us the date again so we can be sure."

"It was two days ago, August third."

They told her she could go home, but nowhere else. She and her estranged husband were possible suspects, and they needed to remain in town where they could easily be reached.

Rich contacted the gas station and was assured they sent the correct tape. They said they would check the tapes from the days before and after to see if there was any sign of Mrs. Torres. They didn't recognize her as a regular customer, but said it was possible since a lot of people pay at the pump, so they didn't have face-to-face contact with every customer.

In the meantime, David was running a background check on Tina Torres, while Rich contacted the restaurant where she'd worked. To his surprise, he discovered she'd been fired the day the children disappeared; she had not quit as she had stated. The manager said she'd been working there for five months when, on the morning of August third, she placed a case of frozen hamburger patties in the trunk of her car when she was on break. She saw an opportunity to help herself to a case right off the delivery truck and was terminated immediately.

David and Rich got into their rental car and went see her. They were afraid that if they called, she would take off before a cruiser had a chance to pick her up.

Tina Torres lived in an older, single-story duplex with gold aluminum siding and dark brick accents around the doors and windows. She shared a driveway, as well as a two-car attached garage, with her neighbors. When they arrived, David heard a dog barking and assumed the sound was coming from the next door neighbor's house.

In contrast to Mrs. Torres's house, the neighbor's had two cars parked bumper-to-bumper in the driveway, and every light in the house seemed to be on. Mrs. Torres' house was dark and looked uninhabited. Fighting with the brush that had grown over the sidewalk, David noticed red, pink, and ripe black pepper vine berries hanging in bunches. When he and Rich knocked on the door, no one answered. As they wondered what they should do next, they heard classical music playing inside.

David decided to see if the neighbors knew anything. They told them a police car had dropped her off a few hours ago, and they had not seen anyone since. The neighbors' medium-sized tan and brown mutt had been the source of the barking they'd heard.

David went back to Mrs. Torres's and told Rich what the neighbor said, and Rich knocked on the door a second time. Still no one stirred. Rich tried to peek through the front window but was unable to see anything. His sixth sense kicked in and he felt something was horribly wrong. The same music was still playing, over and over again. Rich recognized it as Bach's Coffee Cantata. He dialed the local police, who gave him permission to kick the door in while they were in route.

David searched for the source of the music, while Rich looked around the dark house. The light switches were not working—there seemed to be no electricity. Once David's eyes adjusted, he found a portable CD player sitting in the middle of the floor in the bedroom. Hanging nearby was Mrs. Torres, with a scarf wrapped securely around her neck, the other end attached to a large hook screwed into the frame of the closet door.

Headlights flashed on the walls, and within seconds, the police were in the house. Mrs. Torres looked peaceful, wearing the same outfit she had on earlier at the police station. Her eyes were closed and it almost looked like her lips were turned into a smile. The scarf was tan and mahogany wool with delicate brown fringe and *C*s printed on it. Nearby was a note.

"I buckled my three babies, whom I love with all my heart, into the back seat of my car and pushed it into the pond on Riley Road. I couldn't support them and their father didn't want them. It was the only way out for all of us."

David looked at Mrs. Torres, who had been so full of life just hours before. He shook his head as he recalled their conversation. No one asked the children what they wanted; no one cared what they wanted. Three little lives had been taken because of their mother's selfish acts. Before David and Rich left for Phoenix, law enforcement officers recovered the three little bodies, still dressed in their pajamas. Mrs.

Torres, so worried about the twins being afraid of the dark, sent them all into eternal darkness.

~

During the flight back to Phoenix, Rich kept turning over the little information he knew about the Torres case in his mind, and something didn't seem right. When Mrs. Torres had proclaimed her innocence again and again, Rich believed her. He usually had a pretty good sixth sense when it came to such things. He discussed his feelings with David, who thought the case was exactly what it appeared to be—a mass murder-suicide. But the more Rich talked, the more David began to change his mind.

"When she was at the police station earlier in the day," Rich said, "she seemed like an upset mother, but there were no indications of depression or suicide. Yes, she was distraught, but her kids were missing. Any mother would be. What I saw was a scared woman who had no idea where her children were."

"Yeah, but maybe it was all an act," David shrugged. "I'm just saying."

"I don't think so. If she killed them, like the note said, why didn't she tell us? The penalties for premeditated murder in Texas are pretty steep; she would probably have gotten the death penalty. If she wanted to die, why didn't she just let the state take care of it?"

"It could take years. Maybe she didn't want to wait that long."

"Not really. If she'd pled guilty and there was no trial, it might not have taken very long. I don't think her hanging was what it appeared to be." Rich released his seat belt and faced David. "Typically when a woman, especially a mother, commits suicide, she does it the cleanest way possible, like by climbing in the bathtub and slitting her wrists, or overdosing on some pills. Hanging just doesn't fit into that mold. There were other things as well."

"Like what? What other things?"

"Like the scarf around her neck. I know you're going to think I'm nuts, but it was a Coach scarf."

"A what scarf?" "

"A designer scarf…an expensive designer scarf. My mom loves the brand and has handbags, scarves, wallets, and jewelry. I'd recognize it anywhere. Mrs. Torres was by no means wealthy; she couldn't buy food to feed her children, so how would she get a scarf that cost over a hundred dollars?"

"A hundred dollars? That scarf cost a hundred dollars?"

"Over a hundred dollars. That's what I'm saying; it doesn't add up. Another thing. I know it was dark in there, but I don't remember seeing a chair or stool or whatever she climbed on to do the deed. My gut tells me she was killed somewhere else, and the body was hung in her house to make it look like a suicide."

"I think you should call the detective when we get back to Phoenix and voice your opinion before they tamper with the crime scene and completely ruin all the evidence. As it stands right now, there were a lot of people walking around there; it may already be too late to salvage anything."

Rich nodded. "I know. I was thinking the same thing."

As soon as the plane landed and they were allowed to use their cell phones, Rich called the police department and found the detective they'd originally been working with was still out. Instead he spoke to the Chief of Police and learned all three children and Mrs. Torres were at the morgue. The chief promised he would go back to the Torres house to see if he agreed with Rich and felt there was more to the case than met the eye. He told Rich he'd be in touch and update him on the outcome.

A bend in the road is not the end of the road...unless you fail to make the turn.

~ Anonymous

Chapter Thirteen

A week after they returned from Dallas, the Chief of Police on the Torres case called Rich and filled him in on what was going on. Rich's instinct was right. The ligature marks on Tina Torres's neck did not leave an inverted *V* bruise, which would indicate a suicidal hanging. After further observation, it was obvious she'd been strangled elsewhere and placed in the house to make it look like a suicide. It seemed she'd put up quite a struggle, which severely damaged the interior and exterior structures of her neck and throat. Also, the scarf was not heavy-duty and was tied in a simple slip knot. If she'd hung herself, it would never have supported her weight as she thrashed around, waiting to choke to death. While the veins and arteries were slowly being compressed, blood would have pooled on her eyelids, lips, and inside her mouth. None of these signs were present; instead, her face and neck were a dark, ruby-red color, indicating venous congestion—and a ligature strangulation.

The final straw, however, was the footprints found on the tile floor in the house. The pepper vine berries had been trampled on, which made for several partial footprints. They were of a Bruno Magli shoe—the same size and type worn by Phillip Torres.

After the evidence had been compiled and Mr. Torres was called back to the police station, he admitted that he'd drowned the children and killed Tina. He said being married was putting a damper on his lifestyle, and he didn't want to divorce her and pay support every month. It was the easiest thing to do. He said he'd forced Tina to write the suicide note, after which he strangled her with the Coach scarf he'd purchased earlier that day. Receipts and credit card transactions verified his story. The Chief thanked Rich for his eye for detail, and told him if he ever thought about going back into law enforcement, he should let him know.

~

In late August, Rich stopped by the post office to pick up stamps. While standing in line, he met a lovely lady three years his junior. Carla batted her milk-chocolate brown eyes, and he thought he saw an angel. He was so smitten he swore she was wearing a halo. Rich commented that her short-sleeved, pastel-yellow sweater hugged her in all the right places, showcasing her ample bosom and tiny waist. Carla, with an armload of packages, became flustered when she saw Rich and dropped them all. Rich rushed to help her and they laughed and started talking, which ended with the two going to a nearby coffee shop for coffee and Danish. They began spending more and more of their free time together.

David and Joshua stayed around the house and the foundation, just talking and laughing about childhood memories and their siblings—well, the other children they grew up with.

"Do you remember when Mom took us to that lady's house in Seattle when John was born?" David asked.

"Yeah, I remember. What was up with that house? Every piece of furniture was covered in clear plastic. I was afraid to touch anything. And the whole house smelled like ripe bananas."

David laughed. "I know! I asked her for a banana, and she said she didn't have any. She kept apologizing because she didn't have any toys for little boys, and we ended up playing with Colorforms. Do you remember that?"

"Those stupid flat dolls with the vinyl clothes? Yeah, I remember. We played with those things for hours. How lame was that?"

"It was lame, but those were good times, Brother, good times." David smiled, remembering.

"I remember she had a television, but she never turned it on. Bea must have told her we weren't allowed to watch TV. Come to think of it, do you have a TV?" Joshua asked.

"Yes, I have one. It's in the living room. I don't bring it up much."

"Bring it up?" Josh was confused.

"I'll have to show you when we go inside." Even though he didn't like the television set, he had to admit it coming up out of the floor was pretty cool.

Josh and David spent a lot of time in the back yard, swimming and barbequing. The swimming pool was kidney-shaped; one end was fifteen feet deep and boasted a diving board. Neither David nor Joshua knew how to swim, so they stayed in the shallow water. On the rare occasion when they did wander to the deep end, they used a floatation device. The barbeque grill was gas, part of an outdoor kitchen, complete with wet bar.

With Rich and Carla out more and more, David didn't like to be far from the foundation offices. The more word spread about their foundation and their successes, the more calls they received. "Never Give Up" was now open twenty-four hours a day, seven days a week, and with the help of Lou Cooper they'd added more operators. Since David didn't think it fair to require the staff to work long hours, he made it a point for him, Rich, or Joshua to be nearby, working the long hours, too. Well, not exactly working, but at least available. In the event of a crisis, they could be contacted at a moment's notice.

"Despite how things ended up, our childhood wasn't that horrible, was it?" Joshua asked.

David answered, "No, it wasn't. Dysfunctional, yes; horrible, no. We had some good times."

When they began to talk about John and Mikey, the mood changed. Their conversation turned to Bea's trial, and Joshua asked David to tell him about it. He was curious about who appeared as witnesses and what was said. David couldn't share much about Aunt Benita's testimony since he'd been in the conference room, but he'd heard the rest and told Joshua what he remembered. David relayed the story Nancy Novak had told about how difficult it was for Charlie, known to them as Mikey, to adjust to his new life. David said her testimony almost brought him to tears.

"How did Bea react?" Joshua asked.

"Completely emotionless. After all she's done, she just doesn't get it. You'd think she'd be more sympathetic."

Both agreed that Bea was especially hard on Mikey, treating him worse than everyone else. David could have told Joshua the events of the day Mikey was kidnapped, but thought it best not to; some things were better left unsaid. Although Bea never physically abused the children, the mind games and the punishments she doled out never, in David's opinion, really fit the crime. They remembered when Bea made Mikey sleep in the rabbit cage for a week when he'd wet the bed. "Even though John stayed with him and held his hand through the wire, I could still hear him crying," Joshua admitted.

"I know. So did I. I knew it was wrong and I knew it was horrible but I didn't know what to do. If the police came and took us away, then what? At least we still had each other," David reasoned.

"Yeah. We were used to the life we had, and we knew what to expect. I think that was something I had trouble with when I returned to my biological parents."

"What was that?"

"The unknown. Not knowing how Mom and Dad were going to react when I did something wrong. Were they going to beat me? Ground me? With Bea, at least you always knew. It may not have been pleasant, but there were no surprises." Joshua shrugged.

"You know, when I was packing up the trailer to move, I found the rabbit cage behind the house."

"What did you do with it?" Joshua asked.

"I set it on fire. For Mikey," David smiled. He still had Mikey's blanket and made a mental note to show it to Joshua later. They decided to try to contact Nancy Novak to see how Mikey was doing. Maybe he could visit. Both David and Joshua admitted they'd love to see him. David had developed a nurturing instinct, wanting to help people and do what he could to make their lives better. He thought if he could see Mikey and talk to him, he could make everything all right. He wasn't sure how he'd do it, he just felt it was something he needed to do, or at least try. He didn't want another outcome like the one with John. David still wished John would have contacted him sooner; if he had, things would have turned out differently. He would have taken him in and provided the love and support he never had with Bea or with his real mom and dad.

With the expertise the foundation had developed, they were able to locate the Novaks relatively quickly. They now lived in Muncie, Indiana. David mentioned he'd run a search on them some time ago but didn't follow up, feeling the time wasn't right.

David was very excited when Nancy Novak answered the phone the first time he called. Putting her on speakerphone, he said, "Hello, Mrs. Novak. This is David Miller and Joshua. We were hoping we might be able to speak to Mikey…I mean, Charlie. We were just talking about him and were wondering how he's doing. He was such a great kid and we miss him."

The other end of the phone went dead.

David furrowed his brow. "Hmm. It looks like the call disconnected, or she hung up, which I can't imagine. Why would she hang up?" He redialed and got her back on the line.

Nancy Novak started crying. "I'm afraid it's not possible for you to speak to Charlie."

"Is he not at home?"

Mrs. Novak explained what life had been like since Charlie had been returned to her. "My husband is in the military, so we move around a lot. No matter where we would go, everyone had seen or heard about Bea Miller and the kidnappings. No matter what we did, or what we tried, they all knew who Charlie was. He just wanted to be treated like a normal kid.

"As you already know, because you heard it at the trial, Charlie had a hard time adjusting. He was afraid of the dark, of being left alone, of cages, of small, enclosed spaces, and had nightmares almost every night. He developed such severe food allergies it was hard to get him to eat for fear he'd have an adverse reaction. I can't tell you how many times we were in the emergency room because his throat almost swelled shut. Finally, they determined it wasn't food allergies, but anxiety."

"Oh, my gosh! I wish I'd have known." David said, interrupting her.

"The kids at school made fun of him. He grew tall, but he was skin and bones, so they called him a lollipop. He was bullied constantly and had such a hard time making friends. More than once he came home with a bloody nose or a black eye. We had non-stop prank phone calls at all hours. When I complained, I was always told the same thing."

"What was that?" David asked.

"The idiots running the school had the nerve to tell me, 'What happens after the last bell rings is none of our concern, Mrs. Novak.' My son was being tortured, and it was none of their concern. At first, I hoped moving to another city and sending him to another school would make things better, but no matter where he went, it was the same. When people found out who he was, and they always did, the bullying and name-calling started all over again. I started home-schooling him, but he became so withdrawn and depressed he never wanted to leave the house. Honestly, I couldn't blame him. What he went through in his first eight years of life, I wouldn't wish on my worst enemy."

"Mrs. Novak, I'm not sure what Charlie told you about his childhood, but it wasn't that awful. I'm the first to admit that Bea wasn't the greatest mother, but she did the best she could with what she had."

"The best she could? Are you out of your mind? Charlie told me about the cage, Mr. Miller. What type of person does that to a child?"

Mrs. Novak had started to cry again. David was speechless for a moment, knowing there was nothing he could do or say. "Did you try sending him to therapy?"

"Of course we did, Mr. Miller. We were willing to try anything. He went to therapy religiously, three times a week, but the therapist told us Charlie never said much. Because he wouldn't open up, it was difficult to treat him. He was on three different types of medication; one for panic attacks, one for anxiety, and another for depression."

"I'm so sorry to hear that. Mikey was such a happy kid," Joshua finally said.

"That's nice to hear, but it's a side I never saw. The boy returned to me was broken beyond repair."

David still didn't think it was that bad. Sure, Bea was hard on him, but he had a loving home. "So, how is he now?" David asked, unsure he wanted to hear the answer. The way Mrs. Novak spoke, he was certain he'd been institutionalized or worse.

"One day not long ago, as a treat, I told Charlie I'd take him to see a movie. He scored really high on a test he was worried about, and I wanted to reward him. He didn't really want to go, but I talked him into it. When the lights in the theatre went down, Charlie freaked out and we had to leave. He kept saying how sorry he was. As soon as we got home, he went to his room, where he spent the majority of his time. Later that evening, I went to check on him and found him hanging by the neck in his closet. He'd used a belt. He left a note that said only, "I'm sorry," and he signed it "Mikey."

David and Joshua were speechless. They didn't know if they should apologize, sympathize, or blame themselves. If they'd called sooner, if they'd known sooner, maybe the outcome would have been different. Charlie Novak was so uncomfortable in his own skin he thought the only way out was suicide. And he took Mikey Miller with him.

"I blame your mother," Mrs. Novak said, loud and clear. "She may not have been there and she may not have done it, but she is responsible. My husband and I are trying to put our life back together and I ask that you never contact us again, ever, for any reason."

Mikey's suicide hit David very hard. His little brother was gone too soon because he didn't know how to live as Charlie Novak. He thought about telling Bea the next time he wrote to her, but decided against it. Knowing Bea, she'd probably be pleased. She'd disliked Mikey from the moment she found out he wasn't a girl.

Rich tried to cheer David up, but nothing seemed to work. He finally decided to invite Carla over for a cookout. Carla, a veterinarian at a local animal shelter, had, at last count, three dogs, six cats, one bird, and a guinea pig, and those were just the animals she called her own. Others came and went because she had a heart of gold. When it was time to euthanize a healthy animal because its time on the adoption register was up, Carla insisted on taking it home and finding it a new forever family on her own time. Rich loved that about her. Since he no longer had Max, he told her if and when a German Shepherd ended up in that situation, he'd be happy to take it. Carla's visit seemed to help a bit as she told stories about the animal shelter.

"We nicknamed one dog Houdini, because he was a master at escaping. He was a dachshund, so we called him Houdini the Weenie,"

Carla smiled. "The first couple of times we found him roaming the shelter, we assumed someone hadn't locked his cage securely enough, and he'd pushed it open. After the fourth or fifth time, we knew something was up."

"What did you do?" David asked.

"We placed a surveillance camera in the room and found that Houdini pawed at the lock mechanism until the door swung open."

"He unlocked the door?" David, never having been around animals, was amazed.

"Yes, relatively speaking. So we placed him in a pen with six-foot-high, chain-link walls and it was constructed on a concrete pad so we knew he wouldn't be able to burrow out. An hour after we put him in there, I turned around and there he was, staring at me."

"Did he jump the fence?"

"No. He shimmied up the corner, front paws on one wall and his back paws on another. It took him less than two minutes to scale the fence and jump over. I ended up adopting him."

David enjoyed the story so much he forgot about Mikey as he laughed and joined in the fun.

Planning to see Bea before the holidays, David made reservations and invited Joshua to join him. Josh, however, decided to go to New Orleans for a visit with his real family.

David and Rich had a small holiday party for the foundation staff. They all looked at the bulletin board that now held twenty-seven pictures of children they'd helped recover. It had been a great year, and David and Rich told the staff how much they were appreciated—not just by them, but by all the families they'd helped. The employees they'd started with were still with them, and they'd added several new faces as they became busier. The team was more like a family. They stood by each other, covered for each other, and helped each other cope with everyday stresses and disappointments. Each and every employee had the same job responsibilities and performed the same function, so when one of them was having a bad day, the others rallied around to make things more bearable.

David had lived in areas where the climate changed throughout the year. Although he hated to admit it, he even missed snow. He was having a difficult time getting used to the Phoenix weather, which the weatherman said more than once was unseasonably warm. David had enjoyed the warm weather at first, but celebrating Christmas in a short-sleeve shirt on a seventy-degree day didn't seem right. He'd mentioned to Rich more than once that they should go somewhere cold for the holidays; someplace like Colorado and maybe do some skiing. However, since neither skied and Rich didn't want to leave Carla, the idea was quickly forgotten.

Better a has-been than a never-was.
But better a never-was than a never-tried-to-be.

~ Anonymous

Chapter Fourteen

In early January, almost six months after David and Rich returned from Portugal, they received a call from the producers at *Good Morning America.* They'd heard about "Never Give Up" and, after doing some research, found out about Beatrice Miller and the kidnappings. They thought David's story would make a wonderful segment. After thinking it over, David and Rich agreed that it would be great publicity. They asked Joshua, who had just returned from New Orleans, to join them. He was hesitant at first, asking who would run the foundation if they all went.

"Don't worry about it. I'll have Lou stop by and check on things. It's a well-oiled machine and can run a few days without us. If anything comes up, the staff knows how to reach us, and we can be on a plane to wherever we're needed in no time," David said, hoping to convince him. They'd never taken vacations while growing up, and David thought it would be nice to have something resembling a vacation with his brother.

David was excited. He'd never been to New York City, and couldn't wait to go somewhere with cooler temperatures. David secretly hoped it was snowing in New York. First on his list was seeing the Statue of Liberty. He'd heard and read so many things about it that he couldn't wait to see it himself. Joshua was equally excited, but Rich had been there before: twice as a child, and once as an adult. His family saw the lighting of the Christmas tree at Rockefeller Center when he was six, and joined the New Year's Eve festivities when he was twelve. Then he went alone, right after September 11, 2001, to help out at Ground Zero. He told David it was one of the saddest times in his life—pulling one crushed, lifeless body after another from the debris, with family members hoping it was their loved one so they could finally have closure, yet hoping it wasn't so they could hang on to the hope they were still alive.

That tragedy didn't discriminate; when the planes hit and the buildings crumbled, everyone was equal. It also confirmed Rich's opinion that in times of crisis, people are generous—some with their time and some with their money—but giving of themselves nonetheless.

Once they landed at JFK, David was relieved that *Good Morning America* had sent a limo to pick them up. The amount of traffic, both vehicle and pedestrian, was more than anything he'd ever seen. Horns honking, people yelling, taxis darting in and out of traffic; he couldn't have imagined it if he'd tried. And the people! All sizes, shapes, nationalities, and colors. They all seemed to be in a hurry and annoyed. Despite the frigid weather, there were hot dog vendors on every street corner, and people playing guitars and violins in the hope of getting donations from passers-by. Skyscrapers, some a block long, made David feel like an ant. Even the air was inspiring and exhilarating. It made David feel alive and energetic, but he didn't know why.

The interview on *Good Morning America* wasn't much different than those they'd done in Phoenix, except that everything was on a grander scale. It was a bigger studio, with more employees, a bigger set, bigger cameras, bigger green room, and a bigger food service area. Rich was star-struck and didn't say much. David, never having watched much television, didn't know who these people were, so he was much more relaxed throughout the entire interview.

The interviewers found David's story fascinating, and he tried to answer their questions as honestly as he could. Of course there were things he didn't know, and he stated as much. They asked him to tell the story of Mikey's kidnapping, and he repeated the same version he'd told in the courtroom at his mother's trial almost a year and a half earlier. He was thankful they didn't ask if he'd heard from Mikey.

David explained who Rich was as he sat and smiled. When David said Joshua, his kidnapped brother, had contacted him and now worked with him, they brought Joshua out, too. They asked him about his biological family, and he made it sound as if being returned to them was a dream come true. He later admitted to David that he didn't want to say anything negative in case his mom and dad were watching.

It was an excellent interview. When it was over, the staff at "Never Give Up" said the phone calls were coming in non-stop, mostly people calling to thank them for what they were doing and telling them to keep up the good work. It wasn't until after the interview that David was informed that *Good Morning America* typically has about four million viewers a day. When he heard that, his palms started to sweat. Rich was well aware of their popularity and said as much when they got back in the limo to go to the Waldorf-Astoria.

After extending their trip for extra couple of days, before they headed home, David wanted to stop in North Dakota to see Bea. Since they were only going to be there for a few hours, they decided to take a taxi from the airport.

Joshua looked out the window at the snow and ice, deep in thought. David asked, "What's wrong, Josh?"

"You know, I thought when I saw it again I would feel like I was home, but I don't. North Dakota isn't home, New Orleans isn't home, and Phoenix isn't home. I don't know where home is anymore."

"I felt the same way the first time I came back. I even drove through the old trailer park just to see if I would feel something, anything. But you know what I found out?"

"What?"

"Home isn't a place, it's a feeling. It's where you feel happy and comfortable. My home is in Phoenix now. Not because of the house or the foundation, but because of you and Rich. You are my home."

~

When they arrived at the prison and David gave his name, it was quite a while before Bea was standing in front of him. As she bit her bottom lip, David could tell she was angry about something. "Mom, what's wrong?"

"Don't you 'Mom' me. How could you?" Bea had her arms crossed firmly in front of her and wouldn't even look at him.

"How could I what? What are you talking about?"

"I saw you, David. I saw you," she said, squinting. "And I'm pressing charges for slander or whatever that's called when you say mean things about someone publicly."

"You saw me? Saw me where? What mean things did I say?"

"You were on TV, talking about me and telling lies, just to make yourself look like a saint and a hero. You and that Rich Butler. Well, let me tell you something. I'm going to sue you for all Aunt Benita's money. And when I win that, I'm going to close your stupid foundation down!"

"Mom, you're talking nonsense. Everything I said on *Good Morning America* was the truth. It's in the court documents, it's public record, and anyone can look it up and see that it's true. If what I said hurt you, I'm sorry, but they asked the questions and I answered them truthfully. I know telling the truth is a foreign concept to you, but it's what most law-abiding citizens do. Besides, I brought Joshua, and he'd like to see you."

Bea's eyes lit up. "Joshua? You brought Joshua? Where is he?"

"He's waiting outside. I wanted to make sure you wanted to see him."

"Of course I want to see him. He is my son, after all…my good son." Bea finally unfolded her arms and relaxed.

"Whatever you say." David turned to get Joshua.

Joshua hesitantly entered, and Bea ran to hug him. "Oh, Joshua, I've missed you so much! Sit. Tell me everything. How is school? Are you still playing softball? Are you still the shortstop? I really miss coming to your games. You were such a natural."

David and Joshua exchanged glances. "Joshua, tell mom about playing softball for Bunting Valley High School, okay?" David said.

Joshua played along. It was if nothing had changed, but at the same time, everything had changed. Bea looked like she'd lost some weight. She also seemed shorter, but that was probably because Joshua had gotten taller. Then, just like that, she started asking about his family and life in New Orleans.

"I still remember the day I found you in the park. You were such a beautiful baby. I still can't believe that stupid nanny trusted me to watch you while she took those whiny girls to the swings." Bea paused as if she was back at that very moment. "But enough about that. Just look at you; you've grown into such a beautiful young man. You still live in New Orleans, don't you?"

"No I don't. I live in Phoenix with David."

"David? In Phoenix? Since when does David live in Phoenix?"

"You know I live in Phoenix, Mom. We talked about this. After Aunt Benita died, I moved to Phoenix. Remember?" David said, calmly and slowly.

Bea didn't agree or disagree, but the rest of the visit was odd. Bea thanked David for the pillow. It had worked wonders, but they were now on to something else. When her dirty clothes were laundered and came back clean in her laundry bag, there were poisonous snakes in the bag that would escape and hide in her cell. Never knowing where they were and when they might strike, she feared for her life. "Next time you come, can you bring a BB gun or a knife? I need something to fend off the snakes. And I may need your help with my laundry."

David promised he would and Joshua smirked, trying not to laugh. When they started to leave, Bea thanked Joshua for coming. As always, Bea said, in David's direction, "Remember David, things aren't always what they seem," and she turned to go back through the heavy white metal door to her cell.

As soon as they were outside, David said, "See, I told you the visits were weird."

"How do you know what to say? I was so afraid I'd say the wrong thing and she'd slap me on the back of the head. What's the story with the pillow and the snakes? Did you bring her a pillow?"

David shook his head and said, "One of the first times I visited, Mom swore they were trying to poison her. She saw them putting a white powder on her donuts and she was convinced it was poison. She begged me to ask the management about it and when I brought it up, I felt like a fool."

"How so?"

"They told me they don't serve donuts in prison, which I should have known. Anyway, at another visit shortly after, she asked if I'd bring her some aluminum foil to keep them from melting her brain. I never brought any, or sent any, for that matter. Then it was her pillow—and now, as you heard, it's snakes. Next visit, it'll be something else. The stories seem to get more and more bizarre each time I come. The sad part is she's dead serious. She really thinks all of these things are happening to her. When I visit, I usually let her lead the conversation and try to ignore her questions, but if I see she's getting upset, I just play along. I figure it won't hurt anything."

"And you've talked to the staff and they think this is normal?" Joshua asked, concerned. Even though Bea was not really his mother, he knew her longer and better than his own mother, and still felt a kinship toward her.

"Yes. They think it's her medication. Each time I speak to them, I end up looking like the crazy one. I guess time will tell."

While David and Joshua visited Bea, Rich paid a visit to his mom and dad. He didn't get home as often as he liked, and his parents were getting older and he needed to start seeing them more often. David said he should invite them to Phoenix; they had plenty of room, and Rich's parents could stay as long as they wanted.

"Thank you, David. That means a lot," Rich smiled. "I'd like them to meet Carla anyway. I'm thinking about asking her to marry me."

"What? Oh, my gosh, this is huge! Congratulations! I can't believe it," David replied. "This calls for a celebration. We need to go out when we get home!"

"Hold on a minute. I haven't asked her yet. I think we need to hold off on the celebrating until she says yes. That's how it usually works," Rich said, grinning.

"You're right. I'm sorry. I've just never known anyone who got married before. We'll have to have a party at the house. This is so awesome! When are you going to ask her?" David wanted all the details.

"I haven't decided yet. I was thinking of her birthday, which is coming up at the end of the month, but I'd rather ask on a day that means nothing so it will become a special day in our lives, something we can celebrate for years to come."

David shook his head as he laughed.

"What's wrong? What's so funny?" Rich asked.

"Sometimes, the things you say, if I didn't know better, I would think I was talking to a girl."

"I just want it to be special for Carla."

"For Carla, huh? You're such a liar. Just ask her already. Do you have the ring?"

"Yes, I have the ring. I bought it during the holidays. I brought it with me to show my parents, but I lost my nerve." Rich pulled a black velvet box from his pocket and popped it open. The ring held a stunning heart-shaped diamond that was neither too big nor too small. It sparkled when it caught the light and Rich grinned again. David could tell Rich was in love. He had only seen this look once—when his dad looked at his mom.

"So what are you waiting for?"

To reach a great height, a person needs to have great depth.

~ Anonymous

Chapter Fifteen

Not long after they returned from New York, the telephone in the house rang. David, Rich, and Joshua were downstairs at the foundation, so Miss Lopez answered and tried to take a message. It was the security guard at the front gate saying the police were there and had a warrant for David's arrest. Miss Lopez was having a hard time understanding what he was saying. However, since the police didn't need permission, they bypassed the guard and were banging on the door before she hung up the phone. She ran to answer it and they shoved their way in.

"We have a warrant for the arrest of David Miller," one officer said, flashing his badge.

Miss Lopez was frightened. "Mr. Miller no here. He at work. Foundation. Basement."

The three uniformed officers pounded through the house, into the garage, and down the basement steps. David was in his office when they barged in. "David Miller?"

"Yes?" David looked up.

"We have a warrant for your arrest."

Rich heard the commotion from his office and saw the staff staring at David's office. He wasted no time. "What's going on?" Rich said as soon as he entered David's office.

"Who are you?" one of the policemen asked, looking in Rich's direction.

"What do you mean who am I? I'm Rich Butler, co-president of this foundation. We've worked with you on many cases."

The police just stood and stared at him.

"Can someone please tell me what the hell is going on?" Rich was livid.

"David Miller is under arrest for the kidnapping and murder of a male newborn," one of the officers said without batting an eye.

"There must be some mistake. Why doesn't everyone just calm down? I'm sure we can get to the bottom of this."

Ignoring Rich, they proceeded around the desk, handcuffed David, and led him up the stairs and out to the patrol car. They read him his Miranda rights as they went. The last thing David said before the patrol car door slammed was, "Call Lou Cooper."

~

About an hour later, both Lou and Rich were at the police station. Since Lou was David's counsel, they allowed him access to his client. "David, are you all right?"

"I guess. I don't understand what's going on. They say I kidnapped and murdered a baby boy. I have no idea what they're talking about."

"I'll find out." Lou left the temporary holding cell and David paced in the ten-by-ten foot space, wondering what was going on. He remembered when he was arrested in Bunting Valley, which didn't seem so long ago. Having that on his record was not going to help matters. *I wish I knew what they were talking about. A baby boy? Where? When?*

Lou returned a short while later and David, seeing the expression on his face, knew it was trouble. "David, it doesn't look good," he said.

"What doesn't look good?" David, feeling a little lightheaded, sat on the bench at the back of the cell.

"Some new tenants moved into the trailer you lived in on Crimson Lane in North Dakota. They only lasted a few weeks, saying there was an odor they couldn't stand any longer."

"I know there was an odor. It was awful when I visited Mrs. Brown early last summer. She said it was a dead body, but it was taken away. Mrs. Brown seemed to think the smell was getting better."

"Regardless, that was the third set of tenants since you moved out who complained of a horrible odor. The landlord tried everything; new carpet, new furniture, new paint, but nothing seemed to work. So he decided to have the trailer hauled away, hoping he could park another one on the site and rent it out." Lou sat next to David on the bench. "During the move, a cooler was found under the house trailer. Inside it was a baby boy, shot once in the head. His body was in a state of decomposition and had been there for quite some time. He'd been wrapped in a plastic bag and was still lying in an infant carrier. The whole thing, carrier and baby, were submerged in ammonia and vinegar in the cooler. The liquid pickled the body, keeping the stench away for a while. But over the harsh winters, the cooler froze and unfroze, and eventually cracked. Then the liquid started to leak and evaporate. And when the body made contact with the air, it began to decompose."

"What does this have to do with me?" David asked.

"Your gloves were found near the cooler along with a faded, barely legible note that read, "I'm sorry, God. Love, David."

"Oh, my God! That's the stupid note I gave Mom when she made me apologize because I wouldn't get rid of Mikey for her. She's framing me!"

"Because of your testimony about how your mother wanted you to get rid of Mikey, it was assumed you followed through the second time."

"The second time? There was no second time, Lou! This is nonsense. Has anyone spoken to my mother? Where's Rich? Send Rich to talk to her. He'll get to the bottom of this."

"Before it gets that far, you're being extradited to North Dakota where the charges were filed. I'll catch a plane and be there when you land. Don't worry, David. I'll devote all my time to getting these charges cleared."

David couldn't believe it. Of all the things his mother had done, this was by far the worst. *She kidnapped another baby boy and killed him, then made it look like I did it. All that time we lived in that trailer, there was a dead baby just feet from us, and she never said anything. How many times did we talk about that smell? It would be gone a day or two later, but it always returned. Why didn't I do anything? Why didn't I call someone? Now I'm being charged with murder. So help me, Mom, if you think I'm going to rot in jail for something you did, your imaginary enemies in prison won't be the only ones out to get you.*

Within hours of his arrest, David was in handcuffs and leg restraints, and he was transported back to North Dakota on a commercial airline with two armed agents by his side. He was getting angrier by the minute as passengers kept looking and pointing at him, then whispering. Being treated in this way for a crime he didn't commit was among the worst things he'd ever had to endure—and with Bea Miller as a mother, that was saying something. True to his word, Lou was at the airport when he was ushered off the plane. David was taken to the federal prison in a patrol car and Lou, with Rich Butler, followed behind in a rental car.

Bond was set at two million dollars. Using Aunt Benita's money, the bond was covered and David was released in the custody of Lou Cooper, with the stipulation he was not to leave town. After Lou met with the judge and explained David's housing situation and that he ran a foundation to help find missing children, clearance was given for him to travel to and from Phoenix, but he had to advise the court where he was at all times and he was to have no direct contact with any minor children. In the event he was late, or didn't show up for his next appointed court hearing, the bond money would be forfeited and he would be forced to remain in North Dakota. He was also advised, because of his arrest, that he was not allowed within five hundred feet of his mother for any reason. He would be removed from her list of approved visitors.

Since David couldn't see her, both Lou and Rich applied to be added as visitors for Beatrice Miller. They were aware that since she didn't know them, they'd have a hard time getting in to see her. It took a couple of days for the approval to come through, but as soon as it did, Rich made plans to pay her a visit. At David's request, Rich wore the wireless earphone walkie-talkie so he could hear the entire conversation and give input if need be.

A little nervous and not sure how she would react to seeing him again, Rich went in while David and Lou waited out in the parking lot in the rental car. Rich had not seen Bea since the trial, and she looked much older. Gone was the brightness in her eyes he saw every time someone mentioned her children or her late husband, Henry. Gone were the bleach-blonde hair and the bright-red lips. There were dark circles under her eyes, and her brown hair was peppered with gray. She was wearing wire frame glasses that were way too big for her face. They looked like safety goggles. "Hello, Mrs. Miller." Rich stood to shake her hand. "Do you remember me?" Rich had decided he wasn't going to tell her his name if he didn't have to. David had filled him in on how Bea reacted when she heard they were business partners.

Bea glanced back at the guard who'd brought her in. "No. I'm afraid I don't. Should I?" She hesitantly offered her hand.

"I work with your son, David, at his foundation." Rich flashed a big smile, hoping to make Bea feel comfortable.

"Oh. How nice of you to come all this way to see me. Is David all right?"

"No, I'm afraid not. He's gotten into a bit of trouble, and I'm hoping you might be able to help us sort it all out." Rich took a seat back at the table.

"Me? What can I do?" Bea asked.

"Do you remember the trailer you lived in on Crimson Lane?"

"Crimson Lane? That sounds vaguely familiar. What exactly is that?" Bea turned up her nose. "That word—crimson. It reminds me of the color of blood."

Rich shook his head. Her memory was much worse than he thought. Last time David visited, he'd said it seemed like she was getting better. "Crimson Lane is a street in Bunting Valley, North Dakota…about seventy-five miles from here. You lived there in a trailer with your children for several years."

"My children? Refresh my memory. How many children do I have?"

"Four boys. David, Joshua, John, and Mikey. Do you remember them?"

"No, I'm afraid not. Are you sure you have the right person? Maybe you're looking for one of the other guests here at the hotel. There are so many of us, and after a while we all start to look alike. I can understand the confusion." At that moment Bea got down on all fours and started barking. Barking and wiggling her butt, as if she were a dog. Sticking her tongue out and panting, she licked the back of Rich's hand.

"I'm sorry to have bothered you. Thank you for taking the time to talk with me." Rich, not knowing what to do, patted her on the head as he rose to leave.

David hated to interrupt, but couldn't help it. "Rich, don't give up. Keep talking. You'll see. She'll come out of it. Talk about something else. Something she might enjoy. Ask about my dad."

"Mrs. Miller?" He turned back around.

Bea was crawling away, still on all fours. She turned around. "Yes?"

"Can you tell me a little about your late husband, Henry?"

Bea was excited to talk about Henry; no one had asked about him in such a long time. "Absolutely." She stood, bending over to brush the dust off her knees. "I always love talking about Henry. He was the love of my life." Bea came back and sat down across from him, placing her hand over her heart.

"How did you two meet?" David was aware Rich knew the details, but it was good he was pretending otherwise.

"He waltzed into my life one day when I was at work. When I looked up and saw him, I thought a movie star had dropped from the heavens. He was tall, dark, and handsome. And his smile was the most beautiful thing I ever saw." Bea's eyes lit up. Rich could tell, no matter how crazy and misguided she was, the love she felt for Henry was true and still very real.

"Where were you working?" Rich rested his head on his upturned hand.

"At a movie theatre. No, no, it wasn't a movie theatre. It was a restaurant. No, that wasn't it either." Bea stopped for a moment and thought.

David, not hearing anything going on, asked, "What's happening? Did she leave?"

Finally Bea spoke again. "Oh yes, I remember now. It was a truck stop right off the highway. Henry came in with a bloody hand, looking for an Ace bandage."

"A bloody hand? What happened?" Rich asked.

"He cut it trying to fix his semi. He was a truck driver. An over-the-road truck driver who wanted a bunch of boys...a bunch of stupid, testosterone-filled boys, just like him."

David interrupted again. "She's getting upset, Rich. Don't get her upset. Ask about Maggie."

"Who is Maggie?" Rich asked.

"How do you know so much about me when I know nothing about you?" Bea inquired accusingly.

"Your son, David, told me. Remember? David and I work together," Rich quickly said, trying to reassure her.

"Oh, that's right. Let's see, Maggie is my daughter. She is the most beautiful little girl...big blue eyes, chubby cherub cheeks, and golden hair. I love her so much, and she's so smart! She's probably still waiting to ride the pink pony."

"The pink pony? What is that?" Rich remembered Maggie mentioning the pink pony. He also remembered Abby Taylor mentioning it a few days after the rescue.

"It's not important, just something I promised her. I always try to keep my promises—especially to the people I love." Bea flashed a gummy grin.

"Where is she now, while you're here at this hotel?"

"I don't know for sure, since they took her away from me. They said I kidnapped her. I didn't. She was out in the lake, about to drown, and I saved her life. They should be thanking me, not punishing me. Her parents didn't want her. They already had one girl...they didn't need another one."

David could tell Bea was gritting her teeth. "She's getting mad. Talk about something else. Ask her about me."

"Tell me about David and the day he was born."

"David was born on September third. He was always such a happy baby and the spitting image of his father. Henry was working at the time, delivering something somewhere. He was so disappointed that he missed the birth. Truth be told," Bea leaned in to whisper, "I'm glad he wasn't there."

"Why's that?"

"Because something went wrong, and the doctor had to remove some of my female parts. I didn't want Henry to know. If he had, he would have left me."

"Why do you think he would have left you?"

"Because I would no longer have been perfect. I knew he wanted more children, and if I couldn't have any more, he'd have left me and found someone who could."

"What happened after that?"

"Henry started saying he wanted another son. That was all he talked about. So when David was two, he and I went to New Orleans and found Joshua in a stroller at the park. He was all alone, so I took him home and told Henry he was ours."

"Ask her again about Crimson Lane," David said in Rich's ear.

"Tell me about Crimson Lane." Rich hoped she wouldn't react adversely.

Just as Bea started to answer, a guard came out and said visiting hours were over.

"Just a few more minutes, please?" Rich pleaded. He was so close to getting her to tell him what he needed to know.

"I'm sorry, but visiting hours end promptly at eight thirty."

David felt helpless listening in on the conversation. He wanted to do something; he wanted to say something. He wanted his mother to admit she killed that baby and stashed it under the trailer.

"Okay, maybe I'll come back another time," Rich said as he stood.

"Please tell David I said hello," Bea said, as she smiled. "Oh, and tell him I said karma is a bitch and things aren't always what they seem."

Rich shook his head as he watched her walk through the white metal door. As soon as he got back to the car, he told them he thought it went well.

"Didn't I tell you? It's the oddest thing. She sounds crazy and then suddenly, she's fine," David said.

"I don't know if you heard, but she was pretending to be a dog." Rich relayed what went on.

"Yes, I heard the barking. That's a new one. Usually she's claiming someone is trying to kill her."

"Well," Rich said, "my guess is that she's not crazy at all. Did you hear what she told me to tell you? She knows exactly what's going on. I think she's pretending to be deranged, and I think her memory is just fine."

"You think so?" David wasn't convinced. He knew his mom was a good actress, but she wasn't that good. No one was that good.

"I'd bet my life on it. I guarantee that Bea is as sane as we are. The longer she has us convinced she's on the verge of a breakdown, the longer we'll walk on eggshells, trying not to upset her. You've been coddling her from the beginning. Well, no more. We need to ask for a psych evaluation, the sooner the better, and insist it be an outside evaluation…someone who's never seen or treated her."

"Since I've been blacklisted, I don't see how I can request a mental evaluation," David pointed out.

"You can't, but we can," Rich said, looking at Lou, who nodded in agreement.

Don't let what you cannot do interfere with what you can do.

~ John Wooden

Chapter Sixteen

Anxious to get back to Phoenix and back to work, David had Lou contact the court to let them know when they were leaving North Dakota, and he contacted them again when they arrived in Phoenix. Since his arrest, the phone lines at "Never Give Up" had been so slow they'd been forced to lay off the second and third shifts. When the phone did ring, it was usually someone wanting to voice their opinion about David being a baby killer. The FBI no longer contacted them, and David was beginning to fear the foundation might be forced to close. He hoped that once he was cleared of wrongdoing, the tide would turn.

Thunderclouds were rolling in and a storm was brewing. The sky mirrored the way David was feeling—dark and angry. Feeling like a prisoner in his own home, with nothing but time on his hands, David grabbed an umbrella and headed to the bank to see what Aunt Benita might have stored in her safety deposit box. It had been quite some time since he found the key in the decorated box, but there had been so much going on at the time, he hadn't thought twice about it. The key had a round metal key tag with the words Safety Deposit Box #211 written in Aunt Benita's fancy handwriting.

He was met by Sam Armstrong, the bank manager, who was a tall, middle-aged man wearing horn-rimmed glasses, a dark gray suit, a white button-down oxford shirt, and a skinny maroon tie. As soon as he saw David, he said, "Mr. Miller, we've been expecting you."

"Really?" David found that hard to believe, and figured it was something they said to all their high profile clients.

"Absolutely. Your aunt was one of our most valued customers. What can I help you with today?"

"I came to check Aunt Benita's safety deposit box."

David was ushered to the back, where the safety deposit boxes were located. Left alone, he carefully twisted the key in the lock. When he opened it, he found a white plastic envelope, inside of which was a small, silver handgun with a white pearl handle. He turned it one way, then the other, looking it over. He even held it up and pretended to pull the trigger aiming at some imaginary target. Puzzled, he placed it back in the bag and returned it to the box wondering why Aunt Benita would store a handgun there. Perhaps it was an heirloom worth hundreds of thousands of dollars. Or perhaps she bought it, but couldn't stand the thought of having a gun in the house. *If anyone knows, I bet Lou will. He knows everything.*

David put the gun back in the envelope, the envelope in the box, and returned the box back to its cubbyhole. He locked it and left the area, thanking the manager on his way out.

"Did you find everything you needed, Mr. Miller?" Mr. Armstrong rose from his desk and shuffled over to David just as he was about to leave.

"Yes, I believe so." David pushed the door open and walked out into the rain that had finally started to fall, great big drops coming straight down. He climbed into his car, turned on his wipers, and headed to Lou's office. David again pondered the gun. *It makes no sense. Why a gun? And only a gun? She rented a safety deposit box for that?*

Always happy to see him, Lou didn't require David to call ahead to make an appointment, especially now, due to the murder charges against him. David bumped into him in the hall, getting on the elevator as David was getting off.

"Oh, Lou, have I caught you at a bad time?"

"I was just heading out to lunch, but if you need something, it can wait," he said, glancing at his wrist watch.

"Are you sure? I don't want to keep you."

"I didn't have an appointment. I was just running out to get a bite. Would you care to join me?"

"Thanks, but I'll pass. This shouldn't take long," David said, "at least I don't think it should. I found a key to a safety deposit box in Aunt Benita's decorated box. It's been a while, but I finally got around to seeing what was in it. All I found was an envelope with a small handgun. Do you know anything about it?"

"She knew this day would come, David. Please come to my office." Lou took his fedora off and draped his raincoat over his arm as they walked. He opened his desk drawer and took out an envelope. "She asked me to give this to you if you ever asked about the safety deposit box," he said, handing it to David. His name was written on the front.

"What's this?"

"She wrote you a letter."

"What does it say?"

"She never told me."

David furrowed his brow. "She wrote me a letter, because she knew I'd be coming to ask you about the gun in the safety deposit box?"

"Yes. As I told you when you first arrived, Benita was a planner."

David stood. "I won't keep you any longer." David held the envelope up to the light. "Will this explain everything?"

"I don't know, but knowing Benita as I did, I'd bet my last dollar on it."

David, baffled, left the building. As he climbed into his car, he thought about ripping the letter open, but decided to stop for lunch and open it at his leisure.

After he placed his order, he opened the envelope. It was a single, handwritten page dated November 3, 2010—just five days before she died.

Dear David,

Let me begin by telling you how much I loved your mother. She was the light of my life and the joy of my world. The six years I spent as part of her life were not enough. I thought of her every single day, wondering where she was and what she was doing. I prayed she was safe and happy, and that my brother, Edward, was taking good care of her. We both know that wasn't the case.

If you're reading this letter, it means you've been to the bank and the safety deposit box. The gun, as you probably know, is the murder weapon that killed a baby boy. Your fingerprints are all over it, as they should be. The murder weapon, coupled with your gloves and the note, are enough to send you away for the rest of your life.

You were key in putting my Beatrice behind bars. I know I was there, as well—but my testimony proved only how horribly my brother treated her, and that none of it was her fault. I tried to let bygones be bygones. I tried to forgive and forget. I even gave you a home and life. Don't confuse it with generosity; it was a necessary evil to bring you to Phoenix so the plan would come to fruition.

Remember this, David; things aren't always what they seem. Never trust someone you don't really know—and, most of all, never turn your back on family. They are all you have.

Aunt Benita

David folded the letter and placed it back in the envelope. He wasn't sure what he should be feeling. Anger? Frustration? Betrayal? Relief? After several minutes of silence, he dropped twenty dollars on the table and left to return to Lou's office. He was absolutely livid. *You bitch! It was all an act! All this time you wanted me to believe you cared about me, when you only cared about her? So much so, you were willing to spend hundreds of thousands of dollars to fool me?*

The ride back to Lou's office was a blur. David didn't know if he ran any red lights or broke the speed limit, but truth be told, he didn't care.

"David," Lou said when he barged into his office. "I didn't expect to see you again so soon."

David was out of breath. He felt like he'd just finished running a marathon. "The letter," he took a deep breath. "It explains everything."

"Yes. I told you it would."

"You don't understand. Not only does it talk about the gun, it also talks about the baby's body under the trailer. Aunt Benita and my mother were in it together. It's in the letter." David plopped down in a chair and, with shaky hands, handed the letter to Lou, who grabbed it and skimmed through it like a speed reader. When he finished, he looked at David. "This letter makes it look like you did it."

"But I didn't. Yes, I went to the bank. Yes, I touched the gun. But I didn't kill a baby. You have to believe me." David covered his face with his hands.

"I believe you. The question is, will a judge and jury?"

"What? You think this thing is going to go to trial? Isn't there something you can do?" David felt like crying.

"Let me make a few phone calls. I can't promise anything, but if it does go to trial, I'll see if I can get it moved up so we can get it over with sooner." David heard him pick up the phone, and soon he said, "This is Attorney Louis Cooper, calling from Phoenix, Arizona on behalf of my client, David Miller. Some evidence regarding the deceased baby has come to light. I believe we have the murder weapon here in Phoenix and need to get it to you. Since I can't very well carry it on a plane, I'd like you to send someone to pick it up. Secondly, I would like to request a full psychiatric evaluation of Beatrice Miller, by an outside physician. And lastly, I strongly urge Mrs. Miller to consult an attorney as soon as possible. My client and I will catch a plane as soon as we can, and will be there to meet with you."

When he hung up, David said, "Who was that?"

"The Bunting Valley Police Department. If we present the letter as evidence and turn over the gun, it will make it look less likely that you did it. Why would you incriminate yourself? I'd like to call your mother as a witness, but first I want to make sure she's sane. If she's not, and we call her to the stand, it will make us look worse, as if we are berating the mentally ill on the witness stand. The press will have a field day with that one."

"My mother will never tell the truth. Don't you see? She wouldn't know the truth if it bit her. She killed that baby and left him there so I would get framed. She's not going to admit she did it. Why would she?"

"I don't know, David, but it's all we have. Go back to the bank, get the gun, and bring it here. I'm sure the police department will send a courier for it. Then go home and pack. I don't know how long we'll be in North Dakota." Lou stood and started shoving things into his briefcase.

"Can Rich and Joshua come, too?" David needed all the support he could get.

"Whoever you need is fine with me. We may need to call Rich as a witness."

~

David did as he was told and went back to the bank. "Mr. Miller? Back so soon?" It was the same man he spoke with earlier.

"Yes, I forgot something." David was taken to the back, and he when he opened the safety deposit box, it was empty. He pulled it out and stuck his hand in, hitting every side, then turned it upside down. He looked at his key and at the number on the box, thinking he may have opened the wrong one, not thinking his key wouldn't fit another box. He was trying to figure out how it could be empty. He quickly found the manager sitting in an office directly off the main lobby, engrossed in some paperwork. "What happened to the contents of my safety deposit box?"

Mr. Armstrong looked up. "What are you talking about?"

"It's empty. I was here a little more than two hours ago, and there was something in it. Now it's empty. What happened to it?"

"I have no idea. Perhaps you took it with you and forgot?"

"No, I didn't take it with me. No, I didn't forget. Where is it?" David placed his hands on the desk, locking his elbows he leaned in, inches from the manager's face.

"I told you, Mr. Miller, I have no idea," he said, pushing on the floor with his feet, backing away. "As far as I know, no one else has been here to check your safety deposit box. If there's nothing in it now, it must have been empty earlier. Things don't just disappear."

"This is bullshit!" David yelled. "Look at the security tapes, and tell me who went into my safety deposit box!"

"Mr. Miller, please keep your voice down. You are alarming the customers unnecessarily."

"I don't give a damn about the customers. I need what was in that box. Don't you understand?" David reached out and grabbed the manager's skinny little tie.

"I can review the security tape, but it will take some time." Mr. Armstrong actually looked scared.

David let go of his tie and shouted, "Go to hell!" as he stormed out of the bank and immediately called Lou.

"Lou, the gun is gone. The safety deposit box is empty. Someone took it."

"Took it? Who could have taken it? Are you certain it was there earlier?"

"Yes, I'm certain. There was a small silver gun wrapped in a white envelope; it was in there earlier and now it's gone. You read the letter. You know there was a gun. I didn't make it up."

"I'm baffled, but don't worry about the gun. We have the letter. We'll do what we can with what we have. I'll call the Bunting Valley Police Department and tell them they don't need to send anyone for the gun. If they ask, I'll tell them we found another way to get it there."

~

Before nightfall, David, Rich, Joshua, and Lou were holed up in a hotel room in Jamestown, North Dakota, the same city where the federal building was located, and where Beatrice Miller was found guilty on two counts of kidnapping not so long ago. By the time their plane landed, they'd established a game plan, and first on the list was to prove Bea Miller was not a lunatic, as she seemed to want everyone to believe.

Even a stopped clock is right twice a day.

~ Marie Von Ebner-Eschenbach

Chapter Seventeen

Word from the foundation was there were no calls coming in at all. David, forced to make a difficult decision, closed "Never Give Up." He thanked the staff for their help, and told them they would receive one month's salary as a severance package and glowing letters of recommendation. If and when the foundation reopened, he would contact them to see if they were available, but he said he didn't know when that would be, if ever.

David was saddened by how quickly the community, and the world, had turned against him. Prior to his arrest, he was one of the most respected citizens of Phoenix. He'd been on countless talk shows, interviewed for many newspapers and magazines, and donations were coming in regularly—several hundred dollars a day. One wealthy gentleman, who'd sat on the board of directors of the Chamber of Commerce with Aunt Benita, left his entire estate of several million dollars to "Never Give Up" when he passed away earlier in the year.

The bulletin board had grown to two bulletin boards, and over fifty photographs were proudly displayed. Now, he was completely ostracized before he even had a trial, and it was heartbreaking. The most disturbing part was that his fate was in the hands of his mother, the person who gave birth to him. But that was where her duty, responsibility, and loyalty had ended. David knew she could care less if he lived or died; her only motivation was to get even. He knew when he'd testified against her that she'd find a way to punish him. The only thing he didn't realize was that vengeance was coming posthumously from Aunt Benita as well.

Lou had met with the prosecuting attorney, Marshall Callahan, for several hours to see if they could reach a plea deal. Short of David pleading guilty, there was no other option. Callahan explained the baby had been dead for over two years, and stated that if David admitted to the murder, he would probably get a lighter sentence. If it went to trial, Callahan couldn't guarantee anything.

David refused to plead guilty to a crime he did not commit, so the search for a jury began and the trial was scheduled to begin in two weeks. Bea Miller had been examined by a psychiatrist, once taken off all her medication, was determined to be of sound mind. She was happy she was needed as a witness, and Lou couldn't understand why. He told David, who shook his head. Knowing his mother as well as he did, he knew that when she opened her mouth, you never knew what you were in for. There was never any rhyme or reason to why Bea reacted the way she did.

Still unable to come within five hundred feet of his mother, David and Joshua hung out together while Rich spent most of his time with his parents. Carla managed to get some time off and came for the trial. She wanted to support David in any way she could. Rich had proposed to Carla, and she had accepted, so while visiting with Rich's parents they were busy talking about the details of the wedding, which Rich and Carla wanted to take place in Phoenix.

As time until the trial shortened, Lou learned Bea had contacted James Monroe, her attorney from the first trial. No one knew exactly why she was meeting with him, but when David heard, he wasn't happy.

"I hated that man the first time. So help me, if he does anything to jeopardize this case, like convincing my mother to lie on the witness stand, I'll kill him with my bare hands."

Lou knew he wasn't capable of murder, but David's statement didn't land on deaf ears, so he decided to do a little digging. Lou found out that James Monroe and Bea Miller were "dating," if you could call it that. Bea had grown very attached to him during her trial and they'd managed to stay in touch. He'd been to visit her many times, but no mention was made of it until now. David could not believe it when Lou told him.

"How can my mother like that slimy bastard? If you ask me, he looks and acts exactly the way my mother described Grandpa Edward." David flipped his hand in the air. "Well, whatever. She's a big girl and certainly doesn't need my permission. What she does in her private life is no concern of mine." Even as the words left David's lips, it still bothered him.

The day of the trial, David wore a new, navy-blue, pinstriped suit. He couldn't wear the one he wore to his mother's trial; it had been purchased by Aunt Benita as part of her sick plan, and the sight of it made him ill. Looking at himself in the mirror, he thought he cleaned up pretty well, and all things considered, he was confident the trial would go well. However, when he and Lou drove up to the federal building, David was not prepared for what he saw. Hundreds of people were standing around holding signs that read "Baby Killer," "Foundation Fraud," "Murdering Miller," and the like. He was having a hard time catching his breath, and all his confidence disappeared.

"The opinions of those picketers don't mean anything," Lou said, trying to reassure him. "It's the opinion of the judge and jury that counts."

Still, it was hard not to worry. If these people had already formed an opinion, maybe the jury had as well. It had been the lead story on all the major networks for days.

"I hope you're right," was all David could say.

When they got inside, David was placed in a holding cell directly behind the courtroom. The bars slammed shut, and David sat down, covered his face with his hands and cried. *How did it come to this? How could everything I worked for and everything I believed in go to hell so quickly? All I wanted to do was help and make a difference.*

Several minutes later David was led from the holding cell to the defendant's table in the courtroom. David was happy to see Lou already seated as he flashed him a friendly smile, and David managed to smile back. Seated in the back of the courtroom were Josh, Rich, Carla, Rich's parents, and Mrs. Brown. He knew Mrs. Brown was probably hoping he'd get the death penalty.

The prosecuting attorney, Mr. Callahan, rose to make his opening statement. Dressed in a beautiful black, pinstriped suit, he looked like he stepped out of the pages of GQ magazine. His brown hair, with golden highlights, was meticulously groomed, and his tan betrayed his love of golf. His smile showed off teeth so perfect and sparkling white he could have been a model for toothpaste.

"We are here today," Callahan said, "to mourn the loss of a newborn baby. A baby shot in the head and placed in a cooler to rot as if his life meant nothing. You will see how David Miller…cold, callous, and calculating…shot and killed that baby, and then left a note telling 'God,' " Mr. Callahan made quotes in the air, "he was sorry for what he did. I'm sure God has forgiven him. Can you?" Callahan paced back and forth in front of the jury, emphasizing the word *you* at the end of his remarks.

Lou Cooper was next on his feet.

"David Miller is not a cold, callous, and calculating murderer, as you have been led to believe. The only thing he is guilty of is not living up to his mother's expectations. She wanted him to follow her in a life of crime and deceit. When he defied her, wanting no part of it, she felt he should be punished. He did not kill that baby boy. Furthermore, he knew nothing of the child prior to his arrest. Returning to his old neighborhood last summer, he was shocked by the stench pervading the area. We now know that stench was of rotting flesh. David Miller had no knowledge of that. When this trial has ended, you will see that my client, David Miller, was framed. Framed by his mother, Beatrice Miller, and framed by his great-aunt, Benita Adams. Do not let what you have heard and read sway your opinion. Here, you will hear the facts of this case. Don't frame David Miller again."

The prosecution called their first witness: Mrs. Edna Brown. David whispered to Lou, "I didn't know she was being called."

Lou responded, "I gave you a list. Didn't you look at it?"

"I guess not." David shrugged, frowning.

After she was sworn in, Callahan began. "Mrs. Brown, please state your relationship to the accused."

Mrs. Brown was dressed in a lavender polyester dress suit with a faux fur collar. The color of the suit brought out the blue in her silver hair, and she looked like an Easter egg. "I was his next door neighbor until he moved to Phoenix in November, 2010."

"And when he was your neighbor, what did you think of him?"

"He was always very quiet. His brother was very active in sports and I read about him in the local paper, but never heard much about

David. I think he assumed the role of man of the house when Mr. Miller died. It seemed like he helped out a lot. They never took very good care of their yard, but when I saw someone mowing it, it was always David. He wore a lot of black clothing as a teenager."

"When was the last time you saw David Miller?"

"He stopped by to see me in July of last year. He said he came to visit his mother, but had some time to kill and decided to pay me a visit."

"How did the visit go?" Callahan asked.

"Good, I guess. He commented on the horrible smell and asked me what it was. He almost seemed relieved when I told him about the neighbor a few doors down who passed away," Mrs. Brown huffed.

"Relieved? How so?"

Relieved? I wasn't relieved, I was appalled!

"I don't know how to explain it. How do you describe relieved? He seemed so worried about the odor, but when I told him about Silvia—God rest her soul—he appeared to relax a little and then he and changed the subject to his mother."

I did not! She changed the subject! She asked about my mother.

"Tell us more about the smell, Mrs. Brown."

"It was awful, like something died and was eaten by something else that died, and both were lying on my doorstep. I called and called and finally they came out and found a dead deer, but when the smell didn't go away and no one at the city would take me seriously, I couldn't even go outside." Mrs. Brown unconsciously pinched her nose.

"When did the odor start?"

"Well, it was there on and off for a while, when the wind would change direction, but it was nothing I couldn't live with. Then shortly after David moved to Phoenix, it got worse. *Much worse.*"

"So David moved in November, and the smell got worse immediately?"

"I wouldn't say immediately, but it was winter and I wasn't outside much. That was when they found the deer. All I know is that, come spring, I couldn't leave my house without holding my nose."

"What happened next?"

"Well, I called city hall again and again. Finally, in early July, they sent someone out to check. Then the health department, the police, and the coroner were there. They found my neighbor Silvia rotting in a black plastic trash bag. The stench was horrendous then. When they hauled her away, it seemed the smell got a little better."

"You said *seemed*. Did the smell get better or didn't it?"

"I wanted to believe it did, at least at first, but as time went on…August, September, October…the smell was still there. Then it got cold again and, shortly after the new year, they discovered the dead baby."

"How do you think the baby got there?"

"I'll tell you exactly how. Bea kidnapped that baby and David killed him…"

Cooper was on his feet. "Your Honor, that is complete speculation. Mrs. Brown has no idea how that baby got there."

"Sustained. Counsel, please rephrase your question so she is stating fact and not just speculation." The judge, with a disgusted look on his face, glanced in the direction of Callahan.

Callahan paced back and forth and then stated, "No further questions, Your Honor."

Cooper walked to the witness box. "Good morning, Mrs. Brown. I've heard so much about you; it's nice to put a face with a name. You were David's neighbor, correct?"

"Yes. I lived next door to the Millers for many years. I bought my trailer with life insurance money left to me by my husband Howard. He passed away in 1999. When I moved in, they were already living there."

"What did you think of David Miller?"

Mrs. Brown shrugged. "He was odd. Quiet and sneaky, like he had something to hide."

"Over the years, how often did you talk to David Miller?" Cooper had returned to his seat and was glancing at his notes.

"I don't remember ever talking to him until the day I saw him outside packing a U-Haul. I went over to say hello and he was very rude."

Liar! You came over to butt your nose into my business like you always do!

"Did he tell you why he was moving?"

"He said something about going to college in Phoenix."

"Did he say he was moving because he couldn't stand the smell any longer?"

"No, of course not." Mrs. Brown looked shocked. "He may be a cold-blooded killer, just like his mother, but he's not stupid."

"I'd like to request that comment be struck from the record. My client is not a cold blooded killer." Cooper looked at the judge.

The judge nodded to the court reporter.

"Tell me, Mrs. Brown, when my client visited with you in July, who brought up the issue of the odor?"

"I guess he did."

"And do you think if he killed a baby boy and placed him under the trailer on Crimson Lane, he would bring the topic up in conversation? Don't you think it would have been more logical if he just said nothing?"

"You didn't live there. You didn't smell it. You have no idea what it was like. There's no way it could have been ignored."

"No further questions." Cooper sat down and put his arm around David. Before Mrs. Brown left the witness stand, she let out a huge sigh, as if she'd been insulted. As she walked past David to find her seat in the courtroom, she said, "The apple doesn't fall far from the tree."

Next on the stand was Rich Butler. He stated his name and said that he and David were business partners who owned and operated a foundation called "Never Give Up," which aided in the return of missing children to their families.

David admired the way Rich spoke, so confident in his words, and hoped to be able to do the same one day. David couldn't think of anything Callahan could ask Rich that would make him look bad in the eyes of the jury. "Mr. Butler, can you tell me how you and David Miller met?"

"Yes. I was employed as a police officer in Bunting Valley, working on a missing child case, and I was the arresting officer when Bea and David Miller were taken into custody in July of 2010 for the alleged kidnapping of Maggie Taylor."

"So, you arrested David Miller for kidnapping, but you trusted him enough to go into business with him? A foundation that, of all things, helps find missing and kidnapped children?" Callahan sneered.

"Yes, absolutely. David was cleared of all wrongdoing in the kidnapping of Maggie Taylor. He'd been coerced by his mother, and was unable to defy her for fear of retribution. David is the most caring person I've ever met. He would never do anything to hurt another human being, and he certainly would not shoot and kill a baby."

Callahan laughed. "Thank you so much for your opinion, Mr. Butler, but honestly I don't really care what you think of David Miller. It's up to the jury to decide. No further questions."

Cooper intended to ask Rich to make a testament to David's character, but he'd already done that. Since he had him on the stand, though, there was no harm in driving it home a bit more.

"Mr. Butler, how long have you known my client?"

"Since July 19th, 2010. I had tried to reach him before that, but never did."

"Reach him? Reach him for what?" Lou and Rich had been rehearsing their questions and answers, and David was amazed by how they managed not to give it away.

"I wanted to ask him a few questions about the disappearance of Maggie Taylor." Rich cleared his throat.

"Please tell the jury who Maggie Taylor is."

"She was a three-year-old girl who was abducted at Lake Gerber."

"And why did you want to talk to David? Was he a suspect?"

"Not necessarily a suspect; some witnesses at Lake Gerber mentioned they'd seen him there the day of the kidnapping, and I thought he may have seen or heard something helpful."

Callahan was immediately on his feet. "Objection, Your Honor. We are not here to discuss the kidnapping of Maggie Taylor; we are here to discuss the dead baby found under the trailer on Crimson Lane, where David Miller lived."

"Stick to the charges at hand, Counsel," the judge said, sitting up straighter in his chair.

"Tell me about the day you visited my client in early November." Cooper pushed up his glasses.

"David was packing that day. He invited me into the trailer for something hot to drink and, as soon as we entered, he told me he'd pinpointed the source of the smell." Rich shifted in his chair.

"Was it bad?"

"Not that bad. There was an odor, but as David told me, you noticed it when you first entered, but quickly got used to it."

"So what did he think the source of the smell was?"

"He pulled back a throw rug and showed me a bloodstain on the carpet." Rich leaned forward.

"A bloodstain? From what?" Cooper asked.

"I don't know the details, but I assumed it happened when Beatrice Miller shot and killed Edward Noslen, David's maternal grandfather."

"What was your reaction when you saw the bloodstain?"

"I told him I'd been around a lot of bloodstains in my years on the force, and had never known one to give off such an odor. Not a lingering smell that stuck around for months. David said something to the effect that he thought perhaps the blood had run through the floor and pooled under the trailer. He didn't think it was the bloodstain on the carpet that stunk, but the pool of blood underneath the trailer."

"What did it smell like?"

"Like ammonia. But then again, it reminded me of pickle juice." Rich wrinkled his nose.

"Pickle juice? How so?"

"Kind of vinegary. Like the smell of coloring Easter eggs."

"So, ammonia and vinegar mixed together?"

"Yes, exactly," Rich nodded. "Almost as though someone was trying to mask one smell with the other."

"Was there anything else?"

"Yes. As David and I walked into the kitchen, I noticed a hole in the wall."

"A hole? What type of hole?"

"A bullet hole."

"Did you ask my client about it, or point it out?"

"No. I thought it bad enough that he found the bloodstain. I sure wasn't going to point out the hole in the wall where, I assume, the bullet that killed Edward Noslen lodged. That's too much for a kid to take, no matter how mature."

Cooper nodded. "After you resigned your position on the Bunting Valley Police Department and moved to Phoenix, did David ever mention the smell again?"

"Only once, when he returned from that visit with Mrs. Brown. He told me about the neighbor's dead body."

"What did you do?"

"I called some of my buddies on the force to find out the facts. They told me about the woman who'd passed away, and how her son had placed her in a trash bag and sat it outside their back door. They assumed the smell would dissipate, although some of her body fluids had leaked through the bag and saturated a large patch of grass. Something of that magnitude doesn't disappear overnight."

"Did you believe them?"

"Of course I believed them. They are professionals, as well as my friends. I had no reason not to."

"Thank you, Mr. Butler. No further questions."

Next up was Beverly Smith. Rich thought it might be helpful for one of the foundation clients to testify on David's behalf, describing their professional relationship and David's character.

After she was sworn in, the bailiff barked, "Please state your name and your relationship to the accused."

"My name is Beverly Eliza Smith. I was a client of Mr. Miller's foundation, 'Never Give Up.' "

Callahan rose to question Mrs. Smith. Of all of the witnesses, she was the one he was least wanted to question for fear she would jeopardize his case.

"Mrs. Smith, can you tell me how you met the accused?"

"Yes. I saw him on a local talk show in Phoenix and he spoke about his foundation. Like pretty much everyone, I had heard about Bea Miller, so when I saw David talking about how he wanted to turn all the horrible things his mother had done into something positive, I was impressed. Having two young girls, I hoped never to need his services, but decided to enter the foundation telephone number in my cell phone, just in case."

"So you never met him, you just saw him on television?" Callahan was feeling a bit more confident.

"Some time later, I required his services. That's when I met him."

"What happened?"

"My family and I went on vacation to Portugal, where my youngest daughter, Eliza, was abducted."

"You decided to contact 'Never Give Up' instead of the authorities in Portugal? Isn't that odd?"

"I talked to the authorities in Portugal but, given the language barrier, we couldn't understand each other. I knew Eliza was in more danger the longer it went on, so I called the foundation. Both David Miller and Rich Butler came to Portugal to help."

"Just like that?"

"Yes, just like that. They never hesitated."

"What did you think of David when you met him?"

"I was surprised by how young he was. But when he started talking and asking questions, his age was inconsequential. His knowledge and experience surpassed anything I expected."

"Did he help you find your daughter?"

Mrs. Smith hesitated before speaking. "No, but it was not because of anything David did or didn't do. My husband sold our daughter to the black market. David could not have changed that. But David was caring and empathetic. He was the one who explained what had happened, and he was as shaken as I was. His love for children was evident."

"No more questions."

Cooper jumped up. "Good to see you, Mrs. Smith. Thank you for coming all this way."

"It's an honor to share my experience with the jury," Mrs. Smith smiled.

"You said earlier that David's love for children was evident. How could you tell during your brief encounter?"

"My communication with David didn't stop when we realized what had happened to Eliza. He called me about once a month, to see how I was doing. He told me several times how sorry he was, and how he wished the outcome could have been different. He even sent my other daughter a gift for her birthday. I found David kind and caring, and could tell he loved children."

"Thank you, Mrs. Smith."

Next on the witness stand was the medical examiner. He stated the facts regarding the corpse found under the trailer. "The child was African American and a day or two old. Because of decomposition, the exact time of death cannot be determined. Some parts of the body, because they were submerged in a pickling agent, are rather well preserved, while other parts are mummified and unable to be examined."

"You have no idea how long the body had been under the trailer?" Callahan wanted a date, and wouldn't stop until he got one.

"I do not."

"If you gave an educated guess, what would you say?"

"I can give an educated guess but it is not scientific and has not been proven."

"Okay, what is your unscientific and unproven educated guess?"

The medical examiner cleared his throat and spoke loud and clear, "I think he was placed in the cooler sometime in late 2009."

David gulped so loud, he felt sure the entire courtroom heard it.

Cooper stood, "Your Honor, as the witness stated, that is an educated guess, not based on fact or scientific evidence. I ask that it be removed from the record."

"Sustained," The judge said, nodding in agreement looking towards the court reporter.

Never deprive someone of hope; it might be all they have.

~ H. Jackson Brown, Jr.

Chapter Eighteen

There was a fifteen-minute recess, during which David was taken back to the holding cell. Lou stayed by his side, assuring him he thought things were going well so far. David felt it was going horribly. The pièce de résistance would come when his mother took the stand.

Just then, a court employee walked in to announce that David was next on the stand. It was supposed to be Bea, but she had not yet arrived from the women's prison, so her testimony would follow his. He had a million reasons to hate her, now it was going to be a million and one.

David was dreading it. Rich told him over and over again to just tell the truth; the truth wins in the end. David was certain that this time, the truth was going to lose. They were going to convict him, toss him in jail, and throw away the key. When he was led back out to the courtroom, Rich came up and touched him on the shoulder. David turned and smiled, thanking him for all the nice things he said about him during his testimony on the witness stand.

"I just told them the truth. Also, you might like to know the police were here and broke up the picketing in the parking lot. Sadly not before the news crews got wind of it. Just imagine how stupid they're all going to look when you're found innocent," Rich said.

Rich leaned over and whispered in Lou's ear, quietly, so David wouldn't hear, "It'll be a miracle if David gets out of this."

Lou nodded in agreement. But David heard what Rich said.

David had felt from the start that the trial was not going to go well, and now his entire support team was in agreement. When his mom came out, it would be a case of "he said-she said," and the jury would believe her. He just knew it. She and Aunt Benita had concocted this whole story and calculated exactly how they were going to pull it off. They knew what they were doing. They'd dotted the i's and crossed the t's. All along he knew he would eventually have to pay for telling the truth at his mother's trial; now he had to wait and see what the punishment would be.

Callahan acted as though he couldn't wait to get David on the witness stand. What he thought he would get from him neither Cooper nor David knew, but the time had come for them to find out.

"David, can you please tell me what your mother asked you do with Mikey when she found out he was a boy and not a girl?" Callahan, holding a fistful of papers, was looking through his notes.

"She asked me to get rid of him."

"And what did you tell her?" Callahan tilted his head and glanced up at David.

"I refused. I told her I wouldn't hurt him, and she'd better not hurt him either or I was going to call the police."

"So, the next time your mother took a baby boy, by accident, did the same thing happen?" Callahan laid his notes on the table and folded his arms.

"There was no next time. The only other time she took another kid was Maggie Taylor, and she was not a boy, nor a baby. I think she was three years old."

"Let the prosecution present Exhibit A." The bailiff carried out the silver handgun with the white pearl handle David had found in the safety deposit box. "Mr. Miller, does this look familiar to you?" Both David and Cooper were shocked.

"Yes! That's the gun I found in my Aunt Benita's safety deposit box."

"Where was that?"

"In Phoenix…at the First National Bank."

"Can you tell me how a handgun, bought and registered under the name of Beatrice Miller, ended up in your Aunt Benita's safety deposit box in Phoenix, almost two thousand miles away?"

"I have no idea, but probably the same way the same gun ended up back in Bunting Valley, when the last time I saw it was in Aunt Benita's safety deposit box in Phoenix, almost two thousand miles away."

"Don't you mean to say you used the gun to shoot and kill that baby boy, then hid it? And when you were packing, you found it and decided to take it with you? And then, when you arrived in Phoenix, you placed it in your Aunt Benita's safety deposit box? Isn't that how it happened, Mr. Miller?"

"No!" David was beginning to lose his temper.

"Can you explain to me, and the jury, how your fingerprints are the only fingerprints on the gun?"

"Yes, I can. I knew Aunt Benita had a safety deposit box, and I went to the bank to see what was in it. When I found the gun, I took it out and held it. That's all. That was the first time I ever saw the gun. I had no way of knowing it belonged to my mother, and I have no way of knowing how it got from Bunting Valley to Phoenix. All I know is that I didn't take it there!"

"Then can you explain how your gloves and a note you wrote that read, "I'm sorry, God. Love, David" ended up near the dead baby?"

"I'm assuming my mother put them there. The note was something I'd written to her when she kidnapped Mikey."

Callahan laughed out loud. "You mean to tell me you called your own mother God?"

"No, I didn't call my mother God. She was angry at me for not doing what she told me to do...to get rid of Mikey for her...so she told me to apologize. I refused. I was not going to apologize for something she did. We had words, and I told her if I owed anyone an apology, it was God. So I wrote the note to God and gave it to my mother. She must have saved it and used it to frame me. I have nothing to ask His forgiveness for. I did not kill that baby. I love children. For God's sake, I started a foundation to help them. Why would I kill one of them?"

"Perhaps you did it out of guilt."

"Guilt? Guilt for what?" David furrowed his brow.

"For killing that baby and placing him under the house trailer like a piece of trash. No further questions." Callahan sat down but not before Cooper could object to his final comment.

"Objection, Your Honor. My client has not been found guilty."

The judge looked at Callahan again, "Counsel, this is the last time I will caution you on stating opinion or speculation. Sustained."

Lou and David had rehearsed his testimony over and over again. They both knew exactly what to say and when to say it. But what they rehearsed was nothing compared to the damage Callahan had done. Their only weapon was to bring out the letter Aunt Benita had written, hoping the jury could read between the lines and determine who was telling the truth.

Cooper began, "Let the defense present Exhibit B...a letter David received, through me, posthumously, from Benita Adams. I gave this to him immediately after he found the gun in the safety deposit box. She wrote it a few days before she died and left it with me, her attorney." Cooper read the letter aloud. Waiting a moment for the words to resonate, Cooper began his questioning. "David, please tell the jury where that letter came from."

"It was given to me by you. When I went to the bank and found the gun, I went to your office to ask if you knew anything about it. You told me Aunt Benita had written me a letter, and asked you to give it to me in the event I asked about the contents of the safety deposit box."

"Was that the first time you saw the gun?"

"Yes. The first and the last. That day, after reading the letter, I went back to the bank to get it, but it was gone. Obviously, someone," David looked directly at Callahan, "had arranged for it to be taken from the safety deposit box and sent back to Bunting Valley."

"Why did you go back to the bank to get it?"

"Because it was evidence. I wanted to turn it in. I've done nothing wrong, and the gun would only help prove my innocence."

"So, you're saying you only saw the gun once."

"Yes, Sir. Until today."

"Did you know Beatrice Miller had a gun?"

"I never thought about it, but she would have had to if she shot and killed my grandpa. I never asked her about it, and still haven't," David shrugged.

"Did you notice the bullet hole in the wall that Rich Butler described earlier?"

"I saw the hole, but didn't think much of it."

"You saw a bullet hole in the wall and didn't think much of it? How can that be?"

"I didn't know it was a bullet hole. The trailer was old and worn; four boys had lived there. There were other dents and holes. One didn't catch my attention more than another."

"What did you think of the smell?"

"I thought it was coming from inside the trailer. It seemed to me when someone mentioned it, it would be gone the next day. I assumed Mom knew what it was and cleaned it up. When I was packing and I found the bloodstain, I was sure that was the source of it, but Rich told me bloodstains don't have a lingering odor. When I went to visit Mrs. Brown, she told me she first thought it was a dead animal, and then told me about the decomposing body of the neighbor. I believed her. I had no reason not to, and I had no way of knowing what it was."

"David Miller, did you use that gun to shoot and kill the baby boy found under the trailer on Crimson Lane?" Lou hated to give him such a hard time, but David knew it was coming.

"No, Sir. Absolutely not. I would never harm a baby."

"No further questions. Thank you, David." David stepped out of the witness box and walked back to the table.

The bailiff stood and announced, "We have just received word the final witness will be here in about fifteen minutes."

The judge said, "We'll take a short recess, and reconvene when the witness arrives."

David paced in the holding cell. The closer his mother got, the harder it was for him to breathe. At one point, he felt like he was going to faint. Lou had him sit and put his head between his knees. It helped, but the lightheadedness started again when they received word she'd arrived.

David wasn't afraid of Callahan, the jury or the judge. He had faith in the justice system, and knew what was meant to be would be. However, knowing his fate was in the hands of his mother scared the living daylights out of him.

"Come on, David. You can do this. You're better than her. Don't let what she might say scare you. You're innocent. You did nothing wrong. Just go out there, put on a smile, and hope for the best."

"Lou, I heard what Rich said to you. Neither of you believe I'm going to get out of this. Why don't you admit it?"

"I admit the evidence and the testimony thus far have been very damaging. It could go either way. But until they read a guilty verdict, I refuse to believe we've lost. Let's see what your mother has to say."

"We're talking about my mother…a lying, serial-kidnapping, cold-blooded murderer. She has no morals or values; she doesn't know right from wrong. I know she shot and killed that baby. This is not going to go well. I know it."

David reluctantly sat at the table again and watched his mother step into the witness box. She was wearing the same suit she'd worn at her own trial, and it was the first time David had seen her with bright-red lipstick in a long time. She smiled at him, and he felt calm—undoubtedly the calm before the storm.

Bea was sworn in and asked to state her relationship to the accused. "He is my son, David. My only biological child." Bea was seated, and it seemed the entire room was holding its breath—including David.

Hope sees the invisible, feels the intangible,
and achieves the impossible.

~ Helen Keller

Chapter Nineteen

Callahan jumped up, almost giddy, to question Beatrice Miller. He'd heard so much about her, and couldn't wait to see what she had to say. "Mrs. Miller, do you know why we're here today?"

"Yes," Bea answered.

"And what is that reason?"

"My son, David, has been accused of murdering a baby boy, and placing the baby under our trailer on Crimson Lane."

"That's correct. What do you think of these charges brought against your son?"

C'mon, Mom. For the first time in your life, do the right thing. Tell them the truth. David closed his eyes.

Bea cleared her throat and said, "I think they're complete rubbish."

Even though this was Bea's opinion, and it had no right in a court of law, Cooper decided to let it slide.

The gasps in the courtroom were so loud, the judge pounded his gavel.

Callahan could hardly believe what he'd heard. "Mrs. Miller, did you understand the question?"

"Yes. I understood it perfectly. I passed my GED, so I'm smarter than I was the last time I was here," Bea smiled. She almost looked human.

"Please repeat what you said."

"I said its rubbish. My son would never kill a baby."

"Then can you explain to me how a dead baby got under the trailer, and a handgun licensed to you ended up in a safety deposit box in Phoenix, Arizona?"

"I'm so glad you asked. Pull up a chair, Mr. Callahan. This might take a while." Laughter erupted and the judge pounded his gavel. "One day in November, 2009, after Papa had been dead for some time and my life was returning to normal, I was in the living room looking out the window on the front door. I saw a pregnant girl walking down the street. She was walking extremely slowly, as if carrying the weight of the world on her shoulders. She reminded me so much of myself at that age…minus the big belly, of course."

"Mrs. Miller," the judge spoke, "answer the questions as presented to you."

Bea sighed and started again. "She looked so lost and confused that I decided to go out and talk with her. If nothing else, maybe I could offer her a cup of tea or an ear to bend. She looked like she had a lot on her mind and needed a shoulder to cry on."

Callahan gulped, but said nothing.

"She told me her name was Melinda, and she lived just down the street from me. She even pointed at a brown trailer about six down from mine. I invited her in. She said she was fourteen years old and due to deliver in a few weeks. I could tell she was close because when she sat down and her t-shirt stretched taut, her belly button was protruding."

"Go on," Callahan said.

"Melinda told me she was giving her baby up for adoption. Her parents were making her. Seeing my opportunity to finally get the baby girl I always wanted, I asked her if she knew what she was having, because I always wanted a girl. She told me the ultrasound showed it was a girl. I couldn't believe my luck. I asked Melinda if she would consider selling her baby to me. I told her I'd be a good mom and she would be welcome to come and see the baby any time."

"You know that buying a baby is against the law, don't you?" Callahan interrupted.

"I didn't care. All I cared about was getting my baby girl. When I asked about buying her baby, Melinda's eyes lit up. 'How much money do you think my baby is worth?' she asked. Never having bought a baby before, I had no idea. But given her state of disarray and her youth, I figured it shouldn't take much to make her interested. I said, 'How about I give you five hundred dollars now and another five hundred dollars when the baby is born and you bring her to me,' holding my breath.

"'One thousand dollars!' she screamed. I couldn't tell if she was excited or offended, so I said nothing. After several minutes, she smiled and said, 'Deal!' She remained on the couch while I went into the kitchen to get the money together. I had money stashed everywhere; in canisters, bowls, bags, cups. I don't know why I did that, but it was always a pleasant surprise when I took a coffee mug or a bowl out of the cupboard and found money in it. Even though it was my money, it still felt like a windfall. I hoped I could find enough to give her five hundred dollars. I was so excited thinking I was finally going to get my baby girl. I didn't have to kidnap her. I didn't have to steal her. Her mother was willing to let me have her, for only one thousand dollars!

"I finally gathered together the money. The last thirty or so was in quarters, nickels, and dimes, but Melinda didn't seem to care. As I counted the coins, she told me her due date was in three weeks, and she would be back to hand over her daughter and collect the last of the money when they were released from the hospital. Three weeks! I was beside myself. I didn't want to tell the boys about their new sister for fear that I'd jinx it."

The silence in the courtroom was deafening. David felt like he was in a dream—a dream in which his mother was normal.

"I went to the bank and withdrew two hundred dollars from David's bank account. There wasn't much more than that in it, so I had to figure out a way to get the rest of the money to finish paying for my daughter. My daughter! It sounded so foreign to me. I couldn't believe it.

"I looked around the house to see if there was anything worth pawning. We had nothing…well, nothing worth three hundred dollars. I looked at my wedding ring, and twirled it around my finger. It was the second ring Henry bought me. The first one was a plain gold band he'd purchased for twenty dollars at a storefront gift shop in Las Vegas. I'm not even sure it was real gold. The second one, the one I still wore,

Henry gave me on our fifth wedding anniversary. It was much more elaborate; it had a single round diamond surrounded by smaller diamond chips. I'd never had it appraised, so I never knew the carat weight, but I was certain it was worth at least a few hundred dollars. Henry had been dead for many years, and I thought he would be okay with me pawning my wedding ring to buy a little girl. As a matter of fact, as I sat staring up to the heavens, I pictured him smiling down at me.

"Once I decided to pawn the ring, I couldn't get to the pawn shop fast enough. The gentleman behind the counter pulled out one of those magnifying instruments to take a look at the stones. I was afraid he was going to tell me the stones were fake and it was worth nothing. After a few minutes, he told me he would give me five hundred dollars for it. Oh, my gosh! I thought I'd died and gone to heaven. With the two hundred dollars from David's account, it was enough to finish paying for my baby girl, and I could get her a few things to boot!

"I was overjoyed when I left the pawn shop, but my finger felt naked. After so many years of wearing a ring, once it was gone it felt funny." Bea paused for a moment and looked at her ringless hand. "I decided to wear my original wedding band. It wasn't worth much, but it meant the world to me. That's what I would have on today if they hadn't taken all my jewelry.

"About three and a half weeks after I made the deal with Melinda, she knocked on my door. The boys were in school, so I was alone. She didn't say anything as I opened the door and she came in. She still looked pregnant as she sat down on the couch and placed the baby, in a carrier, on the floor beside her. The carrier was tan plastic, with no padding or pillows. Melinda looked very sad, and for a moment I almost felt sorry for her. But when I remembered I was finally getting my daughter and Melinda was getting one thousand dollars, I felt better. I went into the kitchen and took the money from a cookie jar. When I walked back into the living room, Melinda was crying. I didn't know what to do. But her tears dried up when she saw the money."

David was sitting with his eyes closed for fear that if he opened them, he would wake up from this dream.

"She told me to take good care of her baby, and said she was very healthy and weighed a little over eight pounds. I asked if I could unwrap her so I could have a good look, but Melinda asked that I wait until she left because it would be too painful for her to see. Moments later, the baby started to fuss. Melinda excused herself, opened the door and walked out. Then I was alone, finally, with my baby girl, bought and paid for! She belonged to me!"

Everyone in the courtroom was sitting completely still, eyes on Bea, waiting for her to continue.

"I removed the blanket to take her out of the carrier, and staring back at me was an African American baby! How was I going to pull this off? What would the neighbors think? She was still fussing so I picked her up to see if her diaper was wet. When I stuck my finger in, I was not prepared for what I felt. It was a penis. Another penis! Another stupid boy! I ripped open the diaper to be sure.

"What was I going to do? I dropped him back in the carrier and opened the door to see if Melinda was on the street, walking back to her house, but she wasn't. I pulled on my shoes and took off on foot. I was not about to let a fourteen-year-old girl take advantage of me. I didn't want her stupid baby boy and I wanted my money back!

"The longer I walked the angrier I became. I'm sure if someone was watching, it probably looked like I was marching, but I didn't care. I couldn't wait to see her face-to-face, give her a piece of my mind, and get my money back.

"When I arrived at her trailer, the shades were drawn and it looked like no one was home. I knocked, probably too hard, but I was angry. A big man, wearing a white sleeveless t-shirt and boxer shorts, answered the door and I asked to speak to Melinda. 'Melinda? There's no one here by that name.'

"Yes there is," I said. "She's fourteen years old and just gave birth to a baby boy. Don't lie to me. I need to talk to her and I need to talk to her now! He said, 'I'm sorry Ma'am, but I have no idea what you're talking about. I don't know a Melinda and she doesn't live here.'

"I was growing madder by the second. I said, 'Don't mess with me, Mister, I'm in no mood. If she doesn't show her face right now, I'm going to call the police.' I couldn't believe it when he said, 'Well, I guess you'll have to call the police, because she doesn't live here.'

"I stepped back and looked at the trailers. They were all starting to look alike. It was possible that I had the wrong house. Ashamed, I said, 'Sorry to have bothered you,' and went to the next trailer and the next and so on until I was back at my own. No one knew Melinda. No one had ever seen Melinda. No one knew what I was talking about. I'd been swindled. At one point in my life, I was the swindler; I could spot a con artist a mile away. Now here I was. I'd bought everything Melinda said, hook, line, and sinker, and I was stuck with another baby boy!

"When I walked back into the house, the baby was screaming and I didn't know what to do. I didn't want another boy. There was only one way out. I had to kill him. I went into the bedroom, pulled on a pair of heavy gloves and grabbed my handgun. This would be the second time I'd used it; the first was to kill Papa. It was something I didn't want to do, but I had no choice. I knew David wouldn't do it."

Callahan stood and picked up the Exhibit A, the small handgun. "Is this the gun you're referring to?"

"Yes. Yes, Sir. That is my gun. I went back into the living room, took a pillow off of the couch, and placed it over his face. He stopped crying and I thought maybe I had smothered him, but when I removed the pillow to look, he looked right at me with those coal-black eyes and started screaming again. So I put the pillow back, placed the gun on top of it, closed my eyes, and squeezed the trigger. I figured the pillow would prevent blood from splattering and muffle the bang of the gun. One gunshot, and he was screaming no more. He was gone. I moved the pillow, and blood was seeping out of a hole in the center of his forehead, running down his nose into his eyes, which were still wide open. When I covered him with the blanket and sat down to think, I noticed the bullet was stuck in the wall about six feet away. It must have gone through his head, through the carrier, and into the wall. I was still wearing the gloves, so I pulled it out and put it into the carrier.

"I had no idea what to do with the body, but I knew I had to get rid of it before the boys got home from school. I found the biggest plastic bag I could find and I put him inside, still in the carrier. I took a cooler and filled it with half ammonia and half vinegar. I even sprinkled in a little salt. Then, I put the baby and carrier into the cooler and took it outside, in the back. I bent back the skirting on the trailer and shoved the cooler under the house, as far as I could. I even sat on the ground and pushed it with my feet. I figured once it started to smell, I could figure out something else. Winter was approaching, and I knew the body would freeze, which would buy me some time.

"I went back into the house, and what I'd done hit me. I started to cry, and then I panicked. I didn't know what to do. After talking with Aunt Benita...only the second time since Papa made her leave...she convinced me to frame David for the murder. 'He's a young boy and won't get in as much trouble. Put some of his things near the cooler. A pair of his gloves and anything else you think might help.' She also told me she'd send someone to get the gun; the further the gun was from the dead body, the better off we'd be. A few hours later, a man in a black trench coat and sunglasses was standing at the door. I handed him the gun, in a white plastic envelope, and he left. I never saw him or heard from Aunt Benita again. She was my angel, always there when I needed her most. She promised to take my secret to the grave."

"So can you explain to the jury why the odor would appear and disappear?"

"Yes. Like I said, the winter did buy me some time. When spring came, the body started to stink, so I transferred it from one cooler to another, filled again to the brim with the same recipe. I was surprised how well my liquid concoction worked. Don't get me wrong, it was disgusting. I didn't open the bag to look at the baby; I had no desire to see what it had become. If it hadn't been for the cooler cracking, I think it would have lasted quite a while. And each time someone mentioned the smell, I pulled the cooler out and dumped more liquid in it. Then I was arrested in July, and couldn't tend to it, so after that, it was what it was."

"Mrs. Miller, do you understand what you're saying?" Callahan asked, his eyes wide.

"Yes I do. I can't watch my son go to jail for something he didn't do. The Beatrice Miller sitting here before you today is different from the Beatrice Miller who killed that baby and proceeded to mount evidence to frame her only son."

David finally looked at his mother.

"Remember, David, things aren't always what they seem." Bea released a huge sigh, smiled, and placed her forehead in front of her on the edge of the witness box.

David couldn't believe it. All that time, when his mother pretended to be crazy, telling him things weren't always what they seemed, she was talking about herself. She wasn't crazy. She was the loving mother he knew she could be. Before they took her away, David hugged her.

Bea said, "I'm so sorry, David. I'm so sorry for everything I put you through. I've always loved you, and I hope someday you'll forgive me."

He already had.

Epilogue

When the trial was over, they headed back to Phoenix. Curious about how the gun got back to Bunting Valley, Lou found out Benita had arranged to pay the bank manager one hundred thousand dollars, to be deducted from her bank account, when David came to the bank to view the contents of the safety deposit box. The manager was given explicit orders to then contact the police and turn over the contents of the safety deposit box, telling them it was, or would be, a major piece of evidence in a murder trial in Bunting Valley. To get his money, he worked around the clock to be sure he wouldn't miss David's visit to the bank. He was thrilled when, a little over a year later, it all came together and he got his money.

Bea, already in jail for at least twenty-five to thirty years, was given a life sentence. David hated thinking his mother would never be free again, but prison was the best place for her. He vowed to visit her at least once a month. After all, she'd saved his life.

Aunt Benita's house had lost its luster. It upset David to know she'd coerced him into living in Phoenix just so she could help frame him for a crime he didn't commit. After a great deal of thought, he knew what he had to do.

"I've decided to put Aunt Benita's house on the market," he told Lou, about a month after they'd returned to Phoenix. David and Lou had become really good friends and on occasion, they met for lunch just to catch up. David looked to him as a father figure, and Lou, having several children of his own, didn't mind.

"I knew that was coming," Lou said.

"It's way too big for me. Rich is getting married, so he already moved in with Carla. It's just me and Joshua since the foundation was forced to close. We don't need that much room. Besides, it doesn't feel the same anymore. I loved that house when I first moved in, but now it's different. I look at it and get sick to my stomach. Not even rose-colored glasses could change that."

"I understand. I'd probably feel the same way. What about the contents? Do you want anything, or are you thinking about having an estate sale?"

"I thought about an estate sale. What doesn't sell can be included with the purchase of the house. Eventually, I'd like to try to reopen the foundation, but I'm not ready yet. Everyone has a bad taste in their mouth about what happened, and if it's going to go well, I need a little time."

"I sent out multiple press releases when you were exonerated, trying to clear your name. What happened to you was awful. I'm sorry to say Benita Adams was one of my good friends. I had no idea she was capable of doing something like that."

"I'm just glad you stuck by me. I was afraid you were going to side with her, out of loyalty."

"Never. My loyalty lies with the truth. From everything you told me about your mother, I'm still shocked at her testimony."

"I know. Me too. I think how different my life would have been if she'd been like that when I was growing up."

"If you sell the house, where will you have the foundation offices?" Lou stuck a forkful of salad in his mouth.

"I could rent a storefront; I don't need anything big or fancy. I still have Aunt Benita's money, so I should be able to find something."

"Are you planning to live in the house until it sells?"

"No. I already found an apartment. It has three bedrooms, and it's perfect for me and Josh. I can't stay there anymore. I'm going to start packing up my things later in the week."

"I'll contact an auction house to get the estate sale underway. As soon as that's over, I'll contact a realtor and get it on the market. We need to see what sells at the estate sale before we can determine a price. Did you need my help negotiating the lease on your apartment?"

"No, I got it covered. It was pretty cut-and-dried. I signed a one-year lease, and we'll see how that goes. If I like it, I may renew; if not,

I'll look for something else. I'm not a teenager anymore. I should start thinking about buying my own house, don't you think?"

"There's no rush. You have a lifetime ahead of you."

~

Rich and Carla planned a beautiful spring wedding and everything turned out exactly how they dreamed it would. It was held outdoors at a park. The center aisle was scattered with pink rose petals, and Carla wore an off-the-shoulder white dress with intricate beading. When he saw her, Rich looked like he was about to burst with pride. Only a handful of guests were in attendance because they wanted to keep the ceremony small and share their special day with the people who meant the most to them. One of Carla's dogs, a rescue from the shelter, was the ring bearer. Once he caught sight of a rabbit, he was off on the chase. Thank God he didn't have the real rings attached to his pillow. By the time the wedding was over he was back, panting and tired as they all laughed.

David was best man. When Rich asked him to do the honors, he said, "Who else am I going to ask, you knucklehead? If it weren't for you asking me to move to Phoenix and help with the foundation, I would have never met Carla. I owe you, Brother; I owe you big time!"

David was overjoyed for them. They took off on a two-week honeymoon inter-island cruise of Hawaii, a gift from David. When he and Carla returned, they bought a home, and Rich decided he needed to find another job. He was certain he would be able to get back into law enforcement in some capacity.

Always having wanted grandchildren, as soon as Rich and Carla were married, his mom was asking when they planned to try for a baby. She was a wonderful woman—kind, caring, and with a great sense of humor. David saw so much of her in Rich it made him realize how Rich turned out so well.

~

Joshua was looking for a job, and was having difficulty finding one without a college education. So he registered for a few classes to see how it would go. His parents, who had visited him in Phoenix, were thrilled to see how well he was doing. They suggested that he major in law, but he suggested that they stop suggesting it.

In all the time Joshua lived in Phoenix, his twin sisters had been to visit only once. When David met them, he remembered Josh saying about how hot they were. He was right; but since they were related to Joshua, it seemed as if they were related to him, too. They didn't stay long, but Joshua was glad to see them.

~

Bea had been moved to another prison in North Dakota. Now convicted of murder, she was considered a dangerous felon. Gone were the craft classes, the cut-and-sew program, and watching TV. She now spent the majority of her time in her cell, reading the Bible or writing. She hoped to write a book about her life one day, to demonstrate that it's never too late to change.

David had been to visit her once, and was planning another in a couple of weeks. She was now sweet, polite, and appreciative of the time he spent with her.

James Monroe visited a few times a week. David had hated him, but when Bea told him it was James who'd suggested she tell the truth on the witness stand, David realized maybe he wasn't that bad after all.

~

Five months after Rich and Carla returned from Hawaii, they announced she was pregnant. Rich couldn't believe his good fortune—to meet the woman of his dreams, and to be able to have a child, something he never dreamed would happen. He told David he hoped it was a girl.

"Oh, my God. Don't you start! Don't even tell me how much a little girl would brighten your life. I've heard it all before, and it doesn't have a happy ending. Trust me on this one." David was teasing. He hoped Rich and Carla had whatever would make them happy. He knew they'd make wonderful parents.

"You don't understand. I want to have a baby girl for a reason."

"What might that be?" David said, waiting to hear the punch line.

"Carla and I have agreed to call her Eliza, after the little girl we tried unsuccessfully to rescue in Portugal."

David was so touched that Eliza's story had made such an impact on Rich that he wanted to name his daughter after her. The only time David had ever seen Rich lose his cool was when he punched Matthew Smith in the nose.

As David thought back to how he felt when Eliza's father admitted selling her into the black market, he remembered again why he wanted to start his foundation. Even with all the horrible, selfish people in the world, once in a while you met the one who changed everything, the one who made you stand back in awe, wishing you could be like them when you grew up. At those times, you knew you should never give up.

David was his mother's son, after all.

THE END

About R.K. Avery

RK Avery, a recent graduate of the Institute of Children's Literature, discovered one thing during her coursework—she loves writing adult fiction, especially fiction that makes you ponder about it long after you've put the book down. R. K. Avery lives in Macedonia, Ohio, with her family, which includes three Morkies and a Puggle. This is her second novel.

CPSIA information can be obtained at www.ICGtesting.com
Printed in the USA
BVOW030000031212

307110BV00005B/8/P